Coffee with Poe

A Novel of Edgar Allan Poe's Life

ISBN 1-58961-104-7

BottleTree Books
P.O. Box 253
Collierville, Tennessee 38027-0253
www.BottleTreeBooks.com

**To Roo and Booga-Boo
for making my life extraordinary one day at a time.**

Special thanks to the Edgar Allan Poe Society of Baltimore for providing the letters contained in *Coffee with Poe*. Bracketed Words and letters denote those that were illegible from the original text or left out. Any mistakes in *Coffee with Poe* are, of course, entirely my own.

Coffee with Poe

1811 - Age 2

Frances Allan once again surveyed the folded page of the *Richmond Enquirer*:

Died—On Sunday last, Mrs. Poe, one of the actresses of the company at present playing on the Richmond Boards. By the death of this Lady the Stage has been deprived of one of its chief ornaments. And to say the least of her, she was an interesting Actress, and never failed to catch the applause, and command the admiration, of the beholder.[1]

She turned to her husband. "My heart bursts for the child. Look at him standing there, his tiny hand on her placid forehead. I can think of nothing sweeter."

"This is hardly sweet. The boy's first memories will be the death of his heart two weeks before Christmas." John Allan leaned back and took in the trefoil archways flanking the choir loft and tracery forms of the reticulated stained glass windows. An oaken cross was carved into the pulpit. Amber light lay across the massive organ pipes exposed in the front wall of the sanctuary, their somber noise vibrating the wooden pew on which he sat.

"If it were not for the caseworkers there would only be the boy. He is the lone family member. The Old St. John's Church has never felt so vacant."

"Death invites the company of fools and the greedy," John Allan said.

"Well our motives are of compassion."

I was standing on my tiptoes on a red velvet chair. The flames atop silver candelabras were prancing in the background from drafts seeping through the limestone walls. Helixes of smoke were spiraling toward the rafters. From the Allan's vantagepoint I am convinced they could see the glints of my tears falling into the casket, staining the heavy rouge of my mother's face. I was beside myself in grief.

"Poor child, orphaned in this cruel world at the age of two."

"Do not forget his sister. Rosalie is only a year old," John Allan remarked, straightening his tie. "Thank goodness she is too small to remember this tragic event *or* the loathsome profession of her parents. William Mackenzie and his wife have already adopted her, under blind eye I am sure."

Frances shifted in the pew and pulled the sleeves of her charcoal-gray wool dress to her wrists. Tissues were balled in one hand along with the article. "I would feel more sorrow if the Mackenzies were not a wealthy Richmond family as we are close to becoming. Rosalie will be brought up in the finest of schools and so will Edgar. Thank you for bringing him into the family on my behalf. When do we intend to adopt Edgar? Sooner than later, I hope. Poor, poor child."

"At the moment he has matured into an upstanding citizen of Richmond and is worthy of our good name. Until this time, the boy's upbringing will be my consuming passion. I have given my word to his grandfather."

"You are so rigid."

Ignoring his wife, John Allan remained face forward in his aisle seat, arms crossed.

Frances hooked one of them. "Edgar's older brother Henry is three and already living with his grandfather. General David Poe and his kind wife will provide the best of homes, but alas not the wealthiest. It's a shame that the daughter-in-law of the great Revolutionary War vetern is lying cold in her coffin, nary a flower to accompany her to the grave."

"Or perhaps it is because Eliza Poe is a disgrace to the proud family, especially after she led General Poe's son off the road of prosperity."

"Money. Wealth. Is that all you can think of at a time like this? Sacrilege, John. How can you speak of the destitute mother of three young children while she is stiff before us? God have mercy on your soul."

"All I am saying is that General Poe wanted more for his son David than gallivanting around America and Europe acting in third-rate theatrical companies with a commoner. Eliza's last performance was at the Monumental Church. Can you believe such an ... an act in a church?" John shook his head. "Painting the face, dressing in scanty clothes, and practicing the so called arts is not a respectable profession."

"You are nothing but strong headed. I swear if they opened your head they would find an anvil inside."

A caseworker glanced back toward the whispering commotion and frowned.

John kept looking forward, jaw muscles popping. Out the side of his mouth, he said, "It is not your place to disrespect, woman."

Frances sighed. She knew her place in his life and it was the size of a postage stamp. "Forgive me, but despite common thinking, poets and playwrights are talen—"

"'Poets and playwrights,'" John interjected, nostrils flaring. "There are no forthright people in the arts. Period."

"And what is Eliza Poe's crime? That of trying to raise her children the best way she knew how? Trying to make a living and then dying of anxiety and exhaustion during the southern leg of her theatrical tour?"

"The crime of this English actress was marrying David Poe, Junior—a promising Baltimore law student—and beguiling him to cast aside an upright profession to join her on stage. It drove the man mad." John backhanded a hymnal slotted in the pew and the clatter was smothered by the music. "Why do you think David Poe deserted his family and died of a drunken stupor a few days ago? The arts made him do it. There is no greater crime than disrespect for profession, self, and family, in that order."

Using both hands, I helped myself down from the velvety chair on which I stood. I stared out into the empty church pews and John Allan motioned me.

The organ pipes stopped reverberating and a great silence blanketed the sanctuary. With a flip of his tails, the organist was gone behind a carved door.

For an instant I remained still, a gothic portrait of a toddler in a black coat, knickers, ruffled shirt, and white knee socks. My hair was dark curls. There was a pout on my lips and puffiness around my eyes. I knuckled away the endless tears.

John Allan waved again and a bonnet-wearing caseworker on the front pew compelled me down from the platform.

I stepped off the chair and just stood there for what felt like hours. Chest slumping, my inner reluctance finally gave in to sensibilities. I walked forward, the shiny buckles on my shoes gleaming under the candlelight as I slowly descended the limestone steps. My footfalls echoed off the walls.

Upon stopping next to John Allan I took to surveying my shoe buckles, hands in pockets. John Allan placed a finger under my chin and forced my gaze upward. "Today you begin your new life, Edgar Poe. Today you come to live with me."

1822 - Age 13

The Joseph H. Clarke Academy was abuzz in the prattle of children on their first day of class. Hard-soled shoes were clopping down the hallway that bifurcated the boys' classroom from the girls'. Books were strapped over shoulders and knocking against the walls. Ponytails were being tugged and arms pinched.

Lost and alone in a sea of strange faces, I made my way down the hallway of the private school. Starting a new school was never easy, especially being friendless, and I had done it countless times. I tried the door to the girls' classroom and quickly changed direction amid a host of giggles. Before entering the open door across the hall, I took a quick glance inside to ensure no further embarrassments awaited me. Boys, all mean-faced boys awaited me, their uniforms in various states of neatness.

Stopping at the doorjamb, I tried in vain to press down my side-parted hair. Long curls made the strands useless to flatten. I was a ball of nerves as I took a deep breath and entered the classroom, expecting the other boys to pause and stare at the new student. Much to my relief this was not the case.

The boys, many extending their summer friendships, continued on with their laughing and paper wad fights. Heads bobbed and ducked.

Scanning the classroom I saw a bank of windows lining the wall opposite the hallway and then a vacant desk. Seemingly unnoticed, I slumped into an empty seat in the back, cognizant that I did not quite fit in, and knowing it was more than my recent years spent in England. I was having difficulty placing it. Maybe the feelings arose from the boys' mannerisms, the way they held themselves even when cutting up, the inflections in their voices. I wondered if the difference stemmed from old money versus John Allan's attempts at self-made wealth.

A sudden grating of metal against the slate board made us cringe as the auditory chill wafted over our desks. At the front of the room stood a block of a lady, her dress the color of a winter sky. She was gripping the wood shaft of a pointer, the far end whittled to a sharp point.

"Edwina Scarsdale. *Miss* Scarsdale to you boys. I am your substitute proctor in place of Mister Jim Clarke who has taken ill. Rest assured that although I am only your substitute teacher, I have been granted full supervisory and disciplinary authority."

Neck craning toward the front of the room, I noticed Miss Scarsdale's hair was pulled off her wavy forehead. Reading spectacles were perched on the end of her nose that bore a striking resemblance to the pointer's end. She was pacing in front of the classroom, slapping the shaft in her palm.

"You are here to learn and pay the utmost attention. This includes outside of class where you will have numerous assignments to complete at nights and on the weekends. And I, in turn, am here to teach you the fine arts of math and science that this institution is founded upon."

"It's an institution, all right," I whispered in the back. A section of boys erupted in laughter.

"Silence!" The class fell tomb quiet. A breeze whispered through the open windows. Miss Scarsdale stopped her pacing, orbs ready to pop from her head. She briefly searched for the offender, then said, "Capital punishment is what this classroom will thrive on ... what I thrive on!" She flung toward us and whacked the pointer across a desk. *Thwack!* At once we all leaned back in our seats. "You, in the front row, what's your name?"

For a moment there was no response and I thought the fellow had been stabbed. "Uh, Robert St-St-St-Stanard."

"Let me tell you something, 'Uh, Robert St-St-St-Stanard,' slouching is not allowed in my classroom and neither are splayed legs. Now sit up and do not let me catch you slipping into the throws of immorality again."

From the back came: "But this is an all boys classroom. What does it matter?"

All heads spun to glimpse the brave soul who would dare talk out a second time against Edwina the Terrible.

Emboldened by my earlier statement, I found that I was gaining favor among strangers. "Way I see it, us boys should be able to sit however we want ... on our heads if we deem fit, just as long as we learn."

"Insolence!" A great fervor overcame Miss Scarsdale and the pointer snapped in half as though a twig. The chords in her neck were strumming. She waddled up the aisle, spilling papers onto the floor and splashing indigo liquid from inkbottles. Before I could move, a splintered edge of the pointer was at the small of my throat where my collar lay open. "What is your name, boy?"

My head was pressed to the back wall, shoulders molded into the seat. If I were to move an inch I would be impaled. It was difficult to speak. "Name ... Edgar ... Allan Poe."

"Ah yes, the middle child of the impoverished *actress* who was taken in by the Allans. Your foster family has been in Europe for the past five years, recently back in America. I saw your profile in the roster. Is that what they taught you in merry ole England, to think you are special?"

"No, just ... to be reasonable," I said with a rasp.

"Then you must have decided on a *reasonable* profession to suit you and the good name of your foster family. Why not tell the class?"

"I have only one desire ... that is to become America's greatest poet."

"America's greatest poet. Pha-tosh! Is that what they taught you in England? Poetry? Poetry in America has its place on outhouse walls, but not among respectable society."

The classroom giggled at this, yet the jagged pointer did not leave my throat. I wanted to swallow, but thought better. "Poetry can be the ... language of love or the specter of death. It is one of our greatest art forms."

"What do you know about art, boy? Poetry is nothing but a tool for iniquity and so are your outbursts. Now fasten up your collar and do not ever let me see as much as one button undone or you will be expelled, at which juncture you will have plenty of time to write your poetry."

Miss Edwina Scarsdale turned to address the rest of the class that was facing the back of the room. She fanned the splintered pointer. "And that applies to all of you. This class shall be one of civility, respect, and learning. Is that understood?"

"Yes, Miss Scarsdale," came the response in unison.

"Disrespect will not be tolerated."

The substitute schoolmarm made her way back up the aisle, knocking desks aside with her hips and sending quills floating about the room. When she barreled past Robert Stanard, he noticed that the ties of her dress had been dipped in ink.

When he looked back, I flashed him a wry smile while massaging my neck.

The first day of class at the Joseph H. Clarke Academy passed slowly. The constant stares of Miss Scarsdale did not help matters. Many congratulatory notes were given to me that day for standing up to her. From their tone, I had become an instant hero.

When the school bell finally rang from its whitewashed belfry at half past three, we hurried from the stifling room, which had fallen prey to the Richmond heat. I was the last to leave, but not before a few handshakes and pats on the back. Outside the door I was met by a group of boys with stern faces; the apparent leader, a freckled-faced kid with fiery hair, stepped to the forefront. He crossed his arms. "Name's Martin Reynolds. I'm the head of our class, got that? Don't care much for you trying to show me up, Orphan Boy."

"Not trying to show up anyone," I responded. "Just trying to put Scarsdale in her place."

"That's my job. What do you say I put *you* in your place?" Martin balled his fists.

The group of boys effaced into a circle. "Get 'im, Martin!" someone yelled. "Show him you're the boss!" screamed another. "Do 'im up right!"

I dropped my books and threw up my palms in defense. "Let's not start trouble."

He circled toward me. "Wha-wha. The poet is a lover not a fighter. Imagine that. Seems you have already started enough trouble in our classroom, Orphie. Are women the only people you stand up to?"

Backing up, I felt hands push me back into the middle of the circle. I braced for the first blow to land in my midsection, but instead I caught a glancing fist across my lip.

From somewhere in the ring of shouting boys Robert Stanard had approached Martin and shoved him into the wall just as he was swinging. "Let him be, Ma-Ma-Martin," Robert said, "or I will tell everyone the sordid details of when I found you this summer."

"You got nothing on me."

"Really?" Robert faced those standing around. "I found Martin here rolling around in the hay with a servant's daughter. He loves the black-n-white swirl!"

Martin was prepared to start another fight at this moment, but then heard jeering laughter rising up from the circle that was expanding with more onlookers by the second. Children of the aristocracy of Richmond were to have no social interaction with commoners, let alone a romance with household servants.

Burnt red was rising from under Martin's chin. His face and hair looked aflame. Robert began a new saying that spread around the ring and soon became a chant. "Martin gets ebony lovin'. Martin gets ebony lovin'."

The enraged boy spun back toward his former supporters in disbelief, then pushed his way past Robert. "St-St-St-Stuttering Stanard."

The circle disbanded as the chanting followed Martin in an echo down the hall. I extended my hand and Robert shook it. "Thanks. I owe you one."

"Consider us even. I owed you one for dipping Scarsdale's ties in the inkwell." While I gathered my books off the floor, Robert asked, "I know you are new. How about coming over to my house this afternoon? I would love to hear about Europe. Never been out of Richmond."

We made our way out of the schoolhouse and down a grassy embankment fronted by a gravel road, its surface pocked by a thousand horseshoes.

"You could have beat Martin," Robert was saying. "You are bigger than he is ... stronger. I can tell." When Robert looked over, I was unbuttoning my collar. Flecks of blood marred its flat whiteness and my upper lip was swelling.

"In my training, only little people fight with their hands. The written word is a much better weapon."

"How did you get your muscles?"

"John Allan, my foster father, makes me work on his land."

"I guessed as much given how callused your hand was when I shook it." Robert scratched his head. "So what about England? Is it all tea and crumpets and haunted castles, like they say?"

"Much different than here. The buildings are hundreds of years old. Things are more settled ... an established government. Lots of tradition."

Robert slung his books over his back and I followed suit as we began walking on the shoulder of the road.

"John Allan had business doings there. When I was a small boy we moved. I attended Misses Dubourg School, which was not an all-girls establishment by the way, and later the Manor House School at Stoke Newington." I could tell from his blank expression that

Robert had never heard of them. "The training there is based more in the arts. I love them, I must confess."

"I'm not a big reader, but my mother is. Have to warn you about her," Robert qualified, "she is not right in the head." He made loops at his temples. "Crazy."

"Hey, I think the same of John Allan some times." I made a deep voice. "He has convictions about turning me into an a high society businessman. But Ma, I mean Frances Allan, is dear to me."

"I am serious about my mother. They wanted to lock her away but Dad wouldn't allow it. They chain people up in institutions, make them wallow in filth."

"So I've heard."

"Mother is outside on Monday afternoons tending her flower garden or I would never bring you over."

A shiny carriage passed us, wheels kicking up dust. We hacked and spat before moving off the dirt road to a skirting field. The brazen sun was merciless, but we didn't care. We were having so much fun chatting.

Robert told me he only stuttered at times of stress and I told him I only dipped schoolmarm's dress ties in ink at times of having a skewer at my throat as we made our way across the large field, weeds and wildflowers rasping against our legs. From afar we must have given the appearance of being afloat, ghostly schoolboy warriors dressed in black uniforms hovering across a sizeable canvass on which the artisan had spilled paint.

"In England I read much of Jane Austen, a local novelist. She is a remarkable writer who can really get the blood flowing if you know what I mean. Hopefully she will get proper recognition over here. She died a few years back."

Robert shrugged. It was apparent he was not a reader. Under a copse of oak trees he spied a mulberry bush slouching over a hump of rounded stones. We angled over and were soon standing in front of it.

"It's an Indian burial ground," I said on inspection. "Bet these berries are full of *blood* sucked up from the ground below."

"Vulgar!" He plucked off a handful of fruit and gave it to me. "Drink of the Injun blood."

I made a gurgle sound as the berries went down and then wiped away the excess juice with the back of my hand.

"Sick!"

We laughed again over Martin's new nickname while Robert snatched off a handful for himself. On we went, talking and joking as if we had known each other our entire lives, tossing mulberries into the air and catching them in our mouths.

The weeds began thinning and we came upon a cobblestone avenue lined with magnificent houses etched in gingerbread. "Tares mine," Robert spluttered through his mouthful of berries, dark liquid dripping from his lips. "Right on the snorner."

A horse-drawn cart stacked with hay bails passed and I focused on a beautiful home rising from the northwest corner. A turret jutted up amongst its varied rooflines and a round stained-glass window was set in the center apex of the highest gable, watching over the thoroughfare. A large expanse of open windows in the upper regions of the home was covered by black sections of material soughing in the breeze.

"Mother's room," Robert confessed. "She and Dad have not slept in the same bed for years. Do not tell anyone, Dad being a prominent judge and all."

We darted across the street and jumped a hedgerow guarding the front yard, then skipped alternate steps leading up to the front porch that formed an apron below the turret and expanse of upper windows. Robert flung the screen door open and held it for me. As I passed, Robert bunched his neck and puffed his cheeks in mocking fashion of Miss Scarsdale. "America's greatest poet. Pha-tosh! What do you know about art, boy?"

Walking through the doorway I did my own impression while pinching my nose to a point. "Poetry in America has its place on outhouse walls, but not among respectable society." I offered a thin smile, which turned wide upon noticing a carafe of tea surrounded by wedges of cornbread on china plates sitting on doilies. The tea was the darkest I had ever seen, and this was remarkable given my time in England. "Art is everywhere," I commented. "Notice the tea and surrounding cornbread make a beautiful sunflower."

"You are artsy, my friend. Even with Mom's strange ideas floating in her head she has not lost her touch in the kitchen."

I nodded that I understood.

"I will get some ice. Father is off pounding the gavel in court. Have a seat." Robert pointed to an arched backed chair with scroll arms in the den.

I tossed my bundle of texts onto a braided rug in front of the chair and collapsed into it. The first day in my new school had been exhausting and my lip felt as though it was ready to burst. After watching Robert disappear into another realm of the cavernous home, I began studying my surroundings, which were nicely appointed in silken tapestries and handcrafted moldings.

"She always has a snack waiting for me," Robert yelled back, head poking from the icebox.

Before I could respond, I heard the rustle of fabric and glimpsed a dress of cascading material coming down the stairway. In it was a sinewy woman. Her body was lost in the chiffon folds, which had splotchy areas. Her makeup was garish and sloppy, as though applied in a speed contest.

I stood to greet her, but she spoke first.

"Hello, young man. Jane Stanard. You can call me Helen. I feel like *Helen* today." Her eyes got big. "Helen of Troy." She pushed her hair on top of her head and cocked her shoulder. "See the resemblance?"

I was taken aback by her appearance. I could tell in the light streaming in from the window behind me that the splotches on her dress were stains. Her eyeliner flared off in curlicues. Powder was indiscriminately applied to her face and a clownlike ring of lipstick encircled her mouth. A wilted hyacinth was stuck in her hair. The smell of fragrance was about her, but doing a poor job at disguising her need for a bath. "H-Helen is a nice name." Now I was the one stuttering.

"Do *you* have a name?"

"Yes, yes, of course. Edgar Allan Poe. Pleasure to make your acquaintance."

"Sit," Jane ordered, taking her place in a velvety chair across from me. "Must be Robert's friend."

"We met at school today."

"Not a very good one if he has yet to offer you sweetened cornbread." Her milky arm reached over, took one of the plates, and handed it to me. "What happened to your lip?"

"Wish I could say I caught it in a cider press."

Jane snickered. "Substitute apples next time. Less painful and better tasting."

After finishing a healthy bite of cornbread, I noticed Jane was clutching a leather-bound book, a lace swatch acting as her marker. There was an odd embossing on the cover. "What are you reading? If I may be so bold."

"*Frankenstein.* I cannot put it down, nor sleep, nor eat. Have you heard of this book?" Jane displayed suspicions pertaining to the reading habits of a young man her son's age.

I surprised her. "Of course. What a magnificent novel! The way Doctor Frankenstein brings the monster to life is terrifying. I have never read such horror! His actions are all the scarier because our doctors are using galvanic batteries to shock people into the living. I believe the story could really happen. People want the book banned. The Church calls it heresy. They say women are frightened to crack the cover."

"Not me! I love this book. The horror of the creation is only superceded by the way the creature is treated by mankind," Jane said, leaning close. Her breath was rancid and I did everything in my power to keep from flinching. "But the story is truly a *love* story, one of pity for those different in our society. You know ... people in this community say I'm different. Can you believe it?"

I choked on my next bite. "No, Missus Stanard—"

"Helen!"

"—I mean Helen ... and I could not agree more," I said, clearing my throat and immediately qualifying, "with your interpretation of the story that is."

Jane swung over, grabbed the carafe, and poured. "Please."

I received the cup and saucer in hand and took a drink to wash down the cornbread. "Uh!" I spluttered. "That's not tea!"

"Of course not, silly boy. It is coffee." She poured her own cup and her shaking hand caused much of it to spill onto her dress, growing the population of stains.

"Who would have cold coffee sitting—" I cut myself off, seeing an intense look overcoming Jane. I positively identified the stains on her dress and pretended to drink the tepid liquid as if I enjoyed it. Unlike most young men my age, I had a fondness for coffee but not in this setting or at this temperature. "Very nice, I mean." I sat the cup and saucer down.

"Coffee is the nectar of the gods, the Grecian gods." Jane's head flittered as she glanced around the den, making sure no one was around. "Edgar, you are the first person to clarify Mary Shelley's wisdom in *Frankenstein*. In my estimation people are missing a wonderful love story through the veil of terror."

"Exactly. The gothic mode of literature is one of the most effective ways to tell a story. I am seeing this more and more. Who would have guessed a female writer of our day would show us this so clearly?"

"Me, for one," Jane offered. "Women writers have a much more difficult time getting published than men, although I believe them to be better storytellers since they are in touch with their emotions. It speaks to our day and the inequities toward women. They want us to be statues." Jane cupped hands at her mouth (crimson surrounded by alabaster) and whispered. "They are out to get me."

"Who?"

"Society at large. Do not tell my husband, but someday I wish to become a free woman, to be able to vote and dress as I please, to burn my corset and drown my sorrows. How about you?"

"No corsets of my own to burn, but I hope to become a poet."

"What a perfect profession for you! Your last name contains three of the four letters, in order!"

"To be honest, I have never thought of it that way, Helen. But I like it thoroughly."

"And I like you thoroughly. Do visit me oft—"

"Mother!" came the shout down the corridor. "What are you doing?"

"What I am doing is having a fascinating conversation with your friend. Finished gardening early." Jane Stanard swiveled back toward me and said in a whisper, "My wishes regarding freedom are our *secret*, right?"

"Right, Helen."

With that affirmation Jane rose and took me by surprise when she extended the back of her hand.

Feeling I had no other choice I kissed it, which sent shivers through me. Random fingernails were painted and a quarter inch of dirt was under the others.

"Mother! Please!" Robert cried in embarrassment.

Jane snatched up her cup of coffee. "I will leave you now, Edgar Allan the Poet Poe. You are quite the Don Juan. And remember, never stop writing. It is the most honorable profession of the arts."

"Thank you."

While Jane headed back up the stairs, Robert appeared from the shadows holding a chunk of jagged ice hacked from a block that was now melting slowly on the kitchen table.

"Forget it," I said, putting my hand over the carafe, "unless you enjoy iced coffee."

Robert gave off a hearty laugh and spoke in a low voice. "I am sorry about my mother. She means well." He made loops at the sides of his head again.

I finished off my cornbread before responding. "I rather enjoyed her company. She is the only adult who has ever encouraged my writing." With that I noticed strands of hair appear from an angled wall leading up the stairs and a finger pressed to painted lips. "Our *secret*, Helen," I called out.

"Helen?" Robert asked. When he spun, she was no longer there.

A dark shadow suddenly overcame me. Before I could turn I heard: "Edgar! Are your chores finished yet? It is nearly high noon on a Saturday."

I glanced up from my stool near the horse's hindquarters and shielded my eyes from the glaring sun. Lye soap was dripping from the crook of my arm next to my rolled up sleeve. A heavy brush was in my hand that I had just taken from a bucket. My arm was sore. "Almost, sir. This is the last of the horses. I will be finished right away, sir."

John Allan stepped inside the gate and walked toward me. He stopped at the horse and smoothed his hand across the animal's coat. "This shall never do. Look at these horses."

"What will never do? I cleaned them just as you taught me. I even rubbed their hooves and the back of their legs."

"How can we impress local businessmen if you do a lackluster job. Businessmen bring business contacts, and business contacts bring financial gain. One feeds the other, Edgar. And once our family has financial gain then we shall be able to afford servants to do this job and to make a roof over our stables. Then you can spend your time becoming a young man of education and honour; a young man who is worthy of my name."

I stood with anticipation. "Is that when you will adopt me as your own?"

"Of course, Edgar. I am a man of my word."

"You have been promising me for over a decade."

He suddenly kicked the bucket over that was next to the stool, sending soapy water coursing over my boots and sloshing up my pant legs. The horse neighed and nearly bucked. "These coats have to *shine*. They need a glossy sheen to be presentable enough for our family to take into town. Wash them all again and do not use dirty water this time."

"But the sun is growing oppressive. Can I finish them first thing to-morrow morning?"

"Do it now, Edgar. Frances and I will be having dinner with some of my associates tonight, and to-morrow morning you shall be in church to repent for your reprobate attitude."

"What do you expect after all the work you make me do?"

"One more word out of you and you shall be cleaning out the stalls on your hands and knees. Now let these horses be a small lesson to you about public perception, Edgar. Society is not accepting of those who are less than presentable. As others see you, so you are."

John Allan spun and left me to my never-ending chores.

1824 - Age 15

I found myself gaining wide acceptance and many friends during my first year at the Joseph H. Clarke Academy. The embarrassment Robert caused Martin Reynolds to suffer on the first day of class silenced his fists, but not his mouth, which degraded me among the growing student population. So many wealthy children from Richmond began attending the school that a new addition had to be built on the west end of the schoolhouse.

Mr. Clarke, our rightful headmaster, returned in the fall. He was a genteel man, tolerant of open collars and slouching posture. Miss Scarsdale was never seen again. There were many rumors surrounding her whereabouts. One claimed she accepted a teaching position in New York or took a position bottling syrup in Maine, but the favorite rumor was the one I promulgated. I claimed I buried her alive in a coffin under the new addition where no one would notice the upturned earth, her only company for all eternity being the broken pointer that was digging into her fat rolls.

My classmates encouraged such tales by requesting even more of them. I often penned sentences or short verses that would inflict outbursts of laughter or terror in whomever was sitting next to me. I could think of no greater satisfaction than to get a reaction from my readers, good or bad. My snippets became so popular the boys would race to class to get a seat next to me. They began to collect them—trade them!

Out of class I began writing Jane Stanard and she answered my letters forthrightly. We developed a system whereby I would slip notes under the doilies upon which the cornbread or crumb cakes awaited on the afternoons Robert had me over. Jane Stanard ("Helen" as she required me to reference her at all times), in turn, deposited responses in the inside pocket of my uniform jacket that I would purposely leave hanging over the back of the scroll armchair in the den. The exchanges were made while Robert was in the kitchen or looking out the window. He finally became more at ease with his mother's presence when I was around after many assurances on my part.

Helen and I reasoned (as our letters increased in length and intensity) that correspondence between a grown woman and a teenager was too risky a venture for either of us. Our age difference, however, was not a barrier to a meeting of the minds. We both knew the other was the one true person we could confide in, which fostered a certainty that our thoughts on women's rights and proper modes of literature had to remain confidential. Confessions in the early nineteenth century were only deemed proper by respectable society when given to a priest behind the closed door of a confessional or while kneeling on a Baptist altar.

And what confessions they were from Helen! She went into detail about which undergarments she wanted to burn or place in the meat grinder. They constrained her no differently than her domineering husband. I blushed when I read the text. "Wire mesh and lacey torture," she called them. If Robert had known about our *secret*, his friendship would have been lost forever.

Helen praised my writing endeavors to no end. Edgar Allan the Poet Poe at first began sending her snippets of prose, which soon turned into whole verses. She was quick to point out my strengths in rhythm and weaknesses in couplets. Because I knew she loved *Frankenstein*, I sent her ideas for gothic horror tales where readers would confront their greatest fears and she gushed over them. She wrote me about the ruminations of my tale *The Premature Burial* (thanks to Edwina Scarsdale). "It nearly made the skin crawl off my bones!"

Helen claimed I could someday equal the writing of Shelley if I worked hard. Of course I did not believe her, but her words of encouragement propelled me toward succinctness of text and clarity of thought. Character generation in my tales began to develop at this young age and my couplets in poetry eventually began to snap like a John Allan bullwhip.

I simply could not get enough of her thoughts and intellectualism.

From the moment we first met I had a connection to Jane Stanard. She exuded an inner beauty under the layers of garish face paint. I wondered if the misapplication was on purpose, done for spite against yet another male imposition on female looks.

We penned a great number of letters to each other during that first year of our acquaintance. In the final waning months Helen's thoughts grew more radical and she seemed to be withdrawing into her own world—a world of seclusion and fears. Robert told me how she was becoming more crazed, but I did not need this update for it was readily apparent from her handwriting, which had degraded into nothing more legible than squiggles. For stretches her correspondence stopped altogether.

I vowed not to stop writing her. Helen needed my words of encouragement as time went on just as much as I needed hers on the afternoon we first met.

Just before the school year's end, Mr. Clarke announced he was heading to Europe. The place was to be called the William Burke School, making reference to its incoming headmaster. The students asked me to deliver the farewell ode. I took this as the highest of compliments and delivered in front of the class eight lines of perfect A-B poetry that I had worked on unceasingly. They garnered an enthusiastic round of applause and a standing ovation from Mr. Clarke who gave me the top grade in English.

Robert approached me the moment the last day of school was finished. Adventure was on his face. "Let's get out of here ... go for a swim in the James River. I am burning up."

"Anything to get this uniform off once and for all."

We hurried from the smothering room and raced each other down the long hallway splitting the boys' and girls' classrooms. Outside the early June day was sunnier and brighter than any we could remember. A band of girls had already taken to playing jump rope and one let off a shrill cry at the opposite end of the schoolhouse.

"That was crotchety Miss Scarsdale," I yelled over my shoulder to Robert as we ran. "She wants out of her coffin!"

"That is disgusting!"

"I heard her beating on the lid. She's coming to get you."

On a dead sprint we scampered across the dusty road and through the field we trotted in every day after school. The berry bounty was starting anew. We thwarted hills and rocky dells teeming with the sounds of summer come alive. I led the entire way and Robert, who considered himself an above average athlete, was having difficulty keeping pace.

"Last one to Ludlam's Wharf is a rotten corpse!" I yelled.

"Watch out for Injuns!"

"They're mad because we drank their blood."

Soon we came upon a cluster of tall reeds growing from a marshland, its water level greatly diminished from when the James River swelled in the springtime. A rush of water could be heard, but not seen from our position.

Skirting carefully through prickly thistles and down an embankment, we came upon the base of Mayo's Bridge, its archway supports plunging deep into the James River. A young boy in overalls had a boat moored to the one nearest the shore of the wharf and was fishing off the stern.

"Any luck?" Robert asked.

"Nope. But goin' to git me a catfish before the day is through."

The academic cares of the world were peeling off us in layers, as were our clothes. My jacket was lost somewhere between the schoolhouse and the wharf. I tore most of the buttons from my white shirt while stripping it off.

"We should've invited some girls," Robert exclaimed, tossing a boot into the brambles. An instant later it came flying back and clunked him square in the head. "Ouch! What the—" Robert spun to see who the perpetrator was and his throat immediately went into stutter mode. "Ma-Ma-"

"Well, well, well, America's greatest poet and the son of Lady Loony Bird." From the underbrush emerged Martin Reynolds and a score of snarling boys. Martin's cheeks were flush from running, making his face one giant freckle.

"H-How did you fi-fi-find us?" Robert asked, sidling toward the river.

"I happened to overhear you at school. Sounded like a party and we decided to join you."

I was going the opposite direction of Robert and found myself in front of Martin. "We do not like trouble."

"How would you like my fist in your face?" This made the group of boys chuckle as they moved closer.

"You know I will not fight you. Fighting is for the delusional."

"Then fight your friend's mom. She's nuttier than squirrels."

Robert spoke out from behind me. "You can take him. Remember, Martin gets ebony lovin'."

"You're next, Stanard." Mere inches apart, Martin locked eyes with me and stuck his finger in my bare chest. "I will pummel you this time whether you fight me or not." He drew back his fist.

"Wait, wait," I said, thinking fast, "I have a much better idea: I will wager that I can swim the James from right here, Ludlam's Wharf, south down toward Chesterfield ... to the old post office."

Robert spoke up. "You joking? That has to be *three* miles!"

"What do you say?" I asked Martin. "If I make it without help, you never bother Robert and me again. And if I fail to make it to the old post office, you can pummel me without resistance and I will give you the most prized horse from my father's stable."

"This is a false bet. His father will never give him the horse," one of the boys said.

"I will let the horse out in the night. I will not need John Allan's blessing."

Martin thought for a moment. "Not good enough, Orphie."

"What do you mean? That horse is worth a hundred dollars, maybe more."

"The horse is fine, but I want you to swim from Ludlam's Wharf to Warwick Bar."

"You're crazy!" Robert blurted. "That's six miles or more. Plus it's upstream the entire way!"

Eyes still locked with mine, Martin said, "That is the bet, take it or leave it."

"I accept!" I began prying off my boots while Robert pleaded with me to forget it, to come to my senses. "No. It is the only way to truly be free of Martin and his thugs."

By the time I had my boots and stockings off, pant legs rolled over my knees, Martin had waded out, untied the fishing boat, and pulled it on shore. He pushed the boy who was fishing into the water. "To make sure there is no cheating, Orphie, me and some of my boys will follow you in this boat."

"I'm going too," Robert said.

"Fine, but not in my boat."

Before Martin could utter another word, I splashed into the water and began swimming upstream away from the archways; deltoids pumping rhythmically in the sun-flecked waters.

A handful of boys, including Martin, piled into the boat and began rowing after me while Robert gave chase along the shoreline.

Immediately those rowing the boat recognized the strong tide and strength of the James River. Stroke after stroke, yard after yard, they struggled after me in the hot June sun, complaining to Martin as they went. For miles we passed shipping yards and boys in striped pantaloons and dented straw hats fishing from the shore. Occasionally there were lavish southern mansions and women strolling beneath parasols to which Robert offered many apologies on his abrupt passing along the water's edge.

The river was clear at first, but within the first mile I came upon a rocky outcropping. Water bubbled and frothed over boulders and through crevices, which forced me to swim diagonally instead of straight.

"Stable boy! Fairy poet! Wimp! Orphie!" For hours I suffered indignities under the catcalls of Martin Reynolds and for hours Robert Stanard urged me onward from the rocky banks.

Tirelessly I outstretched my arms and kicked my legs, muscles rippling in the sunshine. The hard work John Allan had forced upon me in his stables was paying off. I was a thing of beauty and grace to watch and this angered Martin even more. I seldom paused to catch my breath because the eddying current would push me back.

The set of rowers in the boat had switched a number of times at this juncture, no set of boys being able to power the boat upstream for more than a mile.

"Not much longer, Poe," Robert called out. "Maybe a half mile! You are going do it. I just know it. You are going to make it! The bet is yours!"

"Shut up, St-St-St-Stanard," Martin barked from his seated position on the stern as the boat skirted portside around a tiny island splitting the middle of the river. These were the first words out of him apart from incomprehensible grumblings for the last two hundred yards.

"Martin gets ebony lovin'!" Robert yelled, his voice belabored and feet raw from exertion, but he exuded a certain confidence toward Martin from his safe position on the shore.

At this area of the James a number of people had stopped their tasks and were pointing at the mysterious figure cutting upstream through the waters. Robert had to climb an embankment to make it around them and for a moment lost sight of me.

Around a few more bends a hanging sign welcomed us to Warwick Bar. I was never so relieved as I slanted to the riverbank and slowly crawled out of the water. My joints and muscles were crying out. From a kneeling position I tried to stand. At first my legs appeared shaky, but the result was from stiffness caused by repetition.

The boat docked a number of seconds behind me.

I finally caught my breath. Within moments I was standing and strength returned to my legs. I flashed a smile at Martin Reynolds. He glared and quickly tramped his way up the embankment, refusing to stick around for congratulations. Perhaps he had become frightened of my display of physical strength. "Never again, Martin!" I shouted in his retreat. "Never again can you or any of your crew bother Robert or me. That was the bet. It had better be gospel in your book."

He stormed off, never speaking to us.

Gasping, Robert hurried over to my side. "That ... was amazing! I have never ... seen such a feat ... in my entire life and I doubt I ever ... will again. Unbelievable! Do you want me to fetch a carriage ... to take you back?"

"I'm fine," I said, slicking my hair. "Let's walk back to Richmond."

"You sure?"

"All the work my father makes me do in his stables has proven good for something," I regretted, swinging my arm around Robert, "but I am worried about you my good fellow."

"No problems with me."

"Your feet are cut and bleeding."

"Like new I am," Robert claimed. He never wanted to act weak around me, especially after this day.

We made our way back into town, Robert treading gingerly.

"I have been meaning to ask you, how is your mother these days? She has not been writing me of late to encourage my poetry. She was clockwork for a while. Oft at night I see her standing at her bedroom window, not moving, watching Nineteenth Street, a lamp in her hand."

"How embarrassing. Father cannot get her to stop. She has been taking a turn for the worse. Doctors visit the house almost daily. She only reads *Frankenstein* as though it were the Bible. The cover is worn thin she has read it so many times."

"I am sorry to hear that. Wish her my very best and let her know that Edgar Allan the Poet Poe has managed to keep his lips out of cider presses lately."

Robert was not sure what I meant, but promised to follow my instructions. We had trod a few miles back in the other direction when Robert said, "You are strong like your grandfather, General David Poe, comrade in arms with General Lafayette."

"Thanks, but he was never actually a general, only a major. People just refer to my grandfather as a general. My brother Henry is living with him in Baltimore."

"By the way, I heard that Byron died fighting in the Turko-Greek War."

I turned, a troubled look on my face, yet no tiredness. "We live in a world where our poets fight our wars and our warriors write our poems."

Deep into the summer I was on my way to visit Robert and to deliver a fresh poem to Jane Stanard when I heard a great commotion coming from the home. I rounded a bend and peered around a copse of trees. The front yard was a war zone the likes of which I never witnessed.

Upon hearing the third or fourth scream, I slowly took the walkway up to the porch. Confusion was about me.

Glass littered the ground and the inclined roof. I stepped over a broken footstool and a shattered makeup kit, and then noticed a corset rack bobbing from a feathery conifer. The black material normally covering the windows was tattered and flapping from what used to be Jane's bedroom windows. Crimson stains marred the whitewashed surrounds and I wondered if it was blood or lip paint.

In my hand was a roll of parchment tied by a scarlet ribbon as I took the steps leading up to the porch. Robert was standing in wait for me and answered the front door with the most sullen of looks across his pallid face. "Mother keeps throwing things out her bedroom window," he said without a greeting. "Even Father cannot stop it."

"Please let me see her. I have written a poem. Should bring her into good spirits and ease her mind."

"Not a chance." Robert glanced behind him as if expecting a phantasm and quickly turned back. He was pulling at his sideburns. "It's not safe!"

From the upper regions of the house an unearthly caterwaul rang out, followed by words of comprehension. "Freedom I tell you all ... freedom from oppression! Prometheus cannot vote and neither can I, you bunch of cretins!"

I jumped next to the doorjamb when an oil lamp came spinning out of the sky and crashed onto the sidewalk in an explosion of glass and amber liquid.

"Doctors treat women less than dogs in this society. They cut my wrists! *Butchers!*"

"I beg you to leave," Robert implored, tear streaking his cheek. He was having trouble breathing though not from physical exertion. "Go and do not return until you have received news from me. Physicians are on their way to apply more sedative and give a fresh round of bloodletting. They say they have identified the vein that helps the mind and are going to drain it of the tainted blood."

I swallowed hard, afraid for Robert, but more afraid for Mrs. Stanard, my Helen. "Tell your mother I came to talk literature and give her this." I handed over the roll of parchment. "The poem is called *To Helen*. Penned by my own hand. If she cannot read it in her state, kindly speak it aloud to her."

From above: "MEN!"

Robert pushed me away and shut the door to a crack. "You *must* go! Wait to hear from me."

"My prayers are with you and your mother." The carved front door snicked closed and I slumped onto the wooden planks lining the porch. In the yard a porcelain washbasin thumped onto the lawn upside down and cracked open like a hatching egg. Thereafter a leather boot with raised heel tumbled from above and got snagged in the conifer near the corset rack, its laces holding onto the end of a bough for a moment before it fell to the ground.

From inside I heard Robert trudging up the steps near the den and afterwards a loud knocking. "Mother, it is I, Robert. My friend Edgar Allan Poe has written a poem for you. If I may, I will read it. He titled it *To Helen*."

Suddenly the yelling stopped in the upper bedroom and items stopped flying out the windows.

A gash of sunshine opened across my body as I listened on the porch to my own words issuing from the broken windows. John Allan had taught me that men of aristocracy never show their emotions in public; nevertheless, my eyes became welling pools of sorrow.

> Helen, thy beauty is to me
> Like those Nicean barks of yore,
> That gently, o'er a perfumed sea,
> The weary, way-worn wanderer bore
> To his own native shore.
> On desperate seas long wont to roam,
> Thy hyacinth hair, thy classic face,
> Thy Naiad airs have brought me home
> To thy glory that was Greece,
> And the grandeur that was Rome.
> Lo! in yon brilliant window-niche
> How statue-like I see thee stand,
> The agate lamp within thy hand!
> Ah, Psyche, from the regions which
> *Are the Holy-Land!*[2]

All I could hear was sobbing, then the clocking of the physicians' boots up the sidewalk. They walked in cadence as if off to battle. Their medicine bags were held in the same arm under determined faces. The regiment stepped over me on their way inside. I was forced to leave when I heard screams from above once again and the physicians' orders to string Helen to the bedpost.

I understood on this day the power of my prose and I vowed to never forsake it. In September the new school year began and Jane Stanard died of congestion of the brain nearly a year after we first met.

Weeks thereafter I visited her grave in remorse. Some days I did not even invite Robert.

1825 - Age 16

The summer of 1825 was blistering in Richmond. I began the season as I had most others, tending horses in John Allan's stables—a hard job that comprised slopping the stalls, tanning saddles, washing hooves, brushing manes, saddling and finally riding the horses for daily exercise. I was told over and over that it would build character, build appreciation for the finer elements of life, and foster manhood at an early age.

Pha-tosh!

One particular June daybreak when the sky was transitioning from auburn to burnt orange, I was cranking a butter churn filled with fresh milk from the morning's delivery when I heard from behind, "My, what big muscles you have." I spun on the bedewed lawn and beheld a flaxen-haired girl who was close to my age, perhaps a year or two younger. I sprung to my feet, swiping my palms on my shirt, and kissed her outstretched hand. The scent of lilacs was about her.

"Sarah Elmira Royster, but you can call me by my middle name. And I take it you, sir, are Edgar Poe."

"At your service"

"With muscles like that, I am sure you can be of service to a woman, Mister Poe."

I blushed at this and found myself struggling to keep the conversation moving. Elmira's hair was glistening in the new light of day, her skin peaches and cream. "Not sure whether I have seen you around town," I lied. I *had* seen her many times and was taken by her natural beauty. Her Southern accent was as thick as the curdled milk beneath me and just as sweet.

"Well, you are about to see me a lot more, especially since we are new neighbors. I am starting upper school with you this fall." She paused.

In the awkward moment I smoothed the grass with my boot, clearing a path in the dew.

"What's a lady supposed to do with a man she has heard more about than seen?"

She called me a man, I thought as I scanned the emerald blades.

"You are a popular fellow, Mister Poe. Many female voices have told me of your poetry and of your astounding physical exploits. Rosalie Mackenzie informed me you swam seven miles yonder up the James River if you swam a yard."

"Ah, you have met my younger sister."

"She hinted you might be found here."

"My foster father will soon be moving us across the street from the Mackenzie's."

"Mercy. Already moving away from me?"

I smirked. "Do not take it personal. I look forward to being close to Rose, who is now in trouble for sending you here. She claims I am too withdrawn."

"Mercy me. I can assure you, I came on my own volition," Elmira said, taking my arm. "If anyone is in trouble, it looks like it's me from the looks of you. I approached Rosalie, not the opposite."

By this time I had forgotten about the morning's task and nearly fell backwards over the butter churn. Elmira held fast to my arm.

"How about breakfast? A woman needs her energy for the coming heat of day. George's Eatery serves a superb cup of coffee and raspberry cobbler that is scrumptious."

"How can I resist?"

We wasted no time in heading down the thoroughfare. The early bustle of Richmond, Virginia had yet to make a presence. We passed a feed store piled with stacks of grain and then a barbershop where a straight-edged razor was being stropped to a delicate edge. I wished there was more activity on the street so I could be seen strolling with Elmira. She was the kind of girl who could get a boy respect for months just from being seen conversing with him. I rolled down my sleeves and buttoned them at the wrists to make myself more presentable as I began talking of our common interest in coffee.

"Any man who loves coffee is a woman's man indeed," she commented. But we mostly spoke of nothingness apart from that. A haberdashery was sporting a sale on caps and derbies. In a corner of the storefront was a panached suit that made Elmira remark, "My, my, Joseph's coat of many of colors must have been excavated and brought to Richmond."

Among her many qualities, Elmira could make me laugh. In the glass reflection I secretively glanced at her and got my first good look. I found to no surprise that she was beyond pleasing in her saffron dress. It was apparent that the shapeliness was hers more than the tight drawstrings and formed wires snaking beneath the material.

Minutes later I held the door for Elmira and a bell announced our entrance into George's Eatery. The air was redolent with freshly ground coffee beans and baked goods. The marble-topped tables were empty and the man behind the counter indicated that we could take our pick.

Elmira angled over to a window seat. "Ya'll hurry back," she said.

I walked to the counter and ordered. "Two cups of coffee, fine sir. Cream in the young lady's, strong and black for me."

"You prefer your coffee like I prefer my servants, son."

The well-worn joke of the owner was lost on me while I tried to remember the cobbler Elmira favored. I struggled for a moment (which I am sure was not the first time a young man had forgotten something in Elmira's presence) as George retrieved a gooseneck bottle of cream from a small icebox behind the counter. I finally remembered and soon joined Elmira at the table holding a tray. "Two cups of steaming coffee, one raspberry cobbler for you and a biscuit topped with cinnamon and spice for me."

"That is darling precious, Mister Poe, cinnamon and spice and everything nice."

I sat down and blew on my coffee, a response failing me, before I took a cautious sip. Upon putting the mug on the tabletop, I remarked, "Coffee is heavenly."

"Like taking a bath on the inside. I love to take long hot baths with lots of suds. How 'bout you?"

Elmira's lips seemed to move in slow motion as she spoke and I had trouble keeping my eyes off them. Shaking my head, I took another mindless sip as I felt my cheeks glow.

"Good heavens, are you shy, Mister Poe?"

"Just quiet in the morning, that's all." I blamed it on the coffee. "This is very hot."

She reached across the table and brushed my palm. I tried not to flinch, to act as though every morning of my existence I meet a beautiful girl who snatches me away to a coffee-house and smells of lilacs and talks of taking long hot baths. But this was another's life, and when I was not working in my foster father's stables, I was writing poetry in a dark corner of the house and living up to my "withdrawn" moniker Rose had branded me with. My hand involuntarily retracted into my lap.

"You *are* shy, Mister Poe."

"Would you stop calling me that? It makes me sound old."

"And just how old are you?"

"Sixteen," I announced.

"Sweet sixteen. Sugar and spice and everything nice. I am fifteen and like older men."

"I'm not that *old*, so please, call me Edgar."

"I think I like Poe. Do you mind if I call you Poe?" Her smile was radiant.

I smiled back. "Sure, as long as there is no mister in front of it."

"Fine then. That is a beautiful ring on your finger, Poe," she said, noticing the elevated ring for the first time. "Excuse me for asking, but is it what they call a death ring?"

I took a deep breath and exhaled. "Yes. I keep a lock of my mother's hair in it. She died when I was two and my first memories are from her funeral."

Elmira grasped my hand firmly and this time I did not flinch away. "Rosalie tells me how you and her and Henry were orphaned at a young age. I am so sorry. Some things are unfathomable."

"She was adopted by the Mackenzies, as you know. My older brother Henry lives with my grandfather and I live with the Allans."

After taking a bite of cobbler, and commenting how she always ate around the edges first to save the middle for last, Elmira asked, "So you were all adopted by different families?"

My head slumped. From most people I had kept the dark secret, but the genteel Southern mannerisms of Elmira Royster had a way of opening me up. A part of me felt relieved by it. "John Allan has been unwilling to adopt me. Says I have to earn his name."

The blunt end of Elmira's spoon cracked the tabletop. "That's absurd. You are top of your class, write beautiful poetry, and can swim like a spawning salmon. What more does he want?"

"Wish I knew. I have tried to please him my entire life. I even use his surname without spite."

"He is unworthy of that honour in my estimation." Elmira took a sip of coffee. After she sat the mug down, she noticed flashes of pain and unwonted hurt about me. "Mercy, let's forget all this talk. How about taking a bite of your biscuit or else I may have to eat it too, and that would not be good because a woman must watch her figure," she said, running hands down her side.

I uttered the first words that came to my mouth: "I'll watch it for you," and in embarrassment partook. Chewing, I surveyed the walls on which were hung various paintings of hunt clubs. Men on horseback were dressed in red coats, holding flintlock rifles in one hand and reins in the other, bloodhounds sniffing at the ground.

"I understand Beethoven's *Ninth Symphony* has premiered in England after being first performed in Vienna," Elmira said. "Rumors have it that his music is so sensuous women swoon in its very presence. There is talk of some villages in Europe banning it. But I tell you this, if the Richmond Symphony Orchestra ever plays one of his concertos, I will be the first in line."

"Music is the most powerful of the arts, but words are a close second."

"So tell me about your poetry. I want to read every word."

"Maybe," I said, knowing Elmira was a person who could not be denied. "Right now I am focussing on the two states of consciousness. One is termed the arabesque, which concerns that of the mind and spirit, while the grotesque is that of the body."

"I find the body most fascinating," Elmira said, finger smoothing her mug.

Over the summer Elmira and I took many trips to George's Eatery and love blossomed in vibrant shades. Our frequent private rendezvous point was the Mackenzie's where we slipped out the back and ran through twisting piazzas and ducked behind border plantings where we would fall down laughing. In the cool of the day, after I had tended the stables, we took walks along the banks of the James River, threatening to push each other in, but neither backing up the promise.

John Allan purchased a brick mansion called "Moldavia" for $14,950, which was located on the southeast corner of Fifth and Main near Downtown Richmond. His business was doing better than ever. He finally got his covered stables and a handful of servants that he bought at auction. My stable duties, however, were not relinquished as he promised. *I am a man of my word, Edgar*, he had said. John Allan now claimed that the increased real estate required a greater work ethic from me for upkeep and neighborly appearances.

Moldavia had a multitude of rooms; upper and lower porticos lined an entire side and gathered the morning sun. Three chimneys poked from the manse's gabled roofline. I had never seen a house so massive and one that possessed such a regal appearance. John Allan's newfound riches and large home did not impress me in the least. My attitude let him know as much.

Elmira called Moldavia "darling precious."

"How can anything the size of the Mayflower be 'darling precious'?" I asked.

After we had moved, I would take breaks from my writing to watch the high society activity happening outside. From my high upper bedchamber I viewed ladies walking down the sidewalks as though colorful mushrooms under their umbrellas. Butcher and baker carts were being wheeled in the front of the large homes of the neighborhood where bells were rung and servants dashed out to the street to get supplies for the daily meals. Following right behind was usually a grinder offering his services to dulled scissors and knives in need. It struck me that one need not leave Moldavia to receive the world's bounty. Modern conveniences of the nineteenth century!

Nearby was the Mackenzie mansion and I welcomed the closeness to my sister, Rosalie, but more so the proximity to my meeting place with Elmira. Yes, she was our neighbor in our prior house, but our families grumbled about us spending too much time together so we frequently met at my sister's home.

I saw her flit inside the Mackenzie's one midday, a blonde blur. My heart was thumping as I finished my chores and cleaned myself up. I immediately made my way to the hall outside my room. In my excitement I did not say goodbye to Ma as I usually did. I flew down a long flight of stairs lined in wood paneling, turned through the mudroom and flew past a fine selection of polished guns. My boots were clicking across the hardwoods as I made my way to the foyer where a hat rack and floor vase (holding a repertoire of canes, umbrellas, and riding crops) stood sentinel at the massive front door.

Stepping onto the porch I heard, "Edgar! Where are you going?"

I stopped cold and rounded to find John Allan in the doorway. "Pa, I did not know you had come home for lunch. I am going across the street to see Rose, having finished my chores early today and in good fashion."

"No you have not. Your chores are never finished, Edgar. They are a continuing obligation."

"In all respect, I will continue my obligations to-morrow at the crack of dawn. I promise. All the earlier. Now if you do not mind, I will be on my way."

John Allan stepped onto the porch, jaw muscles popping. "I most certainly *mind* and I know why you are going across the street. It is to meet that Royster daughter, that ... that girl who is rumored to be unchaste. Do not deny it, Edgar, for my confidants have seen you most every day squandering your time on boyhood fancies when you could be learning a

business trade or at a minimum helping the servants. Moldavia's upkeep does not magically happen and neither does gaining the respect of those around us."

"First, Elmira is not unchaste and second, it is summertime. While other young men my
age are travelling or enjoying leisure, I am working in the stables."

"The only matter you work hard at is writing your nonsense and disgracing my name. I
have even moved you across the street from your sister and in repayment you give me
disrespect."

"No, Pa, you moved to Moldavia to be in the wealthiest neighborhood in Richmond, to
get invited to social functions and débutante balls where you seek to gain business contacts
or an offering to visit the Hunt Club on Saturday. Forgive my honest thoughts, but my sister
has nothing to do with it!"

John Allan snatched me by the lapels and began to shake me. My chin was forced to the
sky. Soon there was nothing under my feet and we were at eyelevel. I twisted and squirmed
to no avail. It was difficult to breathe.

At the moment when I thought he might slam me on the ground Ma appeared in the
doorway and put her hand over his shoulder. "Unhand him. Please, John, let him go visit
his sister."

"This is none of your business, woman."

"They have lived apart their entire lives. I have checked the stables myself and they are
in fine order. Please."

Blood slowly drained from Pa's face. "You try my longsuffering goodness, Edgar. Afternoon." He loosed my collar and I crashed to the floor. While I brushed myself off he turned
and pushed past Ma back into the house.

"Now run along, Edgar," Ma said.

"Thank you so much," I said from over my shoulder as I hurriedly made my way down
the curving flagstone sidewalk that cut through the front yard. Fright had turned to elation.

From behind I heard a bark: "Frances get in here," then shouting from inside Moldavia—
the wax and wan of heated voices. They fell away as I unlatched the iron gate that guarded
the grounds. Seconds later I rose up the wide steps fronting the Mackenzie home, which
were hewn of Italian marble.

Elmira let me in the door and greeted me with a hug. We had no sooner said our hellos
and taken a seat on a blue fainting couch in the living room when Rosalie appeared from her
bedchamber at the end of a long corridor. She passed room after room and the encroaching
sunlight revealed her at the open doorways facing south.

"Rose is as usual wearing an old-fashioned dress and a coiffure. Her appearance is like a
poorly wrapped parcel," I said to Elmira who offered a giggle. "Give your sense of style to
my sister if you give her nothing else."

Rose sleepily made her way into the living room. "Almost noontime and I am just rousing," she said, rubbing an eye.

"As if today is different from any other," I said. "I work hard all day and you work hard at sleeping."

"A life to which I aspire," Elmira informed.

Jane Mackenzie, a plump kind woman who always wore her hair clipped off her forehead, entered the living room. Behind her was a servant lady carrying a lavish tray of food, cups, and silverware. "Lunch is ready," Jane said as the tray was placed on a serving table near the fainting couch. "We have cheese sandwiches, crackers, and a selection of fresh tomatoes. The garnishing flowers are edible. I hope the food is to your liking."

"Perhaps you should have breakfast prepared for my sister," I joked.

"I would pour your beloved coffee over your head if I did not know Elmira wanted it," Rose said.

"Bickering," Jane said, "the true test of sibling blood. It is great to have you across the street, Edgar."

"That makes one of us," Rose said.

"So cute. If it were not for my stingy husband, I would have adopted you both."

"I wish you had," I confessed.

Jane ruffled my curly dark hair. "Well, enjoy the lunch and holler if you need anything else. Lemon pie is for dessert."

"Thank you, Missus Mackenzie," Elmira said. "As always you are a most gracious host. Darling precious to the nth degree."

When Jane and the servant had left, the three of us began speaking of the Union and of what I called the "New England Paradigm" regarding the architectural styles being constructed in town. I had yet to drain my first cup of coffee when I turned the conversation to the latest in literature and which modern writers I relished and which I thought were frauds.

"You speak as though you were a famous writer yourself," Rose commented, rolling her eyes.

Before I could respond, Elmira exclaimed, "Someday he will be."

"Not if my father has his way."

"John Allan is not your *father*," Rose scolded. "He is barely human by my standards. The way he treats you is deplorable. Your father, *our* father, was a brilliant thespian who—"

"—happened to abandon Mom when she was strapped with three young children," I interrupted.

"Enough, Brother, you are upsetting my lunch."

Elmira snuggled close and I smoothed her hand. She looked beautiful as usual. For how long we stared at each other I do not know, but I then noticed my sister mulling over the tray of food. Her hair was mussed, pins haphazardly stuck into it.

"Your head resembles a pincushion."

She made a twisted face at me while taking a cracker. She was endearing in any state of appearance.

"Rose, in all kindness, why do you wear your hair in such an absurd style when the lady of the house can provide you with every accompaniment of our society?"

"You know I am not one given to the latest fashion trends, Brother."

"How about the trends of this century? You're so ... so seventeen hundreds."

"That is the problem when has one been awoken abruptly after having been asleep too long in the style of Europeans."

"In the style of Rip Van Winkle is more appropriate!"

To this Elmira laughed aloud and Rose crinkled her nose before yawning. Rose, having yet to sit down, shrugged into the rococo mirror hanging before her. "I am just myself and I know you love me for it."

"He certainly does," Elmira said, offering her assistance before taking a bite of cheese sandwich. Cheese was a delicacy in Richmond and only the wealthiest homes had it.

I stood and took Rose's hand. "I most certainly do and I plan to visit you all the more for it now that we are practically neighbors."

Elmira joined us and fluffed her golden hair in the mirror. "It is too nice a day to be inside. I intend to sweep your opinionated brother away so he cannot make any further comments about your lifestyle or the literary figures of our day."

"Thank you. And I will enjoy my lemon pie in peace and quiet."

I said: "And a good nap after that, I am sure."

Elmira took my arm and whisked me toward the back of the manse. After skirting an ornately carved table in the dining room and darting through the kitchen where black and white marble tiles were trampled underfoot, we burst into the bright sunshine and headed on our usual course, twisting through a sun drenched piazza and around variegated border plantings.

A few hundred yards later I noticed the stickiness of the August day. I suddenly stopped. "Forget running in this heat. Let's take my father's horses."

"You serious? Mercy."

I was bursting inside. "I have to be alone with you far away from here."

"And I will go anywhere with you, Poe."

We trailed back along the side of the mansion and dashed across the street. I prayed John Allan did not see us as we ducked inside the iron gate and ran along the porticos, then rounded the back of Moldavia. We found ourselves at the newly renovated stables. The barn was painted the color of brick with white accents. Sleek horses brayed at our presence.

The alabaster orbs of Obadiah (a servant near my age that I had become friends with as I worked the land of Moldavia) appeared from the nether regions of the stable. A startled look was across his face as I kicked open the swinging gate and entered the long passageway that separated the stalls on either side.

I placed finger to lips, reached for two saddles hanging from posts, and heaved them onto the backs of the first two thoroughbreds on my right. The silent Obadiah hustled over and buckled the silver clasps to secure them and afterwards bridled the horses. He opened the gates to our respective stalls. "Enjoy, massar."

"Will you be able to ride?" I asked, the thought just crossing my mind that Elmira may not know how to work a horse or, even if she did, was not dressed for the occasion.

"The question is not whether I will be able to ride," she enlightened, "but whether *you* will be able to keep up with me." That being said, Elmira hiked up her dress. I glimpsed the slender flesh of her thigh. Hay particles floated aimlessly in a shaft of light cast down from box window overhead. She placed a foot in the stirrup and swung atop the nickering horse.

"I should expect no less from Sarah Elmira Royster," I said, mounting my animal. I glanced over at the coat of dark sheen and rippling muscles under Elmira. "That is my father's best steed, the quickest. Are you sure about this?"

"The faster the better," she winked, leading the steed from the barn. Before I could say another word, she healed it into a quick gallop that soon became a dead run past the carriage and servant houses, and John Allan's small counting house.

I made my way after her flailing the reins in unrelenting fashion.

Eight hooves thundered away from Moldavia with me seeing nothing in front but the bob of Elmira's golden locks in cadence with the swish of her horse's tail. The sway of her hips was amazing and I knew there were worse sights to behold.

We tore into a field of heather and tussocks. A cloven path soon churned beneath us and Elmira chose the fork that branched off to the east, which led through an expanse of young birch trees and slender poplars. The wind was at our faces, branches slapping at our legs.

Elmira looked back and waved me forward. "If you catch me you can have me!"

Her horse was indeed the quickest in John Allan's stables. I found it difficult to catch her no matter how hard I rode. "Ya!" I snapped the reins and hunched low.

The eastward path began clearing, trees becoming sparse as the field transitioned to a prairie of rolling hills. In the distance a steepled Baptist church stood out against the base of the foothills. My steed whinnied and I finally pulled along side Elmira, fell back, then pulled even again. "To me you are the sweetest honey, an apple at harvest."

"Our romance is so ripe, Poe, but can it run on airy wings?" Elmira let her frilly handkerchief fly into the air and it caught my nose before fluttering away. For a brief second I smelled a whiff of lilac perfume and breathed deeply. Looking up I noticed she had again pulled ahead.

The pathway flattened into a dell guarded by a foaming river that eventually fed into the James River. A weeping willow stood off to one side, its trunk the color of granite, its girth wide. Around its soughing boughs were wild azaleas in late bloom.

The horses slowed to a canter and Elmira checked her steed at the riverbank. I followed suit. "That was some display of horsemanship," I told her in a pant, trying to catch my breath.

"Horsewomanship," she corrected, hopping down from her saddle. "I most certainly could have jumped the water, but I wanted to give you a chance at catching me." Elmira handed me her reins, ran fingers through hair, and took off running.

I jumped into the tall grass and lashed the horses' bridles about a hefty, but low hanging oak limb. "Then I will take full advantage of it now." I rushed after the screeching and laughing young lady.

We darted a good ways under the welcoming branches of the weeping willow and fell arm-in-arm into the tall meadow. The shade was welcomed and a slight breeze found its way under the tree. We rolled in the high grass like mechanical threshers, Elmira tickling me in places I had never been touched. I felt embarrassed by the unfettered way in which I was chortling in a high voice. Before I realized what had occurred, I found myself pinned by Elmira.

She hovered above me with hair shimmering, hands pinning my wrists to the ground. Her chest rose and fell with the taking of hurried breaths. The wide cusp of her dress fanned over the lower part of my body. "Who has caught whom, Mister Poe?"

"I told you not to call me that."

"Mister Poe, Mister Poe, Mister Poe!"

A thrust of my hips sent her spilling onto her back and before Elmira could react, I was on top of her. The position was secondary as long as we were together in this scenic place, as long as her body was against mine.

Silence ensued, only the trickle of water in the background and the rasp of leaves. The horses stared in wonder. The day burned on. A droplet of sweat dripped from my nose. I watched it in horror land on Elmira's upper lip and explode.

Just as I was about to wipe it off, her tongue slid from her mouth and in slow motion I watched in amazement as she licked the droplet off. I leaned down and began kissing her, for I could not contain myself. I took in the taste of her skin—her untamed scent—and it gave sustenance to my very being.

Elmira gandered deep into my eyes and uttered words of surprise: "That was my first kiss and, given the young man I enjoyed it with, they were both beyond my expectations. It was all I had dreamed about and even better than those in *Pride and Prejudice*, which you have me reading."

I silently cursed John Allan's words that claimed she was unchaste.

For a great length of time we caressed and held each other—playful rustles in the meadowlands. The horses neighed in their puzzlement, but remained at their post. The muscles in my back and arms were hard and angular even through my clothes. For a moment I thought I was dreaming.

Her touch was silken and hair a golden frame for the artwork of her face. I could not get enough of her. I blurted: "Marry me, Sarah Elmira Royster."

Her eyes grew wide and response deliberate. "Are you mad? We just met this summer."

"Who cares? Seems like years ago."

"My parents *care* for one. I am but fifteen and you still having schooling."

Church bells could be heard off in the distance and I wondered if this was a precursor of things to come. For a moment we peered out from our rolled culvert of grass.

I sat back on my haunches, thinking my mouth had betrayed me in the moment, but yet I knew the words were heartfelt. "I plan to enter college in the winter. Within the year, when you graduate from high school, you can join me on campus. You act as though it is unusual for people our age to get married, when it is not."

"Yet people in the Richmond society in which we live rarely do get married this young. That is for the commoners. Our families demand that we are the five percent of young people that actually attend college because they have money to support us in that endeavor."

"I assure you, we can do both. Be mine forever."

Elmira scooted back against the willow's trunk. "Father is very strict. If he had the chance he would arrange my marriage as though I were from India. I have told him many great things about you this summer, Poe, how you are strong and intelligent and artsy. I have even told him that I love you."

"And I have told Ma the same but not John Allan. Seems we only converse in heated words these days. Please understand when I tell you that I did not plan this proposal—" While I talked on in nervousness, Elmira's face transitioned from one of meager apprehension to happiness as she thought. I did not detect her affirmations until the third annunciation sizzled through the breeze.

"Yesssss! I will marry you, Edgar Allan Poe."

1826 - Age 17

Valentines Day. I could think of no worse time to leave Elmira and start college at the University of Virginia—the college that Thomas Jefferson had started March 7th the year before.[3] There I planned to study languages, along with my father's requirements of the hard sciences and business courses. The language of *love* was what I really sought to study, and Elmira and I had done just that for over six months since our impromptu engagement. Elmira's father, an astute businessman of Richmond who had inherited his line of work from his grandfather—an early settler—did not accept our engagement and neither did John Allan. I sought to please my foster father to no end regardless of his treatment of me, and did not fight the decision for me to attend the University of Virginia, which was far away from Elmira in Richmond. My thinking was that the schooling would bring me into the good graces of Mr. Royster.

That Valentine's Day I found myself being whisked off to Charlottesville by one of my father's carriages after I had given Elmira a long poem and we had stolen many kisses inside a vacant room of the Mackenzie's. The hundred mile journey on harsh roads, which consisted mostly of gravel and frozen wheel-ruts compliments of the weather, took the entire day.

On our approach I saw from the carriage window the university's fluted colonnade sitting beneath a magnificent pediment. Red-tinted brick of fine workmanship fronted the university along with large trees. Wings were still being added onto the sides and scaffoldings framed the Rotunda.[4] It was apparent construction had slowed during the winter months at Jefferson's Academical Village.

A stream of boys was funneling under the large pediment. The way in which they were dressed told me many originated from wealthy families. Perhaps a few had made the journey from New York or Philadelphia. Young ladies (as Elmira had informed) were nearly absent and I had no doubts this would put her at ease with my being away from home. She vowed to join me the following year. After being out of her presence for a day, I relished the mere thoughts of having her near. Robert Stanard had planned to attend with aspirations of becoming an attorney like his father, but decided to stay in Richmond and work as a law clerk till at least the fall.

My father's carriage angled in amongst the others parked at the roadside arching before the university and the horses were reined back. A scattered group of boys in drab greatcoats were at play on the Lawn like a flock of pigeons. Obadiah untied my luggage from the roof and handed them down to a servant I had never seen before the journey. Father was doing so well at the time he was acquiring new servants at auction every month and I could no longer keep track of them.

"Weez ready now," Obadiah said, opening the door for me.

"I am worried. Pa has sent me here with one hundred and ten dollars[5] to my name."

He referenced me like it was the most money in the world.

"The low estimates are that it costs three times that much to attend this place for a year."

"Massar Allan send more. No worries."

A few of the boys watched us as we ambled over to the West Range. Obadiah helped me inside the dorm hall. He could not enter because no coloreds were allowed. I ordered him to wait outside a half hour before returning to ensure all was in order with my admission. He gladly obliged. "I'm heres for you."

The moment I entered the dorm hall I was deafened by the noise. The head resident—a man of short promptness and harsh glares—escorted me to my room after checking me off a list and I had paid fifty dollars for board.[6] Nearly half my money was gone and I had not even entered my room.

The head resident did not offer to help with my bags. I asked if there was a celebration going on as we made our way down a long corridor (me bumping bags against the walls) and received a smug shake of the head.

Boys (and I call them such because they did not appear to be young men) were running down the corridor in droves. Pillows were being tossed. Wads of paper thrown from doorways were bouncing off sconces that lined the walls. A wad caught fire on one of the lamps and the head resident quickly tramped it out over warnings of expulsion to a burly kid named Charles Wickliffe. I glanced back and saw a brawl ensue among half a dozen boys, Wickliffe seemingly the start of it.

Wondering if I had checked into a halfway house instead of an institution of higher learning, I was shown to Room 13 that was sparsely furnished with a twin bed, a small fireplace, and a corner writing table that sat in front of the solitary window. From the lack of ink stains on the table's surface I could tell it had never been used.

Within minutes I had mostly unpacked, left the riotous dorm, excused Obadiah who was shivering at his post, and found my way to the registrar's office just before closing time. There I was forced to pay another sixty dollars.[7] To my surprise there was no degree being offered in literature, so I chose classes in the Schools of Ancient and Modern Languages[8] to assist my writing, including Latin, French, Italian, and Spanish.[9] I excelled in them and am convinced a large part of it was due to the lack of interest in studies shown by most of the other students. They had wealthy family businesses waiting for them after graduation and were not compelled to learn at a stressful pace. Conversely, I was determined to make a career in writing without John Allan's help.

Speaking of writing, I wrote Elmira constantly during those first weeks, telling her about life at the university and how the students drank and fought on a whim; how they ran with frenzied passion across the campus and through the dorm at all hours. There was even a riot and the offending students were put on the sheriff's list.[10] A stone hit one student and he drew a pistol in defense only to have it misfire at the other's head.[11] I told her I was trying desperately to not get dragged into this lifestyle and that I missed her from the depths of my soul. I also expressed disappointment in learning that Thomas Jefferson was too sickly in his retirement to invite any more students up to Monticello for dinner. It would have been special meeting the elder statesman. Joining the Jefferson Society Debating Club was the closest I came to knowing him.

I knew Elmira would be surprised that our classes only lasted from 7:30 to 9:30 each morning and that I had the rest of the day to read in the temporary library while I hoped for the beautiful Rotunda to get finished. There were many wonderful books housed there that provided enlightenment in the Greek tragedies, Shakespeare, and the writings of Voltaire. I was beside myself in the tomes each afternoon after I had penned my usual letter to Elmira and the occasional letter to John or Frances Allan.

A handful of students from Richmond, whom I told horror stories to every Friday evening in what I claimed to be my haunted Room 13, had heard of my swimming exploits on the James River and often invited me to play sports on the Lawn as springtime approached, though it brought me little pleasure. Writing was my pleasure—oh blessed writing—and I began penning a long poem in the afternoons that would eventually be titled *Tamerlane*. I wrote most of it under a red oak tree where I could overlook the games on the Lawn. Much of my inspiration was taken from Byron and although I realized some would claim *To Helen* was inspired by the Grecian architecture at the school, I had written the prose years before Thomas Jefferson started work on his Academical Village. As I sat there and wrote beneath the hushed splendor of playful squirrels, I knew Elmira would be pleased at my most ambitious poetry effort yet. She was receiving the serialized version in the mail. She inspired a number of the poems and I vowed to publish it someday for the world to read.

Day after day I unrolled my sheath of foolscap and wrote Elmira, pouring out my heart. How could I fully express that each breath was a struggle without her? As the summer progressed, and I made up the classes I had missed at the university in the fall, her letters became less frequent, until they stopped altogether. Week after week I awaited her response but received none. Each empty trip to my postal box in the dorm hall caused my heart to die a more fervent death than the day before. The U.S. Postal Service is unreliable at times, but surely it could not have failed to deliver so many letters of mine to Richmond, especially when I received responses from Pa and Rose.

Any indication that Elmira had read one of my countless letters would have been heaven; a sentence, a word, a blank letterhead scented with lilacs! The longest, coldest summer of my existence passed at the University of Virginia no matter what the temperature outside.

On July 4th both John Adams and Thomas Jefferson died. The coincidence was unfathomable. When I heard Jefferson's nearly two hundred servants screaming (some for joy, but most in agony) that morning from the hills of Monticello, I knew what had happened. A palpable sorrow was cast over the university that day. The fireworks display that evening seemed a constant muted drone no matter how lavish given the fiftieth anniversary of the Declaration of Independence.[12]

My letters to Elmira continued, though less frequent than before. I wrote Rose at the Mackenzie's. She told me Elmira had oddly broken off all communication with her, also. My depression grew by the moment and I could not wash from memory her face or that of Mrs. Stanard or my mother as she lay in the coffin. In my head they were all linked and in my nightmares they sometimes merged into a singular face having the most pronounced qualities of each. Sleep became troubled and infrequent for me as a result.

Room 13. *Room 13!*

As fall approached, I buried myself in studies and writing to lessen the pain. I wrote Pa on September 21st to give him an update of my ambitiousness before finals.[13] I had been studying a great deal in order to be prepared, and hoped I would come off better than the rest. I also let him know that the Rotunda was nearly completed and that the front pillars were finished. Of course, I could not end the letter without updating him on the behavior of the boys. *We have had a great many fights up here lately—The faculty expelled Wickliffe last night for general bad conduct—but more especially for biting one of the student's arms with whom he was fighting—I saw the whole affair—it took place before my door—Wickliffe was much the stronger but not content with that—after getting the other completely in his power, he began to bite—I saw the arm afterwards—and it was really a serious matter—It was bitten from the shoulder to the elbow—and it is likely that pieces of flesh as large as my hand will be obliged to be cut out—He is from Kentucky—the same one that was in suspension when you were up here some time ago.[14]*

As hope of hearing from my love dwindled, so did the money Pa was sending. I only had enough to pay for classes, room, and board. The lesson he was trying to teach me about manhood was a mystery. Instead of reading in the afternoons I visited the Village of Charlottesville where I played hands of Seven-Up and Loo. My steel-trap memory served me well at cards and I won enough to support a new set of clothes and linens, but the gentlemen (and I use the term loosely) at the saloon turned wise to my aptitude and began stacking the deck.

It was then that my fortune turned for the worse. I swear I was forced into these acts out of necessity. My gambling continued in the dorm hall and I dare say my loosing streak continued under the unlucky number that hung outside my room. I was soon indebted more than a year's tuition at the university and in dire straights.

In December of the year I was forced to leave UV because of my debts.[15] John Allan sent a carriage to remove me during the thick of night. Obadiah and another servant of my father's whisked me from my room as though I was a prisoner being taken to the gallows. There was no food waiting for me in the passenger compartment and I scolded Obadiah for this. He would not look me in the eyes.

The ride back to Richmond was wrought with fear, me imagining what John Allan would say upon my disgraceful return. Lanterns knocked and swayed atop the carriage, and sleet pricked at the windows as I lay curled in a ball on the rear seat. The passenger compartment was cold and forbidding, hollow like my feelings for Pa. The roads were treacherous and there was no sleep for me that evening on the bumpy return back to Richmond.

When I arrived at Moldavia, John Allan was pacing in front of one of its many fireplaces, a riding crop slapping against his leg.

"Hello, sir."

"Sit down, Edgar!" He stopped his relentless gait and stared at me in furor. "Just when I thought you were beginning to become respectable, you pull this ... this fiasco. You showed your true self once again. Local Charlottesville merchants have issued warrants for your IOUs in excess of two thousand dollars![16] I should send you back after the holidays with even less money."

"Please do. I will gladly return before my peers to whom I am indebted and continue my education. I will find a way to repay my debts. I am capable."

The riding crop was bent into a U-shape. John Allan's face was devilish under the backdrop of flames. "I should sit you on the Lawn in Charlottesville and let your creditors ravage you, but I have decided not to let you leave Moldavia in your state of mind—in your state of betrayal. Perhaps I should make you rot in jail for what you have done to my name."

"But I was forced into gambling because you did not provide—"

"Do not speak another word! You shall never be anything but a disgrace!" Before I could react, John Allan took hold of the arms of my chair, firelight pulsing at the back of his head, spittle dappling the corners of his mouth. "You are nothing but an embarrassment to the surname Allan and to Moldavia. My peers consider you a debauchee and I should send you back to the gutter from whence you came! I'm sure the orphanage would take you in or maybe they shall be disgraced by your presence, too."

I flinched as he rose up and flew back the riding crop to strike me. "No, please. You gave me little support."

"And you have given me much humiliation."

As I braced for the blow, I heard Ma crying out. She burst into the room wearing her nightgown. "John, please!"

"My discipline is none of your concern, woman! Spare the rod, spoil the useless child. Now get back."

She flung at the riding crop with both hands and latched onto it. John Allan was caught off guard and she managed to tear it away. "Striking this boy is not discipline, it is abuse and I will not stand for it." For a moment I thought he was going to backhand Ma or push her into the flames, but instead he turned back and stuck a finger in my face.

"Consider yourself fortunate, derelict. And know that I refuse to pay your gambling debts now or ever. But from the goodness of my heart I shall give you an opportunity to make it back. From this day forward you shall earn a living as a clerk in my counting house. You will learn business skills even if they come at the expense of raw fingers and a stiff back."

"I do not want to be a businessman. My talents lie in the written word."

"If I ever catch you wasting your time writing again, Edgar, I shall destroy the worthless paper on which it is penned." He addressed Ma with a click of his heels. "And you, woman, have a treacherous mind for someone so barren as not to grant me a *real* son."

Ma tossed the riding crop on the ground as John Allan tore out of the room. "You have a monstrous temper, John, that you need to get under control."

I spun from the chair and screamed: "As others see you, so you are!" I quoted his words back to him of so many years ago. "So you are!"

The remaining hours until daybreak passed in waves of heated words between Frances and John. Oaken doors slamming in distant regions of Moldavia were thunderclaps in the night. John Allan channeled his distaste for me on dear Ma, and although I cannot verify whether he raised hand to her, he berated Ma at length. "You have kept me childless for the last quarter of century, woman."

"As if it was my choice to be barren."

"You know I desperately want my own flesh and blood child, not a disgrace of a foster child."

"Edgar is a wonderful young man with many redeeming qualities."

"It is you who forced me into this arrangement against my wishes. It is all your fault and that orphan is at the root of all my problems."

Shuddering from my bed I watched the light turn brighter shades of gray through my curtains as the cloudy morning seeped around the edges of the draperies. I was still dressed in my travel clothes and did not bother to change them before heading across the street. If anyone held clues to Elmira's anchoress behavior, it would be Rose.

To no surprise Mrs. Mackenzie had to wake Rose, but first she offered me freshly baked Christmas cookies and showed much joy at seeing me home. I had no heart to tell her I would not be going back. I was thankful that John Allan had not gotten to her to spread ill will about my University of Virginia predicament. A part of me expected him to mount a sign outside Moldavia telling the world of my perceived insolence or to nail a banner to the home that would wave from the porticos. He seemed to revel in my missteps; any excuse driving me further from adoption.

Rose entered the living room in her nightgown and stocking cap, sleep enveloping her. Upon seeing me her eyes lit and she gave me a big hug. "Brother! It is so nice to see you again at this festive season." She stepped back and took a good look at me. "And you talk of *my* rumpled clothing."

"It is so nice to see you, Rose. I have had the most terrible of experiences and have slept in these." Before going further I noticed Mrs. Mackenzie was still in the room and I gave her a polite look that had 'moment of privacy' written all over it, which shooed the plump woman away. Rose took a seat on the blue fainting couch and I told her everything about my time at the university and violent return.

She was nonplussed at John Allan's behavior. "But why did he—"

"Forget him," I said kneeling to eye level and taking her by the shoulders. "What have you heard of Elmira? Please tell me something about her, at least that she is alive and well."

"That she is, but as I said in my letters, Elmira is rarely seen around town."

"There has to be more information than that in my absence."

"You are in luck, Edgar, for I hear from a connected source that the Roysters are throwing a holiday party this very evening at their home. A gala affair."

"That's great! Are you invited?"

"No one from this household, that is set in stone."

"Surely there has been some mistake. Yes, yes, she is unaware I am in town." I thought for a second. "It has been near a year and a half since our engagement and months since we have communicated. I intend to surprise her tonight!"

"By interjecting?" Rose asked with a mix of concern and glee.

"I would rather call it a self-invite. Once she sees my face again and hears the call of my voice, all will be remembered, right?" I noticed I was shaking Rose and the ball at the end of her stocking cap was bouncing off her forehead. I sprung to my feet. "I have to find an answer as to why my dear fiancée forgot me upon my departure from Richmond. Was it her father? Have I been played for the world's biggest fool?"

"Wish I knew, dear brother."

Fists were clenched at my sides. "Our love was true and I will go to my grave believing it. Why did Elmira forsake our love, *why*?"

"Only God knows, but I suspect you will find out tonight, just be prepared for the worse."

"What could be worse than losing the love of one's life without reason?"

My afternoon was spent getting ready for the gala affair as though I were a girl preparing for her first ball. My hair was dark stubborn wisps, but combed as best I could in a gentlemanly fashion. I dressed in my best suit, starched tab collar shirt, and bow tie. I simply had to demonstrate to Elmira that she was making a huge mistake in forsaking me.

I left Moldavia without telling John Allan where I was going and headed up the thoroughfare. I found it impossible to keep warm in the face of a northeastern wind. Hardened sleet was crunching under my boots as I fought toward my old neighborhood. My ears were crystal ready to shatter at the slightest touch. The party had already begun when I finally approached the Royster's home, vaporous breath roiling out behind me.

An early December nightfall had overtaken the neighborhood, yet bright hope was in my heart. Green candles flickered in each window, filling the abode with warm light. Large red bows were tied on lantern poles that flanked the walk leading to the front steps. I heard festive music and saw the shadowy outline of violinists working their bows in the keeping room—grasshoppers in the verdant light.

A servant in top hat and tails greeted me at the door and let me inside. To my relief he did not have a guest list at the waiting, nor did he recognize me. He took my greatcoat and stowed it in a large walk-in closet along with the other greatcoats and furs of those in attendance. I glimpsed a row of storage boxes below the coats on which the residents' shoes and boots were parked.

A throng of merry people was mulling about, drinks in one hand and jovial stories being gesticulated with the other. I knew a few of them (most powdered members of the Whig party), but kept a low profile as I sidled into the hearth room and the music of the violinists grew louder. A number of fresh Christmas trees decorated the lower level of the home, strands of colored beads festooned the inner branches and glinting ornaments were dripping off the boughs.

I warmed my hands at the roaring fire, my back to the revelers, while I thought uselessly of words to say upon seeing Elmira. How many times had I rehearsed my introduction that afternoon only to be at a miserable loss inside her home?

There was a possibility she would not be in attendance, and the granite section of my heart that had hardened over months of non-responsiveness to my letters wanted this to be the case. Emotions of every sort welled as I stood there transfixed by the licking flames.

"—and her bonnet took flight over Mister Schuler's barn," a lady behind me was saying on the way past, "only to have it uncovered when Schuler dug up his turnips in the summer!"

"—when the hard candy did no less than roll under the pew and continue the length of the aisle to the alter. Thought it was going to repent," someone voiced from another group that cackled as they strode by in the hallway.

I faced the partygoers and propped my arm on the mantel off which Christmas stockings hung. Statuelike I searched for Elmira among the Christmas tree boughs and silvery trays of hot drinks that were floating about with a steaming purpose. I listened for the unmistakable drawl of her voice, a "darling precious" here or a "mercy me" there.

Out of nowhere a commanding male voice ordered the attention of all and the angling bows in the keeping room froze on their strings. "Merry Christmas and thank you indeed for coming to our house on this special occasion. You are all our dear friends and welcome here anytime. Now, before the food and drinks cool off, I take great pleasure in announcing my beautiful daughter, Elmira."

An arm rose above a circle of heads and pointed to a stairway that curved down into the great room. I saw the stairway through an open door in the hearth room. Globes of hewn wood marked the beginning and end of the large banisters. A garland of fresh-cut ivy was draped from them and snaked around the balustrades and the railing spindles.

Elmira emerged from an upstairs room in a flowing off-white dress, like a specter come to life from my past. Curls of spun gold danced over her shoulders and silken gloves adorned her hands. A round of applause and cheers was given. I stood transfixed. She smiled at the top of the stairway and I had forgotten what perfect teeth she had. Floating on air she made her way down the steps. By the time she had reached the middle, I could no longer contain myself and took off running through the clusters of people.

Drinks were spilled and a tray of food tossed in the air, which rained carrot sticks and mushrooms down on those in close proximity. "Elmira!" I shouted, jumping and waving while pushing my way to the front. I found myself speaking from instinct instead of rehearsal. "Over here, Elmira my love!"

People were moving aside and I was attracting much attention in my excited rush to greet her. When the last row of attendees parted, I was face-to-face with Elmira at the bottom of the stairs. Her venerable father was next to us sporting a hoary beard. Our eyes met and I felt a coldness issue from Elmira that I had never experienced. An awkward silence floated over the great room and she finally questioned, "Why did you not write me, Mister Poe?"

Never had my name sounded so formal and cold. I took her gloved hand. "B-but I did write you! Every day for months. It is *you* that did not respond to my—"

A strong hand gripped my forearm and tore it away from Elmira. A middle-aged man was standing there with hair parted in the middle. "Unhand my fiancée," he said in a heated tone.

"Excuse me? Sarah Elmira Royster is *my* fiancée. Tell this insane man the truth, Elmira. Tell him he is ruining your Christmas party."

Mr. Royster stepped in front of me. "This is not a Christmas party, sir, this is an engagement party, and this gentleman that you have addressed in such a reprehensible manner is Alexander Shelton, to whom my daughter is happily engaged and who is already an established and wealthy businessman."

I sought an answer over his shoulder and Elmira nodded despondently from the first step, her eyes cast down in hurt. "But he is too old for you."

"No, Edgar," Mr. Royster said, "it is you who is too young for my daughter. Elmira does not have any future with a stable boy whose foster father will not adopt him because of disgracefulness."

"That is a falsehood! I have a bright future and have excelled at the university as proof."

"I myself have approached John Allan and he has informed me in no uncertain terms of your lax character and questionable aspirations of becoming a writer."

Hate boiled through my veins; yet I could not pry myself away from Elmira. I pushed her father aside and gasps of surprise came from the ladies around us. "I am forthright in my intentions, Elmira, and I *did* write you constantly. Do not make this mistake. Our love is true, you cannot deny it in front of me. I refuse to leave until I hear that you do not love me from your own mouth."

Alexander lashed me about the neck with his arm and began pulling me away from her in a chokehold. My bow tie dug into the small of my throat. I wanted to reach back and pluck out his eyes for viewing my true love in a romantic way. Servants hustled over and wrestled control of my arms. When Alexander let go they began escorting me out of the great room under the stern commands of Mr. Royster. The audience was aghast at my behavior.

I tried to squirm away from the servants, kicking and twisting. "But I love you, Elmira! You have got to understand. I never once stopped loving you!"

The front door flung open and a charge of frigid air greeted me. Thinking of anything to remain in Elmira's presence, I said, "I am not leaving without my coat!"

The servants slowly let go of me, but stood close guard as I fixed my suit and went into the walk-in closet. Another wave of anger struck me and I began kicking at the storage boxes on which the shoes rested out of anger and frustration. I flailed with such furry that I ripped a large hole in one of them. Rectangular objects fell out in the relative darkness. For reasons still unknown to me, I reached down and examined one. To my great surprise I found it to be an envelope ... an *unopened* envelope sent from the Village of Charlottesville and addressed to Miss Sarah Elmira Royster in *my* handwriting.

I tore it open and pulled out one of my letters dated April 14, 1826, a mere two months after I started at the university. My stomach felt as though a millstone had been dropped in it. I tore open the rest of the box and countless unopened envelopes spilled onto the closet floor. Grabbing handfuls of them I shot into the entranceway. "Look here, Elmira, I hold in my hands proof that I wrote you from the university. Unopened letters! Your father has been hiding them from you to break up our engagement."

Calls of surprise wafted over the lower level while Elmira and a group of consolers rushed toward me. Mr. Royster led them.

By this time I was reading one aloud to the entire household. "'Oh that I could be in your sweet embrace, dear Elmira, and that we could be together for just one moment to hear our hearts beating as one!' Dated: March twentieth of this year!" I tore open another. "'Dearest Elmira, my sleep is greatly troubled for I am receiving no response from you. What have I done to vex you so?' Dated: May first of this year!"

"Yes, I did intercept those letters," Mr. Royster claimed, "because you are too young for Elmira." He ordered his servants to act. "Never step foot in his house again!"

They were forcing me out the door as I tossed the letters to Elmira. She glanced at them for verification and tears streamed down her cheeks.

"Break off your engagement, Elmira, and return to me!" I screamed half out the door.

She took my outstretched hand and said, "I am so sorry, Poe, for it is too late with the plans for the wedding being set. I love you."

I grabbed onto the jamb screeching incomprehensibly and more servants had to force apart my grip that was pressing into the wood. "*NO!*" I was tossed into the yard and landed with a *tha-thump*. The breath was knocked out of me as I sprawled across the lawn and came to a sliding halt.

The front door slammed and I heard the bolt slide into the striker plate. Grass and dirty ice stains besmeared by suit as I lay there exposed to the winter without my greatcoat. The cold air was a dagger to my battered lungs.

When I turned in my sorrow to catch one last glimpse of Elmira, I saw Mr. Royster in the window madly throwing the box of letters into the fire with Elmira pleading from behind.

1827 - Age 18

The ensuing holidays were contentious betwixt John Allan and me and so was my eighteenth birthday in January. To think that at one time not too long ago I called him "Pa" is beyond comprehension or the worthiness of a so-called man who has toiled to see the downfall of anything pleasurable in my life.

Months of winter bore onward and so did the tedium of working in the small drafty outbuilding that was his counting house. My daily routine was never changing. In the mornings I awoke before dawn to chop firewood so that I would have heat for the day and then I would churn butter for Moldavia's daily provisions. Obadiah would next prepare a breakfast of oatmeal, eggs, and biscuits on which my butter was used. John Allan and I had little contact apart from him barking orders to me for accounting matters that needed to be transacted in his precious counting house after breakfast. "Balance the ledgers. Not a penny out of place. Balance the ledgers!"

Each day was a struggle for my creative mind, bound by a prison sentence of monotony and repetitiveness and deep feelings of loss for Elmira. I had no contact with anyone in the counting house behind Moldavia, apart from Obadiah who would sneak me an occasional ration of cornbread in return for help with his English. For the most part I sat alone, which was punishment itself as my inventive mind turned against me and tortured me while maple wood popped and syrup fizzled over the fireplace's ad irons and wind cracked against the thin walls.

To save me from my own mind, I wrote in my boredom when I was finished with the accounting transactions. My sharpness with numbers, which served me well at many university card games, allowed me to finish my profit and loss sheets early and turn to poetry. I spent the winter months working on a selection of other poems to accompany *Tamerlane* and soon had an entire drawer full of text in the Spartan office in which I worked throughout the day.

In the evenings my chores were still not finished. The stables had to be tended. I often spent time in the carriage house where I would wash mud from the sides of lacquered vehicles due to the unkempt roads in the winter months. One evening I was doing the later when I heard the side door of the carriage house fling open. At first I blamed it on the howling March winds, but detected the clomp of heavy boots against the floor's planking.

Startled, I stood to glimpse the outline of a man enshrouded in shadows, his jet coat swelling up behind him. I held my lantern before me and called out: "Who's there?"

The figure said nothing as he approached, ominous in stride and stature. A pall of fear overcame me and I backed against a carriage.

Wavering candlelight diffused across the figure and I saw that it was John Allan. He approached me. In one hand was clasped a roll of papers. "What is this?" he asked, holding them up.

"What is what?"

"This ... this poetry I have found in a search of your desk at the counting house, some of the ink still wet. I even found a useless copy of *Don Quixote*." Before I could answer he snatched the lantern from my hand and opened its swinging door. In went one end of the roll.

"No!" I screamed, lunging for it.

A hard kick caught me unexpectedly in the stomach and I slumped breathless against the front of the carriage. When I looked up, the lantern shone from the ground and my poetry on which I had worked so diligently was burning torchlike in the air.

John Allan hovered over me and held it up as though a blazing sign of his light in my life. "How dare you, boy, take yet another advantage of my goodwill by creating this worthlessness!"

"Please, my writings!" I reached up, but he kicked me again back to the floor as charred swaths of parchment flaked off, burning and smoking onto my clothing. I swatted at the embers as they lit but did not dare move against John Allan's wrath.

His index finger ran along the carriage's side. "And here is yet another example of your poor workmanship."

"I am convinced nothing I do will ever meet your standards. Nothing! You only look for ways to keep me under hardship."

Arms spread wide he turned toward the mullioned windows and remarked, "Look outside, Edgar, do you call living in Moldavia a hardship?"

"Ask your other servants what they think? The only difference between them and me is skin color. You even put them in charge of me as I do my chores. Look at my hands and tell me if these are not the hands of servitude."

"Moldavia is an American palace."

"Moldavia is no different than the workhouses of England but with gold trim and tapestries."

He threw the burning paper torch into my midsection. I scrambled to bat it away, then stamped it out with my palm. Months of work were ruined.

"You eat with the beak of idleness and squawk in disrespect. Your imagination is even greater than I thought. Perhaps it can appreciate that I have nurtured you from the impoverished son of a theatre harlot and a drunken excuse for a father, yet you are nothing but an ingrate!"

"Is that why you are not man enough to adopt me, because of your own moral pretensions?"

"I am loath to adopt the child of two theatrical players who chose a life of immorality by making a living in the arts. And even if that were not the case, I would never adopt you as my own because you shall never grow into a businessman that I deem fit to share my name. Your embarrassing stint at the university proved as much."

"May Satan himself deliver you to Hell in a hand basket!"

In the trembling candlelight I saw John Allan grab an instrument off the wall. Its handle was thick and bound. Its end snaked on forever. "Remove your coat and take your punishment like the man you shall ne'er be."

"In your troubled dreams!"

Thwaack! John Allan popped the whip in the air before bringing it down across my chest near the heart. The burn felt as though a branding iron had been pressed lengthwise across my shoulder.

"Frances is not here to save you this time, boy!"

"And Christ himself will never save you."

Again the whip sang through the carriage house. *Thwaack!* The entwined leather tore across my chest again and I felt my skin rip open. "No! What have I done to deserve this?"

The uncoiling snake of leather missed me the third time and wound itself around a wheel spoke. Before he could draw back the whip again I latched onto its tail and with strength that can only manifest itself when one's life is in danger, ripped it from his grasp and tossed it into the dark regions of the carriage house.

Struggling to get up, a heel knocked into the side of my head and pain exploded through my skull. When I opened my eyes, light from the glowering candle was reflecting prismatic, far above in the rafters of the carriage house. Trusses were crisscrossing and carriage wheels churning in place next to me.

I began to crawl when another heel crashed into my temple like a lightning bolt coursing from one ear to the other.

The sheer force of the impact sent me rolling under the carriage, which I realize now saved my life. I somehow uttered over the pain, "I know what you did to Elmira. I know ... of the lies you told her father to ruin our relati—"

The enveloping darkness was the most complete and all encompassing I had ever experienced; darkness so replete that my mind could not interpret a dream through its gloomy veils, nightmare or otherwise, the coal blackness being so thick it shut down my sight, hearing, taste, and mental imagery. I was cast into a great void. I had *become* a great void; a pit of nothingness as I lay there under the carriage.

When I thought all my senses had forsaken me, just like my foster father, a bolt of pain emanating in my head sent a twitch down one side of my broken body. It felt as though needlepoint was being practiced between my temples, jet-black stitches of agony being woven.

Lightlessness and pain were all I could sense.

I tried desperately to focus on something else. The twitch was there nonetheless. I was *not* paralyzed. Even if I was, I knew at a minimum my eyelids would operate. Before the next suture of pain I tried to lift them. They were not so much heavy as stuck together, upper lids fused to lower. Had the needlepoint sown them shut?

My jaw dropped and brow rose. Slowly one eye opened and I saw a peculiar thing: A kitten playing near my head, then another came into view. I had my sight!

My eye closed as another tremor of pain weaved through my skull. *Where am I? How long have I been here? Hours? Days?* There were no dogs or cats at Moldavia for John Allan did not deem pets as having any place in upper society.

Kittens? Has Obadiah been hiding them?

Catching my breath I noticed my tongue was dry and heavy, mouth feeling as though I had been sucking on wheat chaffs. A bone chill had overtaken me. The smell of dust and grease was redolent. My senses were back and I was sorry for it.

My hand reached up and freed my other eyelid from a sticky substance. A pinwheel of light shone across my chest and the encrusted underpinnings of the carriage still hung over me. How long I had been there was a mystery. John Allan had left me for dead in the frigid carriage house. Certainty he would blame my death on a servant, perhaps a few. Most only spoke broken English and their defense in accusatory situations was inadequate with court-appointed attorneys and Richmond juries of whites.

Off to one side candle wax had flowed out the bottom of the lantern and congealed on the floor; a yellow tumor. The dirty brown felines were still there and most playful, lapping up a substance from the planked floor. The next wave of hurt oscillated at my temples and when it had finally passed, it occurred the kittens were staying close to me when Elmira and John Allan had not. I focused on them instead of the pain. It was then to my horror that I noticed they were licking from a pool of blood from my chest wound, blood that was on my face and filled my ear. *My* blood!

As my hearing wavered, I heard squeaks instead of meows; and as my shaky vision came into focus I glimpsed long hairless tails on the kittens and buckteeth. *Rats!*

For another hour I lay there until I found the impossible strength to wriggle from my makeshift tomb and lurch from the frosty carriage house. The sun was rising and the fiery ball forced me to shield my face, but its heat was welcomed. As I fled I heard: "Good morning, Edgar." The unmistakable tone of the abuser's voice. John Allan was at the stables. "Rough night of sleep?"

I spat in his direction and said, "That is what I think of you and your wealth." I then stumbled across the street where Rose tells me I collapsed by the front door. Mrs. Mackenzie and my sister nursed me back to health that afternoon. They were frantic at the sight of me. I begged them not to tell John Allan where I was recovering for fear of my safety after the violent altercation.

The moment I was able, however, I wrote John Allan and instructed Rose to mail the letter from the center of town so he could not tell my whereabouts. I knew it would discomfort him to hear from me and that gave me pleasure. I felt compelled to address our outstanding issues under circumstances where a boot was not being applied to my head.

Richmond Monday, March 19, 1827

Sir,

After my treatment on yesterday and what passed between us this morning, I can hardly think you will be surprised at the contents of this letter. My determination is at length taken — to leave your house and indeavor to find some place in this wide world, where I will be treated — not as you have treated me — This is not a hurried determination, but one on which I have long considered — and having so considered my resolution is unalterable — You may perhaps think that I have flown off in a passion, & that I am already wishing to return;

But not so — I will give you the reason[s] which have actuated me, and then judge —

Since I have been able to think on any subject, my thoughts have aspired, and they have been taught by you to aspire, to eminence in public life — this cannot be attained without a good Education, such a one I cannot obtain at a Primary school —A collegiate Education therefore was what I most ardently desired, and I had been led to expect that it would at some future time be granted — but in a moment of caprice — you have blasted my hope sed because forsooth I disagreed with you in an opinion, which opinion I was forced to express —

Again, I have heard you say (when you little thought I was listening) and therefore must have said it in earnest) that you had no affection for me —

You have moreover ordered me to quit your house, and are continually upbraiding me with eating the bread of Idleness, when you yourself were the only person to remedy the evil by placing me to some business — You take delight in exposing me before those whom you think likely to advance my interest in this world —

You suffer me to be subjected to the whims & caprice, not only of your white family, but the complete authority of the blacks — these grievances I could not submit to; and I am gone [.] I request that you will send me my trunk containing my clothes & books — and if you still have the least affection for me, As the last cal [call] I shall make on your bou [nty], To prevent the fulfillment of the Prediction you this morning expressed, send me as much money as will defray my the expences of my passage to some of the Northern cit[i]es & then support me for one month, by whic[h] time I [sh]all be enabled to place myself [in] some situation where I may not only o[bt]ain a livelihood, but lay by a sum which one day or another will support me at the University — Send my trunk &c to the Court-house Tavern, send me I entreat you some money immediately — as I am in the greatest necessity — If you fail to comply with my request — I tremble for the consequence.

Yours &c Edgar A Poe

It depends upon yourself if hereafter you see or hear from m[e.][18]

Apparently John Allan knew where I was staying, for the next morning a trunk was found on the Mackenzie's doorstep instead of the Court-house Tavern near town. Perhaps he followed my blood trail across the street.

Inside the trunk was a black frockcoat with a white shirt and a black cravat, a black vest, gloves, and (compliments of dear Ma) a fine selection of writing quills, parchment and a hundred dollars. The following letter in John Allan's pen was also contained therein.

March 20, 1827
Sir

Your letter of Monday was received this morning, I am not surprized at any step you may take, at any thing you can say, or any thing you may do, you are a much better judge of the propriety of your own conduct and have general treatment of those who had the charge of your infancy & have watched with parental solicitude & affection over your tender years affording you such means of instruction as was in their power & which was performed with pleasure until you became a much better judge of your own conduct, rights & priveledges than they, it is true I taught you to aspire, even to eminence in Public Life, but I never expected that Don Quixote, Gil Blas, Jo: Miller & such works were calculated to promote the end.

It is true and you will not deny it, that the charge of eating the Bread of idleness, was to urge you to perseverance & industry in receiving the classics, in presenting yourself in the mathematics, mastering the French &c. &c. how far I succeeded in this you can best tell, but for one who had conceived so good an opinion of himself & his future intentions I hesitate not to say, that you have not evinced the smallest disposition to comply with my wishes, it is only on this subject I wish to be understood, your Heart will tell you if it is not made of Marble whether I have not had good reason to fear for you, in more ways than one. I should have been justly chargeable, in reprimanding you for faults had I had any other object than to correct them.

Your list of grievances require no answer the world will reply to them—& now that you have shaken off your dependence & declared for your own Independance — & after such a list of Black charges—you Tremble for the consequences unless I send you a supply of money.

Jonathan Allan[19]

Having no place to go, but knowing forthrightly that I had to leave the bitter memories of my forlorn life in Richmond, I set off to Boston, my birthplace. I rented a small room above a fish cannery (the smell was gagging at times, but the room very cheap because of it) where I worked feverishly on recompiling *Tamerlane* and my other poems burned at the hands of the monster. *'[T]he bread of idleness ... ?'* Drivel! I would show John Allan my feast of industriousness. *'[Y]ou have not evinced the smallest disposition to comply with my wishes ... .'* Only at every scrub of your horses and churn of your butter!

It was impossible to write in my room from the fishy stench rising up from below, so I stowed away in a corner of the nearest coffee house and wrote for days on end, caffeine and my will to succeed my sustenance. I got to know the owners and I am sure they viewed me their worst customer because I would pay for a cup of coffee and get free refills throughout the afternoon and into the evening.

Once my rewrites were finished, I immediately made arrangements to have *Tamerlane* published by one Calvin F. S. Thomas, who gushed about the collection. The deal struck was this: I would pay for the entire printing costs and Thomas would market the book. We would split the royalties. Thomas assured me that self-publishing was the only way for a young, unknown author to get his name out in New England. Fair enough.

A month later I had the book. Self-published or not, there was no greater experience than feeling the leather cover in my hands for the first time, to see the embossed title and neatly printed words inside. My imagination had come to life, but not my name. Thomas insisted on having the collection published under the name "A Bostonian" to pique the interest of the residents and to make me appear as a local.

To my dismay, *Tamerlane* was largely ignored because Thomas, the small, inexperienced publisher that he was, could not get it reviewed in any of the Boston papers.

Penniless and unable to support myself on writing (but with resolve to make it on my own), on May 26th I enlisted in the U.S. Army under the alias "Edgar A. Perry" for a five-year stint. I could not stomach being associated with the name Allan any longer.

1829 - Age 20

On New Year's Day, a year and a half after I joined the Army, I was promoted to the rank of Sergeant Major of the Regiment of Artillery. I found the discipline of the Army easy to endure given my upbringing and I excelled over my less hardened peers. Military life centered on exercise drills and barrack duty, which I found easier than the lightest chore John Allan forced me to undertake. Migraine headaches were my constant companion thanks to him and my ear would often discharge matter after military drills or a hard night's sleep on an even harder pillow. At times I had balance problems as a result of my severe headaches, which sometimes made me lose the drills to other cadets although I was faster and stronger. The beating had also left a scar across my chest.

Many afternoons and evenings I found time to write and began working on a poem called

Al Aaraaf, a fantasy poem where I longed for another realm that outshone the harsh realities of my life, which was tenfold more engrossing than anything the military could offer. On moonlit nights I would tell enchanting tales to the other cadets. This gave me a chance to try out the stories floating about my brain before writing them.

Once again it was my writing (and few games of cards in the barracks) that got me into financial difficulties as I committed to another self-publisher. Even in the face of my promotion I could not afford to pay my commitments, voluntary or otherwise. I realized I had to seek John Allan's help, and to do this I had to impress him that I was aspiring to "public life" in a grand fashion. The common man's Army would fall short of evidencing these aspirations. I knew I had to get accepted at the Military Academy at West Point. For this, however, I had to seek my discharge from the Army.

As my legal guardian, John Allan held the key to my freedom, a bitter irony. I had just turned twenty and had not contacted the monster in nearly two years. It took all my courage and pride.

Under full awareness of how my life had changed for the worse because of my foster father, I begrudgingly took quill in hand and requested my discharge from the Army. Perhaps this would make me worthy of his so-called "good name" and free myself from the Army while increasing my status in both our estimations.

Fortress Monroe February 4th 1829,

Dear Sir,

I wrote you some time ago from this place but have as yet received no reply. Since that time I wrote to John Mc Kenzie desiring him to see you personally & desire for me, of you, that you would interest yourself in procuring me a cadets' appointment at the Military Academy.

To this likewise I have received no answer, for which I can in no manner account, as he wrote me before I wrote to him & seemed to take an interest in my welfare.

I made the request to obtain a cadets' appointment partly because I know that — (if ₮ my age should prove no obstacle as I have since ascertained it will not) the appointment could easily be obtained either by your personal acquaintance with Mr Wirt — or by the recommendation of General Scott, or even of the officers residing at Fortress Monroe & partly because in making the request you would at once see to what direction my "future views & expectations" were inclined.

You can have no idea of the immense advantages which my present station in the army would give me in the appointment of a cadet — it would be an unprecedented case in the American army, & having already passed thro the practical part even of the higher partion of the Artillery arm, my cadetship would only be considered as a necessary form which I am positive I could run thro' in 6 months.

This is the view of the case which many at this place have taken in regard to myself. If you are willing to assist me it can now be effectually done — if not (as late circumstances have induced me to believe) I must remain contented until chance or other friends shall render me that assistance.

Under the certain expectation of kind news from home I have been led into expences which my present income will not support. I hinted as much in my former letter, and am at present in an uncomfortable situation[.] I have known the time when you would not have suffered me long to remain so.

Whatever fault you may find with me I have not been ungrateful for past services but you blame me for the part which I have taken without considering the powerful impulses which actuated me — You will remember how much I had to suffer upon my return from the University. I never meant to offer a shadow of excuse for the infamous conduct of myself & others at that place.

It was however at the commencement of that year that I got deeply entangled in difficulty which all my after good conduct in the close of the session (to which all there can testify) could not clear away. I had never been from home before for any length of time. I say again I have no excuse to offer for my [con]duct except the common one of youth & [folly]s — but I repeat that I was unable [if] my life had depended upon it to bear the consequences of that conduct in the taunts & abuse that followed it even from those who had been my warmest friends.

I shall wait with impatience for an answer to this letter for upon it depend a great many of the circumstances of my future life — the assurance of an honourable & highly success-ful course in my own country — or the prospect — no certainty of an exile forever to another[.]

Give my love to Ma —
I am Yours affectionately
Edgar A Poe[20]

John Allan at first did not respond to my letters, but quickly warmed upon believing my sincerity. To my consternation, I learned Ma was deathly ill and that she greatly desired to see me. I wasted no time in securing my temporary leave from the Army, but it took nearly a week of bureaucracy while the request made its way up the chain of command. When it was finally secured, I left Fortress Monroe and rushed back to Richmond. The thrill of having sweet Ma's arms around me once more propelled me deep into the night.

I arrived at Moldavia the first week of March and let my knapsack drop to the floor as I rushed through a maze of corridors into Frances Allan's chamber. "Ma, it's Edgar! I am home, Ma!"

The canopied bed was empty, coverlet neat and straightened and smelling as if freshly washed. A selection of medical instruments rested on a bedside tray, cold and metallic. John Allan was sitting lifeless on the mattress's edge, head buried in a pillow. He did not rise or so much as turn his head to greet me.

"Where is she? Where is Ma?"

No response. A group of chambermaids would not acknowledge me.

I took John Allan by the shoulders and shook him. "If she is not here, then what hospital is she in? I must see her!"

"Frances Keeling Allan is dead," he told me, peering up with rheumy eyes. She died on February twenty-eighth; buried yesterday afternoon."

"No ... NO! That is not true! It cannot be true." I fell against the paneled wall in agony. John's head returned to the pillow. "She is buried in Shockoe Hill Cemetery."

Obadiah tried to greet me in my return, but I pushed him aside while stumbling incoherently out of the manse, knocking portraits off the walls.

I dashed toward the cemetery with the world crashing down upon me. Ma's grave was easy to find, the mound of upturned dirt being the freshest. Her tombstone was simple and I remember feeling that John Allan had not given her proper respects. His wealth was not reflected in her death.

Under a slate March sky I wrapped my arms about her meager gravestone and wept, regret and remorse mixing an evil potion within the cauldron of my stomach. I kneeled there in agony blaming myself for leaving Richmond, blaming the medical practitioners who could not treat her, blaming the Army for not releasing me sooner, but most all, blaming John Allan.

There is no wonder why those of this age are transfixed by death and its surroundings. It is all around us, as common as the air we breathe. Sometimes I feel it a curse to be on the living side of the grave.

I am told that Obadiah had to assist me from the graveyard in my sorrow that day, pry me from the mud patch in which I wallowed for hours. I am also told that I wrenched the flowers on the grave into pulp as I grieved. And for days thereafter I lay in my old bed in Moldavia, bewildered by grief and the doom that was inevitable for every female in my life.

John Allan confessed the next day that Ma had made him promise to provide for me on her deathbed. That, coupled with my desire to enter West Point, got us talking freely once more. He seemed to have a spark of compassion for my undertaking and a twinge of pride. After a few more days I had convinced him of my sincerity and he agreed to help me gain the Army dismissal and use his business contacts to bring about my Military Academy appointment. Surprisingly, he also forgave my wrongdoings of the past.[21]

When I returned to my regiment, I learned seventy-five dollars was needed to buy a substitute for my leave. John Allan was displeased that I had not told him of this at Moldavia, yet I did not know. He claimed more deception on my part, but reluctantly paid this amount after I reminded him of my strong desire to enter West Point.

On April 15, 1829, I was released from the Army after having fulfilled the obligation of providing my substitute at no expense to the government. I then returned to Moldavia. Once I was armed with a commendation letter from John Allan, whose wealth seemed to be growing by the hour, I made a journey to Washington and met with Secretary Eaton who informed me there were forty-seven other young men on the West Point waiting list ahead of me.

I digested this news harshly as I traveled to Baltimore at the suggestion of Rose to meet my older brother Henry and some of my birth father's relatives to which I had never been introduced. Rose thought this would be therapeutic for me after Ma's death. I was excited at the notion. Moldavia held too many bad memories.

When I reached the city I checked the address on the crude map in my hands. I looked around to get my bearings. The battered sign above read AMITY STR. I made my way up the thoroughfare. Alternating on either side of the street were a candle maker shop, an iron works, a butcher's store with a green-and-white striped awning, and a drug store that by the looks of the metal sign was having a constant sale on castor oil. A sea-flushed captain who had taken leave in the countryside after porting in the Inner Harbor, I assumed, passed me with a rusty tin box of his ship's vital documents and a mermaid-shaped pipe curving out his mouth. He wore a leather patch over his right eye. Bedraggled guttersnipes were playing catch across the street in their tattered clothes. One had a sizeable knife strapped to his arm.

This was another planet compared to Moldavia's neighborhood. I felt unsafe and wondered if the milkman was so bold as to make door-to-door deliveries here. Sorrow overcame me for my relatives while I approached a small two and a half-story brick duplex where Henry was supposed to be staying with my aunt—Maria Clemm.

I knocked several times on the door to no answer. I checked again to ensure this was the house at No. 3 Amity Street. My knuckles rapped once more and I surveyed the neighboring duplexes. Some were painted brick, but most others were left to disrepair. The one before me was somewhere in between.

No one was detected as I peered in the dirty windows. I was late, but my relatives were supposed to be waiting for me no matter the hour of arrival.

Hearing voices, I walked around back. Clotheslines were strung with multicolored garments flapping like flags in wait of a foreign dignitary. A row of purple tulips was swaying in the spring breeze under a white lattice fence that guarded the opposite end of the garden. In front of them I noticed a rather chubby woman, folds of skin about her neck, planting a garden in a yellow sundress. She was a stocky woman, solidly built.

"Pretty flowers," I said, approaching from behind. "Any idea where I might find the woman who lives in house three?"

"Maria Clemm?" She stood and faced me with glee on her face. "You must be Edgar!"

I removed my hat and nodded. "And you must be my aunt."

She motioned to shake my hand but hers were full of mud, which she besmeared on her dress, creating a Chinese character. Before she could invite me inside a sinewy girl who I guessed to be eight, came bounding over the fence and landed right on the row of flowers, crushing a few underfoot.

"Virginia! How many times have I—"

The girl darted under a sheet snapping in the wind and pranced straight for me. "Hello, Edgar. I'm Virginia. Couldn't help but overhear."

"She's good at that," Maria said.

Virginia's hair was shorn at the neck and lank so that it bobbed and weaved when she talked. "Pleased to meet your acquaintance."

"I'm more than an acquaintance, I'm your first cousin, silly bird. 'Bout time you came to visit. Henry and Granny have been living with us for months. Where ya been?"

"Yes, brother, I would like to know the same." I heard a voice call out from above. Shielding my eyes, I glanced into the sun to see Henry with his head poking out a second story window of the duplex.

"I am afraid the military has kept me from visiting anyone."

"Likely excuse. I see the military has also kept you from getting flabby like me."

"Now get down here so I can greet you formally. It has been a long time."

I must have been delirious from my long journey, for when Henry disappeared in the window I noticed a cluster of daisies growing from a crook in the roofline near the chimney, but quickly blamed it on the sunspots in my eyes.

Henry came into the backyard and we hugged and laughed. It was so great to see him. While we spoke, Virginia played among the hanging clothes, lifting them and sticking her tongue out at every chance. A big smile always ensued. To her great embarrassment she noticed some of her undergarments waving off a clothesline and pulled them into the house where she remained, face pressed to the glass. I soon made my way inside with Henry and our aunt.

At the kitchen table we arm-wrestled as only two brothers can and I told military stories to anyone who would listen. Once all had warmed to each other, I engaged Maria about my father and what she knew of my real mother. She had a wealth of information regarding her brother when they were growing up together. To think that he and some friends started their own drama club! She assured me David Poe, Jr. was a highly intelligent man who could have chosen any lot in life and my resemblance to him when he was my age was uncanny.

I asked Henry about the daisies on the roof, thinking he would deem me half mad. "I grew them up there," Virginia blurted, catching me off guard. I had forgotten all about her. She had a way of hanging around with all the ability of clothes on the line.

"How, may I ask, did you get flowers to grow on a shingled roof?"

"I threw seeds up there last fall, silly bird. Mom says the trapped dirt from passing barouches and coaches on Amity Street must have allowed them to grow with a little rain and sunshine this spring. So there." With that said, young Virginia stuck her tongue out and was gone once more, but I knew she would always be in earshot.

Over many carafes of iced tea the three of us adults talked well into the night about nothing but blood relatives. To think that my real mother was critically acclaimed in the theatre circuit and close to garnering the lead in certain Richmond plays at the time of her death. I had never felt a closer bond to my real family, nor had so many mysteries been solved that had caused me sleepless nights. Learning about my parents, whom I had never known at any level, touched my soul, expanding my being as each story unfolded. I had never suspected that I had Irish blood in me from my father's side of the family. Late in the evening we sang a few Irish folk songs. What a grand time!

Weeks later (head brimming with stories of my parents) I returned to Washington for another appointment with Secretary Eaton who let me know I was now eleventh on the West Point waiting list! That summer I also managed to publish *Al Aaraaf, Tamerlane and Minor Poems*[22] under terms more advantageous to myself than I had received in Boston. Many hours were spent sipping coffee at local cafés as I put the finishing touches on the manuscript. The money I made off the book was encouraging, yet far removed from the financial wellbeing that could support my writing endeavors.

By the end of the year, long after I had returned to Richmond, I learned of my official acceptance to West Point and John Allan was ecstatic. His dreams of me becoming a young man of discipline and business were in reach.

1830 – Age 21

My first year at West Point required tenfold the intensity of studying as that in the Army. The training was never ending. I managed to excel in French and mathematics, and some-how, *somehow*, continue writing in the brief and seldom moments of my spare time in Room 28 of the South Barracks.

My fellow cadets loved my tales told by firelight on wintry nights. When I would take a moment to look out at their wide-eyed heads during the stories, it was as though I was viewing a set of finely cropped bushes. I am not sure whether it was my current distress or my keen desire to cause reaction from my listeners, but my tales grew morbid by the day.

At times we gave an effigy to our hated professors by making a crude figure stuffed with straw that we burned or hung from Room 28. One fine evening we even ate the head of our most despised and gray headed professor. My roommate, Mr. Thomas W. Gibson, tells the story best seeing how I made him the designated murderer!

It was a dark, cold, drizzling night, in the last days of November, when this event came off. The brandy bottle had been empty for two days, and just at dusk Poe proposed that we should draw straws—the one who drew the shortest to go down to Old Benny's and replenish our stock. The straws were drawn, and the lot fell on me.

Provided with four pounds of candles and Poe's last blanket for traffic (silver and gold we had not, but such as we had we gave unto Benny), I started just as the bugle sounded to quarters. It was a rough road to travel, but I knew every foot of it by night or day, and reached my plane of destination in safety, but drenched to the skin. Old Benny was not in the best of humours that evening. Candles and blankets and regulation shoes, and similar articles of traffic, had accumulated largely on his hands, and the market for them was dull in that neighbourhood. His chicken-suppers and bottles of brandy had disappeared very rapidly of late, and he had received little or no money in return.

At last, however, I succeeded in exchanging the candles and blanket for a bottle of brandy and the hardest-featured, loudest-voiced old gander that it has ever been my lot to encounter. To chop the bird's head off before venturing into barracks with him was a matter of pure necessity; and thus, in fact, old Benny rendered him before delivery. I reached the suburbs of the barracks about nine o'clock. The bottle had not as much brandy in it as when I left Old Benny's; but I was very confident I had not spilled any. I had carried the gander first over one shoulder and then over the other, and the consequence was, that not only my shirt-front but my face and hands were as bloody as the entire contents of the old gander's veins and arteries could well make them.

Poe was on the look-out, and met me some distance from the barracks, and my appearance at once inspired him with the idea of a grand hoax. Our plans were perfected in an instant. The gander was tied, neck and feet and wings together, and the bloody feathers bristling in every direction gave it a nondescript appearance that would have defied recognition as a gander by the most astute naturalist on the continent. Poe took charge of the bottle and preceded me to the room. 'Old P—' was puzzling his brains over the binomial theorem, and a visitor from the North Barracks was in the room awaiting the result of my expedition.

Poe had taken his seat, and pretended to be absorbed in the mysteries of 'Lecons Francaises.' Laying the gander down at the outside of the door, I walked or rather staggered into the room, pretending to be very drunk, and exhibiting in clothes and face a spectacle not often seen off the stage.

'My God! what has happened?' exclaimed Poe, with well-acted horror.

'Old K—! Old K—!' I repeated several times, and with gestures intended to be particularly savage.

'Well, what of him?' asked Poe.

'He won't stop me on the road any more!' and I produced a large knife that we had stained with the few drops of blood that remained in the old gander. 'I have killed him!'

'Nonsense!' said Poe. 'You are only trying one of your tricks on us.'

'I didn't suppose you would believe me,' I replied, 'so I cut off his head and brought it into the barracks. Here it is!' And reaching out of the door I caught the gander by the legs, and giving it one fearful swing around my head, dashed it at the only candle in the room, and left all in darkness, with what two of them believed to be the head of one of the Professors. The visitor leaped through the window and alighted in the slop-tub, and made fast time for his own room in the North Barracks—spreading, as he went, the report that I had killed Old K—, and that his head was then in Number 28. The story gained ready credence, and for a time the excitement in barracks ran high. When we lit the candle again 'Old P—' was sitting in one corner a blank picture of horror, and it was some time before we could restore him to reason.

The gander was skinned—picking the feathers off was out of the question—and after taps we cut him up in small pieces and cooked him in a tin wash-basin, over an anthracite fire, without seasoning of any kind. It was perhaps the hardest supper on record, but we went through it without flinching. We had set out to eat old K— in effigy, and we did it; whether he ever learned of the honours we paid him that night I never learned.[23]

In dire straights for money, I managed to convince half of the two-hundred and thirty-two cadets to ante up a dollar and a quarter each so that I could publish my collection titled *Poems, Second Edition.* They felt sorry for my constant migraines, but the writing is what they cared about most. This verified the text had its place on the bookshelves of America if I could just gain readership.

The patched relationship between John Allan and myself took a turn for the worse when I learned from Rose and Mrs. Mackenzie that he had remarried Louisa Gabriella Patterson, a woman twenty years his junior to whom I had never spoken. To no surprise I was not invited to their wedding at the Old St. John's Church or to the lavish reception on the grounds of Moldavia. In my estimation his remarriage was not worthy to be had in the sanctuary where my dear mother lay dead when I was two. John Allan immediately fathered a son with Louisa with the ink still wet on the marriage certificate. Apparently his desires were not marred by Ma's death or perhaps the act was to prove to all that she was the one unable to bear fruit, not him.

Letters exchanged between us became terser. John Allan suddenly did not care how well I was doing at the academy. At the end of the year he had sent me what he termed his "final" letter, telling me in no uncertain terms that he was cutting himself off from communication with me.[24]

1831 - Age 22

The workings of John Allan's new wife Louisa were apparent, and although I had never met the woman, there was no question she was trying diligently to destroy the last vestiges of affection John had for me. Louisa and the children from her first marriage, coupled with their new son, left no room in John Allan's life for the orphan boy he never found suitable to adopt.

My stored emotions became so great at these further injustices that I let them all out in one fury of a letter after another holiday suffered alone and with little money to care for my own person.

West Point Jany 3d 1831

Sir,

I suppose (altho' you desire no further communication with yourself on my part,) that your restriction does not extend to my answering your final letter.

Did I, when an infant, sollicit your charity and protection, or was it of your own free will, that you volunteered your services in my behalf? It is well known to respectable individuals in Baltimore, and elsewhere, that my Grandfather (my natural protector at the time you interposed) was wealthy, and that I was his favorite grandchild

— But the promises of adoption, and liberal education which you held forth to him in a letter which is now in possession of my family, induced him to resign all care of me into your hands. Under such circumstances, can it be said that I have no right to expect any thing at your hands? You may probably urge that you have given me a liberal education. I will leave the decision of that question to those who know how far liberal educations can be obtained in 8 months at the University of Va. Here you will say that it was my own fault that I did not return —

You would not let me return because bills were presented you for payment which I never wished nor desired you to pay. Had you let me return, my reformation had been sure — as my conduct the last 3 months gave every reason to believe — and you would never have heard more of my extravagances. But I am not about to proclaim myself guilty of all that has been alledged against me, and which I have hitherto endured, simply because I *was too proud to reply. I will boldly say that it was wholly and entirely your own mistaken parsimony that caused all the difficulties in which I was involved while at Charlotte[s]ville. The expences of the institution at the lowest estimate were $350 per annum. You sent me there with $110. Of this $50 were to be paid immediately for board — $60 for attendance upon 2 professors — and you even then did not miss the opportunity of abusing me because I did not attend 3. Then $15 more were to be paid for room-rent — remember that all this was to be paid in advance, with $110.—$12 more for a bed — and $12 more for room furniture. I had, of course, the mortification of running in debt for public property — against the known rules of the institution, and was immediately regarded in the light of a beggar. You will remember that in a week after my arrival, I wrote to you for some more money, and for books — You replied in terms of the utmost abuse — if I had been the vilest wretch on earth you could not have been more abusive than you were because I could not contrive to pay $150 with $110. I had enclosed to you in my letter (according to your express commands) an account of the expences incurred amounting to $149 — the balance to be paid was $3[9] — You enclosed me $40, leaving me one dollar in pocket. In a short time afterwards I received a packet of books consisting of, Gil Blas, and the Cambridge Mathematics in 2 vols: books for which I had no earthly use since I had no means of attending the mathematical lectures. But books must be had, If I intended to remain at the institution — and they were bought accordingly upon credit. In this manner debts were accumulated, and money borrowed of Jews in Charlottesville at extravagant interest — for I was obliged to hire a servant, to pay for wood, for washing, and a thousand other necessaries. It was then that I became dissolute, for how could it be otherwise? I could associate with no students, except those who were in a similar situation with myself — alho' from different causes — They from drunkenness, and extravagance — I, because it was my crime to have no one on Earth who cared for me, or loved me. I call God to witness that I have never loved dissipation — Those who know me know that my pursuits and habits are very far from any thing of the kind. But I was drawn into it by my companions[.] Even their professions of friendship — hollow as they were — were a relief. Towards the close of the session you sent me $100 — but it was too late — to be of any service in extricating me from my difficulties — I kept it for some time — thinking that if I could obtain more I could yet retrieve my character — I applied to James Galt — but he, I believe, from the best of motives refused to lend me any — I then became desperate, and gambled — until I finally i[n]volved myself irretrievably. If I have been to blame in all this — place yourself in my situation, and tell me if you would not have been equally so. But these circumstances were all unknown to my friends when I returned home — They knew that I had been extravagant — but that was all — I had no hope of returning to Charlottesville, and I waited in vain in expectation that you would, at least, obtain me some employment. I saw no prospect of this — and I could endure it no longer.*

— Every day threatened with a warrant &c. I left home — and after nearly 2 years conduct with which no fault could be found — in the army, as a common soldier — I earned, myself, by the most humiliating privations – a Cadets' warrant which you could have obtained at any time for asking. It was then that I thought I might venture to sollicit your assistance in giving me an outfit — I came home, you will remember, the night after the burial — If she had not have died while I was away there would have been nothing for me to regret — Your love I never valued — but she I believed loved me as her own child. You promised me to forgive all — but you soon forgot your promise. You sent me to W. Point

*l[ike a beggar.] The same difficulties are threateni[n]g me as before at [Charlottesville] —
and I must resign.*

*As to your injunction not to trouble you with farther communication rest assured, Sir,
that I will most religiously observe it. When I parted from you — at the steam-boat, I knew
that I should nev[er] see you again.*

...

*I have no more to say — except that my future life (which thank God will not endure
long) must be passed in indigence and sickness. I have no energy left, nor health, If it was
possible, to put up with the fatigues of this place, and the inconveniences which my absolute want of necessaries subject me to, and as I mentioned before it is my intention to resign.
For this end it will be necessary that you (as my nominal guardian) enclose me your written
permission. It will be useless to refuse me this last request — for I can leave the place
without any permission — your refusal would only deprive me of the little pay which is now
due as mileage.*

*From the time of writing this I shall neglect my studies and duties at the institution —
if I do not receive your answer in 10 days — I will leave the point without — for otherwise
I should subject myself to dismission.*

E A Poe[25]

With third year cadets marching in cadence outside my windowpane under a flurry of
snow, I took the crimson candle burning next to me and dripped its refuse onto the envelope, then bound it with a waxen seal of my hurt.

Wishing to escape the oppression of West Point and to spite John Allan, whose lack of
monetary support once again left me destitute among my peers, I refused to attend classes
or church. The surprised, helpless look on the officers' faces who had belittled us at all
hours of the day gave me satisfaction to no end. A court martial found me guilty of being
wanton in my duties, and my dismissal was shortly thereafter. With my newly published
volume of poems in tow and shame on my head, I ventured to the publishing capitol of
America—New York City. Upon my arrival an illness once again forced me to write the
miserable foster father who had abandoned me.

N. York Feb 21, 1831

Dear Sir —

*In spite of all my resolution to the contrary I am obliged once more to recur to you for
assistance — It will however be the last time that I ever trouble any human being — I feel
that I am on sick bed from which I never shall get up. I now make an appeal not to your
affection because I have lost that but to your sense of justice – I wrote to you for permission
to resign — because it was impossible that I could [stay] — my ear has been too shocking
for any description — I am wearing away every day — even if my last sickness had not
completed it. I wrote to you as I say for permission to resign because without your permission no resignation can be received —*

*My reason for doing so was that I should obtain my mileage amounting to $30,35 —
according to the rules of the institution. In my present circumstances a single dollar is of
more importance to me than 10,000 are to you and you deliberately refused to answer my
letter — I, as I told you, neglected my duty when I found it impossible to attend to it, and the*

consequences were inevitable — dismissal. I have been dismissed — when a single line from you would have saved it — The whole academy have interested themselves in my behalf because my only crime was being sick — but it was of no use — I refer you to Col Thayer to the public records, for my standing and reputation for talent — but it was all in vain if you had granted me permission to resign — all might have been avoided — I have not strength nor energy left to write half what I feel — You one day or other will felll [feel] how you have treated me. I left [West] Point two days ago and travelling to N. York without a cloak or an[y] other clothing of importance. I have caught a most violent cold and am confined to my bed — I have no money — no friends — I have written to my brother — but he cannot help me — I shall never rise from my bed — besides a most violent cold on my lungs my ear discharges blood and matter continuall[y] and my headache is distracting — I hardly know what I am writing — I will write no more — Please send me a little money — quickly — and forget what I said about you —

God bless you
E A Poe

Do not say a word to my sister. I shall send to the P.O. every day.[26]

Receiving no support or response from John Allan, my motto became *"Tenui musam meditamur avena,"* which is translated from Latin to mean, "We cultivate literature on a little oatmeal."

I found little success in selling or marketing my *Poems, Second Edition* in the big city and I truly believe it was because I was not from a wealthy family in the city or part of the "Literati of New York" as I called them. Quickly having run out of money, I wrote to Maria Clemm and was greeted with graciousness into her Baltimore household, for I had no other place in the world to turn.

A fortnight's journey from New York brought me to Amity Street once again with its weathered and mismatched buildings that may as well have been transported and placed there from random cities. I made my way along the cracked sidewalk with its sprouts of grass that fronted row upon row of tightly knit duplexes. A knapsack from the academy was crisscrossed over my shoulders and I was dressed in the only civilian clothes to my name: a black frockcoat with a white shirt and a black cravat, a black vest, black boots and gloves, which were sent years ago in the trunk the morning after my altercation with John Allan. The frockcoat had kept me from the wintry cold as I strolled the byways of New York peddling my tales although I had told John Allan otherwise in my last letter.

Spring came early to Baltimore that year, cheery azaleas and tulips were bursting with color and erasing any memory of the melancholy winter I had suffered. As I approached my aunt's rundown duplex, I saw Virginia waving and jumping on the front porch.

We greeted each other and she whisked me inside. "You have let your hair grow. You look like a bristle brush."

"The day I cut it again will be the day they let women into West Point," I said, placing my knapsack on the parlour floor. Through the doorway I saw Maria poke her head around the kitchen corner.

"What a blessing to have you come stay with us again," she exclaimed. "Please excuse me, I am up to my elbows in muck from planting."

"I am beginning to think you enjoy the mud. The Orientals say it is therapeutic for the skin. You should try taking a bath in it."

"Things will be vivacious around here with you, Eddy." She immediately paused. "It is okay if I call you 'Eddy'?"

"You can call me anything but late for lunch! I am famished from my journey."

"Eddy Poe," she said, "I like it."

"Muddy Clemm. I like that, too."

"Dirty hands, clean mind. This is going to be fun," she called out.

"And vivacious," Virginia said with a giggle. I could tell she was not entirely sure what the word meant.

To Virginia, Muddy said, "Show him to his room while I fix lunch. I have the attic pegged for you, Eddy. A writer needs a good view of the world."

"And food in his belly."

The house at No. 3 Amity Street was a small two and a half story brick duplex that in its entirety only contained five rooms. On the first floor were the parlour (front) and kitchen (rear), each having its own fireplace and overhanging wooden mantels, which were so plain in appearance that I wondered if a railroad tie had been cut in half and distributed to each. The interior walls and ceilings were whitewashed horsehair plaster. All doors, mantels, baseboards and related trim were wood.

The stairway leading to the second floor was narrow and winding. "Glad I have barely eaten in the past few days or I would never make it around the bend," I said, taking my knapsack and starting up.

Virginia grabbed my shoulder. "I must warn you about the second floor. It's Granny. The stroke she had at the end of last year has not left her well."

"And I heard not a word of it at the academy?"

"We did not want to trouble you with all you were going through."

Bumping and knocking, I trod up the steps and found my grandmother, Elizabeth Cairnes Poe, near seventy-five years of age, lying in one of the beds in the front bedroom directly above the parlour. A tiny hearth sat off to one side, sharing a chimney with the one below. I remember thinking that most logs would not fit in these fireplaces, whereas a carriage could have been driven into those at Moldavia.

My eyes strained into the bedroom. Hazy light was across her withered face, eyes retracted into their sockets. Her mouth resembled a drawstring purse that had been pulled tight and one side of her face sagged as if invisible weights were attached. I stepped over to her bed and took her knotted hand in mine.

"She is an invalid, Eddy. Bedridden. No longer speaks. Mom used to sleep in the back bedroom with me, but she moved in here to take care of Granny. Henry switched to my room and he snores like a barnyard animal. *Snawkkk, snawkkk, heww,*" she grunted.

After taking a deep breath, knowing that my grandmother teetered on the edge of the afterlife and knowing the last thing I needed was to have another female figure in my life die, I kissed her lined cheek and said a quick prayer.

Next Virginia showed me to the rear bedroom above the kitchen. It also had two beds, but no fireplace. The bed on the right was covered in an array of hand-sown dolls, tawny yarn for hair, red-stitched lips, buttons the color of Robin's eggs for eyes.

"How old are you now, Virginia?"

"Ten, and growing taller every day, thank you very much." She stood on her tiptoes next to me. "Can run like the wind, too. Want to race?"

"Only if it's a race to see who can eat the most food."

"Come on up to the attic and see your room," she said, but not before sticking her tongue out at me. She tugged at my arm and in one long stretch we found a door that opened to another winding stairway narrower than the one leading to the second story. The planks bemoaned as we climbed our way to dizzying heights. The smell of dust and mould invaded us.

At the top of the stairs was a tiny room cut from low hanging rafters. A twin bed sat opposite a dormer window that looked out onto Amity Street. The shape of the window reminded me of an ivory broach Ma used to wear to dinner parties. A crisscross of sunlight was branding the front of a three-drawer dresser on the other side of the room that had its legs sawn off to fit low in one corner.

"Great view of the countryside if you look over the duplexes across the street," Virginia said.

"As long as the flowers growing on the roof do not get in my way." I bumped my head on an overhang when I tried to stand erect and shockwaves quavered down my neck.

"Watch it," she informed a second too late.

"Thanks," I droned.

"If I keep getting taller I will hit my head in here, too."

"Lucky you."

A bank of amber candles was suspended in air, hanging off the rafters by J-shaped holders. Hatboxes and a selection of rusting garden tools were piled under an armless chair upon which I slung my knapsack. I panicked when I saw no writing table, but Virginia pointed out that the dresser was low enough to enable me to write on its top surface while seated.

"This is where I practice my singing so I keep from disturbing the others." Virginia shuffled her feet and a glum look came over her.

"Well nothing is going to change now that I am here. You can sing at any time, even when I am writing. It might help."

She brightened. "Thanks, Eddy. Mom says I have a church choir voice. Says if I keep practicing I can make money off it just like her brother did in the theatre." She thought for a moment. "Guess that would be your father."

"Sure was," I verified. "Is singing your dream?"

"More than anything."

"There is nothing more fulfilling than chasing one's dreams, Virginia. Never forget that."

Forenoon. We no sooner sat down to lunch when Henry traipsed inside, overalls and hair flecked in whitewash. "Brother!"

From my seat at the table, I hushed him. "Do not say that too loudly in your state."

"See you still have your sense of humor."

"And you your sense of untidiness. I swear you and Rose must have come from a different set of parents than me."

Henry entered the kitchen and Virginia gave her impression of him sleeping: "*Snawkkk, snawkkk, heww.*" My brother flipped his nose at her.

"It's only been a year since I have seen you, but you sure have aged, Henry. Your hair has gone white."

"That's what painting fences will do to you." He faced Muddy. "Not to worry, Aunty Maria, I dried off on the way here."

All she could do was grin, while I remarked, "Better than being splattered with mud," to which I received a spoon handle in the ribs.

When Henry came toward me I smelled the pungent vapor of alcohol and noticed his eyes were red and swollen. I prayed it was paint thinner that I detected, but then noticed the outline of a whiskey bottle in the front pocket of his coveralls. His face had aged a decade since I last saw him, skin creased and saggy, which made me regret my quip about him getting old. There was no question that strong drink had overtaken Henry's life.

I surveyed the table: meatloaf, freshly made biscuits and gravy, mashed potatoes, and a bowl of green beans Muddy had canned last summer. A giant pitcher of iced tea was in the middle. With the three of us sitting round the table and Henry standing because Muddy would not let him sit in a chair until she was sure the paint had dried, we served the food family style, which could not have been more appropriate. They were in awe that I knew all dishes should be passed counterclockwise around the table and that the fork and knife should never touch the table while one is eating; both pieces of etiquette that one naturally knows growing up in high society Richmond.

Virginia made a face at the beans as they were passed, which meant more for me. While waiting, I heaped meatloaf and then biscuits onto my plate.

From above Henry spoke, his slowness of speech was evident. "Not only did they treat my brother wrong at the academy ... they failed to feed him."

Muddy shook her head with concern at his intoxication. I silently vowed to have a talk with my brother after the meal. Once I had filled my plate, I spied a spinning wheel next to the parlour fireplace and asked about it.

"Mom is a seamstress who weaves cotton and wool," Virginia informed.

"She can apparently stitch together a pretty doll, too," I said in reference to what I had seen on Virginia's bed. "And you, Henry, are still working your odd jobs?"

"They are not odd to me. I like changing them often to keep them fresh and to get a wide range of experience. That way, if one industry fails, I can work in another."

"Is that how it is?" Pointing at him with my fork, I said, "You change jobs with the frequency of your undershirt."

"Almost as often as you change addresses, brother."

"That's enough out of you two," Muddy said. To Henry, she added, "And you are drinking *tea* this afternoon, right?"

"Of course, Aunty."

I finished chewing my biscuit, swallowed, and asked, "No offense, but with Virginia and Granny not working, and Muddy sewing and canning the bounty of her garden, how do you tend the rent on this place?"

"Will you explain, Henry?" Muddy asked as she got up from the table.

Henry slyly spiked his tea with whiskey while Muddy was away, winked, put his arm around me, and began massaging my neck. His breath could have peeled the varnish off a church pew. "We are living on Granny's substantial government pension. Grandfather received it for being a decorated Revolutionary War veteran. She also receives a small pension from his time spent as Quartermaster General for the city of Baltimore after the war."

This was surprising and welcomed news. I had never thought of a government pension. A cool spring breeze was kicking up the cottony material ornamenting the kitchen window and I took a deep breath of freedom, freedom to work on my life's passion without the restrains of counting house boredom or the monotonous grunts of a military officer snapping orders.

Light of spirit, we had the best of times at lunch that afternoon. Not a sad word was mentioned of my situation or of Henry's vice, or even of the cholera epidemic that had begun in India and was spreading into Russia and Central Europe. I felt more at home with my brother, aunt, grandmother, and cousin in the cramped old duplex than at any time under the slate roof and gold trim of Moldavia. At the same time I found it oddly refreshing not to have servants catering to my every whim, following me around to clean up after me or asking if they could polish my shoes upon each scuff.

Out of the corner of my eye I noticed Muddy scraping paraffin wax off a purplish-red container. She announced, "Desert is canned blueberry jam on slices of bread."

"From you I was hoping for mud pie," I said with a chortle.

"Be careful, Eddy, or I might feed you the real thing."

Never had my self-promised talk with Henry (through every hurt-avoidance fault of my own and knowing I was susceptible to downing a few beverages from time-to-time myself) and his drinking became worse with each downturn of Granny's condition. He stayed in a constant stupor and often I would hear him spewing outside after an evening on the town or a long workday.

One afternoon, six months after moving to Baltimore, I left the attic to go for a walk and to clear my head after finishing a poem. On the second floor I found Henry and Muddy standing outside Granny's door. I distinctly remember that my brother's index finger was stuck in an empty whiskey bottle that was dangling at his side.

"How can you do this to Granny?" Henry was asking Muddy.

"Do what? I am giving the best of care. I tend to your grandmother night and day in slavish fashion."

"That is just the point, you are taking great care of her so she does not perish." To my shock, Henry invasively brought his face to Muddy's. "You are keeping her alive as long as possible for her pensions, her income."

"You are forgetting that she is *my* mother. And I refuse to let her whither away in bed. What is so difficult to understand about that?"

Henry lost his balance, but caught himself on the doorjamb. Whiskey vapor was fumigating the confined space between the bedrooms.

I took a hold of Henry's collar and steadied him.

"Here comes my brother to save the day like a narrator in one of his tales."

"Muddy has sacrificed a lot for Granny, more than you know," I said.

"Granny is an invalid who cannot communicate with us. How do we know she is not in agony? I have seen the bedsores with mine own eyes!"

"I know you hate seeing the woman who raised you in this condition, we all hate it, but we cannot just let her die. That is murder, Henry."

"No, what is against the laws of God is letting a person suffer in pain. You cannot tell me she is without hurt in that state."

"Keep your voice down, please," I said in a whisper. "How do you know she cannot hear us?"

At that moment Henry stared at me with the presence of one who had a well-reasoned plan that only made sense through the wavering logic of intoxication. "Let the woman die in peace, in dignity. We can suffocate her in a minute and no one will ever know. A pillow to the face."

"If that is your desire," Muddy said, "then leave my house and never return. It is not safe to have you here."

I had never seen Muddy so infuriated and I was flabbergasted at his suggestion.

Henry turned toward his bedroom in the back of the duplex and flicked the empty whiskey bottle off his finger. It clattered onto the floor and bounced against the wall. "I will leave in the morning and you will never see me again. This is not *your* house by the way. The proud woman in that bed sustains it. She is paying for it with her helpless nobility!" He slammed the door and the bottle clinked into spinning motion.

"Please, Henry," I said. "Let's talk about this."

That evening was frightening. Henry did not leave his second story bedchamber. During supper we took turns standing guard. That night Virginia slept with Muddy in Granny's room. They had strict instructions to wake me at the slightest approach from Henry.

Matters were strangely quiet in Henry's room that night, and I know because I barely slept a wink. At daybreak I knew why after finding two more empty bottles in the bedroom along with a stash of others under his bed. I called to him for nearly ten minutes before entering. Henry never had a chance to leave the duplex as he promised. He died that evening of intemperance. He was a vaporous lump, twisted under the covers when I found him.

1833 - Age 24

I had been living in the Baltimore duplex for years and heard not a peep from John Allan. Perhaps he had not received word of my first short story publication called *Metzengerstein* in *The Saturday Courier*.[27] Louisa may have hid it from him—a common pattern among those who seek to keep me from their loved ones in Richmond. No matter. I continued to publish tales, but nothing of note that would get me recognized among the Literati of New York.

In Baltimore, as Granny's paralytic condition worsened along with my migraines, I feared for the state of our wonderful household. If she should expire, so would her pensions and our financial well being. The day was coming fast and our family would be left penniless. So one particularly gray spring day, sitting at my dresser, I cast aside my latest story and penned a letter to John Allan under hopes that surprise alone would gain his sympathy.

Baltimore April 12th 1833

It has now been more than two years since you have assisted me, and more than three since you have spoken to me. I feel little hope that you will pay any regard to this letter, but still I cannot refrain from making one more attempt to interest you in my behalf. If you will only consider in what a situation I am placed you will surely pity me — without friends, without any means, consequently of obtaining employment, I am perishing — absolutely perishing for want of aid. And yet I am not idle — nor addicted to any vice — nor have I committed any offence against society which would render me deserving of so hard a fate. For God's sake pity me, and save me from destruction.

E A Poe[28]

I received not a single line of response from him. For all I knew Louisa burnt my letter just as Elmira's father had done. I did not realize it at the time, but paranoia was creeping into my very soul and would never leave.

Rose sent me word that John Allan sold much of the artwork from Moldavia on the advice of Louisa; the paintings that had been chosen by Ma. The very name made my skin crawl. *Louisa*. LOUISA!

A steady rain was pattering against the dormer window in my room, smearing the countryside into green-brown streaks. I crumpled my latest poem in anger just as Virginia appeared in the doorway. She was eleven now, a tomboy to the hilt.

"What ya doing, Eddy?" Before I could answer: "Let me guess, writing?"

"You know me too well."

"I believe that stylus is attached to your hand."

The hem of her bright, floral print dress stopped at mid-shin. Its cheerfulness was out of place for the day. "If your mother catches you going outside in such apparel, you will be grounded."

Phssspht! she spluttered as her tongue vibrated between her lips. "My dress is not short, I am getting tall. I will be hitting my head on the attic rafters soon. Besides, I am not going out on such a dreary day because you are going to tutor me."

"That's news."

"Foreign languages. I want to learn all you know about Spanish and Latin. Oh, and French too. *Oo, la la.* The language of love. *Amour.*"

"And you will speak the language of sadness if Muddy catches you talking like that."

Virginia moved into the center of the bedroom and rain began slapping the roof in a fit. "Eddy, Muddy, Granny, all these nicknames. I think I would like one." Her chestnut eyes grew to the size of walnuts. "You are a writer, Eddy, so think of a nickname for me. A grand one!" Virginia twirled, flowers spinning everywhere, then curtsied and made a face.

Droplets pelting above us, I thought for a moment. "You are prissy, and you're like a sister to me." I thought some more. On Amity Street horses and slicked carriages were spraying water behind them. The sidewalks were barren.

"Let's hear it already."

"How about Sissy, a combination of both?"

"Sissy with a Y?"

"Sure thing."

"Hoom? I think I like that. Sissy. Miss Sissy. Queen Sissy to you."

This time I extended my tongue.

She held onto a rafter and swung there as the boards creaked and lamented. She had coltish legs that were becoming womanly. "Well? Am I going to get tutored in the languages of Europe?"

My fingers strummed on the makeshift desk as I thought. "All right, I will tutor you if you take it seriously and show more patience than you have just now, but only in languages, not singing. I have trouble carrying a melody in a pail."

As October leaves changed to blotches of vibrant color along the Baltimore countryside the language lessons continued. They were going as well as could be expected and Muddy was pleased. This teaching kept any pressures off me—likely self-imagined—for bringing in little money from selling a few short tales and poems. Muddy was supportive of my art form beyond belief.

The lessons caused Sissy and me to spend many afternoons together after my writing was finished for the day. The duplex was close to the valley of Gwynn's Falls in Baltimore County and we would go there for walks, growing in the strongest of cousinly bonds.

One fall evening after learning the phonetic equivalents of common verbs in French, we were sitting at the kitchen table. A mug of coffee was steaming before me, beating back the draughts that were seeping through the walls and biting at my ankles in the duplex. Sissy was quaffing her own cup but I truly believe it had more cream and sugar in it than coffee. She was trying harder and harder to impress me as evidenced by Sissy's new adult dresses. A month prior she had given away her entire doll collection to a little girl four duplexes over. Muddy protested this because she had made them by hand, but the deed was done.

At the table Sissy referenced giant sunflowers poking out of a cylindrical piece of earthenware in the corner. "Those are the last of the season from Mom's garden. She brought them back from the brink."

"I hear over-watering is the most common killer of plants."

"Especially when they're watered from the dogs next door. The sunflowers are pretty but I would not touch them. The dogs kept tinkling on them so Mom had to run chicken wire to keep them away."

I nearly spit my coffee on the table. This was but one of many instances Sissy made me laugh in fits. Her sunny disposition was oft at odds with my melancholy attitude, which seemed to float about me like a dense fog for days on end. How I found her refreshing. How I began to depend upon her conversations like a cool breeze in summer.

From the hidden seat of a neighboring chair she pulled a pumpkin up by the stem and sat it in the middle of the table with a thud. A dollop of coffee sloshed from our mugs. Sissy pulled two sharp knives from a drawer and brought them over along with a towel that I used to wipe up the spill. I then slid it under the pumpkin and held my knife high in the air, letting the wavering firelight glint off its metallic sheen.

"Stop, Eddy. You scare me sometimes just like your stories."

"That is the goal." I smiled and put down the blade. "I hope the neighbor's dogs were not privy to Muddy's pumpkin patch or I will get some gloves."

"Oh no, orange scares them."

I figured this puzzling statement did not merit a response. Next to me was a manuscript that I had nearly finished, entitled *Manuscript in a Bottle* and I grabbed a stylus lying atop it. I dipped the stylus in ink and began outlining the wickedest face imaginable on the pumpkin. The brows flared and twisted at the ends, set over dark slits for eyes. The nose was all hard lines. From the mouth sprouted vampiric teeth and the lips were fiendishly curled.

"Dreadful!" Sissy exclaimed. "I love it!"

"A face to make Bram Stoker proud."

We began carving by removing the stem as the sunflowers lolled over us. Sissy folded up a sleeve and plunged her hand into the head of the bloodthirsty monster. She pulled out handfuls of seeds and rind, flinging them in an untidy manner (more on her arms and table than towel).

"Out come the innards of the vampire!"

"Eddy, that is sick!"

I warned her not to get any on my manuscript. I had another copy upstairs, but this was the one I was going to mail to the *Saturday Visiter* the following morning for entrance in a contest. John Allan taught me in the carriage house—if he taught me nothing else—to keep a copy of my corpus at all times. I hid my manuscript as the seeds were divided out and salted. We next slid a tin tray into the licking flames of the hearth for baking. Over cupfuls of coffee we sliced out the facial features and were later staring at a gruesome appearance. Sissy found a stubby candle in another kitchen drawer, which we lit and placed in the bottom of the pumpkin. The evil face glowed to life.

"In my studies at the university I learned that some cultures believe a scary face will ward off evil spirits from a household."

"Then Moldavia must be free of them," Sissy remarked, which caused me to almost choke on my last sip.

Minutes of joking passed between us. When Sissy got up to check on the pumpkin seeds, I turned the conversation to Nathaniel Hawthorne.

"Nathaniel who?" Sissy asked.

"In my humble estimation Nathaniel Hawthorne is the best prose writer in America."

She returned to the table and held the jack o' lantern up, the glowering candle inside making the jagged teeth appear to grow longer and champ down on unseen flesh in search of blood. From across the table I saw a thin young lady with a glowing orange face on her shoulders. "What of *The Legend of Sleepy Hollow*," the pumpkin asked, "when the headless horseman throws the carved head and it explodes in a fireball at Ichabod Crane's feet?

The story of the horseman will be remembered through the years, I just know it. What is your impression of Washington Irving?"

"I enjoyed *The Legend of Sleepy Hollow* thoroughly. The Galloping Hessian is a wonderful invention, but Washington Irving and the rest are commonplace when compared to Hawthorne."

"Such a bold statement for an up and coming writer."

"Hawthorn is not without exceptions. I find Longfellow's poems perfect in their kind."

Sissy's response was, "So are my sunflowers."

Although Sissy read most of my works, she displayed no tendency toward literature or intellectualism, which were traits I sorely missed from Elmira and Mrs. Stanard. Sissy was concerned with girly fancies and play, which I should have expected from a young lady of her age and common upbringing.

She began to show more interest a few weeks later when I won the first place prize of fifty dollars in the *Saturday Visiter* contest, which published the manuscript under the title *MS. Found in a Bottle.* That singular prize was the most I had received in my writing career and I was gladdened to no end. The income was more than Muddy could make in three months of sewing.

To celebrate, I took them to one of the best fish restaurants in Baltimore. Our next-door neighbor watched over Granny. While Muddy was talking to me, Sissy said, "Would you look at that?"

I was amazed to see a floating bottle in the Inner Harbor. A note was inside! Sissy pulled the bottle out, removed the cork in the end, and extracted the parchment.

"Read it already," I implored. The coincidence astounded me ... for the moment, that is.

"I can't. You read it." She smirked at Muddy while handing it over.

Dear Eddy,
Thanks for taking care of our family and congratulations on your first place award.
Love, Muddy and Sissy.
P.S. Stop scaring us so much!

1834 - Age 25

I was always pleased to receive word from Rose, but the letter forwarded early in the year was troubling. In short and directed prose she told me John Allan had taken gravely ill. Prominent Richmond doctors were seen coming and going from Moldavia at all hours. Louisa was sparing no expense in getting a multitude of opinions and treatments.

A part of me prayed bloodletting was draining him dry. Bizarrely, another part of me was struck with sudden remorse in learning that the man who had raised me—for better or worse—was sick unto death, the man to whom I had not spoken in years and to whom a gulf of hard feelings divided us. I realized it would behoove my conscience to pay him a visit in his last days.

Without haste I traveled to Richmond under full determination to bridge this chasm and repair our damaged relationship. I was now a quarter of a century old; more willing and able to forget the wrongs of my past. As I approached Richmond (hitching rides with strangers in various carriages), I vowed not to leave Moldavia without John Allan's blessing, if nothing else. I could forgive him if he could do the same.

A distant part of me longed for what I had sought since a child—adoption, even if it was just for one day or hour. As I left my carriage and walked toward the heart of Richmond, I was conscious that I never wanted nor needed his money other than to sustain my writing. Like death spires, the three massive chimneys of Moldavia appeared over a ridge, so tall as to cause an impasse for the low hanging clouds, which turned my thoughts to Louisa and what her reactions would be upon my showing up at the doorstep.

I did not stop at the Mackenzie's to see Rose, instead making my way right for Moldavia. Time was of the essence. I opened the wrought iron gate and made my way up the flagstone walkway. The deep shadows of Moldavia overcame me along with a lifetime of emotions. I felt like the prodigal son returning home, although I had certainly not spent John Allan's fortune and knowing there would be no feast upon my arrival.

I clacked the brass knocker. A male servant answered the front door. "Excuse me. I am Edgar Allan Poe, foster son of John Allan and former resident of this household. I would like—"

The whites of the servant's eyes grew large. It was then that I noticed the man was Obadiah. We shared a brief smile and a hug. "Massar Edgar! How is you?"

"I am fine and you appear well fed, for which I am pleased. We will have time for conversation later. I heard of Pa's sickness and have traveled a great distance to wish him well. Would you let him know that I am here to see him?"

Obadiah swallowed, and responded, "Yas, sir. He real sick like. Moment pleez." The huge door swung shut and I heard faint voices conversing inside. Before I could step back, the door flung open again and a finely dressed woman appeared who did not look much older than me. There was no need to inquire of her name, for I knew who she was.

"Well, if it is not the fabled and much maligned Master Poe. In the flesh," Louisa said. She was a salamander-faced woman, lips razor thin. It did not appear her mouth was moving when she talked. Her hair was greasy ... slimy.

"Do you always greet those who have been raised by your husband with such disdain?"

"Only those who were undeserving of such an honour."

I stood my ground physically and conversationally. My journey left me many hours to think of such a confrontation. "How could I be the subject of your contempt when we have never met until now?" My hand rose. "Regardless, I am not here to see you, but John Allan whom I understand has taken ill. I request the briefest of interviews."

Not the slightest bit of compassion softened her features as she glanced over my worn apparel. "He is very sick and is in no shape to receive visitors, especially one who would upset him so and who may be the carrier of other diseases from parts unknown."

"The only disease I have is that of mistrust and I caught the virus from you long ago without feeling the heat of your breath."

She sneered at this, but had no retort other than: "Say what you will, I must return to his bedside. Good day." Louisa Patterson Allan (to think we had a common last name) slithered inside and pushed the door closed.

I jammed my boot against it and raised my voice. "If you shan't grant me an interview, then I ask that John Allan is at least informed of my presence. The decision on whether he is well enough is his and his alone. Pa will undoubtedly see me. I spent twenty years under his care and you have spent one tenth that. I dare say I know his wishes better than you."

"You know nothing of *his* wishes. You came here to get a share of the inheritance at the last second. I knew your motives the first time I learned of your miserable existence."

"Nothing could be further from the truth," I told her. The Spanish Inquisition had finally been suppressed, but I felt I was under it when standing on Moldavia's doorstep.

Somewhere in the foyer Obadiah called out. "Ma'ams, you alright? Massar Poe?"

"Then what do you want?" Louisa asked, paying Obadiah no regard.

"To see him one last time. I want to make amends." With that I pushed past Louisa and Obadiah who offered me no resistance. I marched down the long hall, past paintings in gilded frames that were foreign to me, and found John Allan in bed. A couple chambermaids were tending him and they spread to the corners of the room when I burst inside. For a brief second I paused. He had physically shrunk since I last saw him. His face was drawn. This was not the man who beat me senseless in the carriage house. "Pa!" I said, approaching.

At first his delirium did not allow for recognition, but then a spark lit his eyes. I knelt by the bed and thought he was going to hug me. "My clothing is not the best, Pa, but know that I come under all due respect to mend our relationship."

The spark in his eyes vanquished into muted shades of hurt and disgrace before transforming into the blackest of coals. John Allan raised his bedside cane and threatened to strike.[29] "Get out!" he ordered.

In shock I immediately withdrew, tripping on the leg of a bedside table, visions of that night in the carriage house dancing in my head. At the doorway I turned back, he swung the cane again with little force, but the intent was there. That was the last time we ever met.

"Good day again, Master Poe," Louisa said with a smirk on my way past in the hall. Tears flecked Obadiah's face on my rush to leave.

The door slammed behind me. I stayed across the street for days under a pall of sorrow. Neither Rose's company nor Mrs. Mackenzie's lemon pie could cheer me. On the fourth day we learned of John Allan's death only by seeing the mortician's carriage parked out front and his stiff body enshrouded in white linens being wheeled from Moldavia.

I sobbed in uncontrollable fits for the broken relationship that could never be mended. Rose and Mrs. Mackenzie comforted me as best they could as I repeated over and over: "In his mind I will always be a failure. In his mind I will always be a failure."

Later that week I returned to Baltimore. When rumors of Moldavia began surfacing in and around Richmond, Rose wrote me. John Allan was buried next to Ma in the Shockoe Hill Cemetery. To no surprise, John Allan had died at the age of fifty-four leaving everything to Louisa and her children. My name was not mentioned in the reading of the will.

1835 - Age 26

The grinding. The pulverizing between my temples. The gnawing at any thoughts of reason. I lay in bed convulsing, or was it my funerary box? It hurt to open my eyes. The slightest bit of movement in any part of my body, but especially my head, filled me with agony.

The proper action for you to take is to ask for Virginia's hand in marriage.

I screamed into the pillow and punched my fist into the headboard. My knuckles felt nothing in comparison. I could not let the rest of the duplex hear me in such distress. After all, I was the man of the household since Henry's death. I prayed to a merciful God for my own quick death. The migraines were growing in frequency and intensity. How many days had I been in this state, unable to write, unable to think with the slightest bit of clarity? How many *weeks*?

The proper action for you to take is to ask for Virginia's hand in marriage.

Is that what Muddy had said the night before? Was it all dreamt from a mind slipping into derangement? My hands clamped down on my ears when I heard the voice again.

She needs a husband, Eddy. How can Virginia go through life without a father figure or husband? To her you can be both. To me you can be everything I've always wanted for her, a son-in-law, a husband. You have my complete blessing.

And I had told my aunt that this was a preposterous notion to suggest betwixt first cousins, unnatural to its core. I had flatly refused. If the prodding had actually happened, I must have refused, right?

When I did force one eye open, pain from the blinding sun filled me as though I were mere inches from its surface. I flinched away from the dormer while the grinding continued behind my nose and cheeks, between my ears.

The gristmill in my head!

From beneath the pillow my hand crinkled something. The noise sounded loud as a roaring bonfire. When I pulled it out I clenched a letter, a letter I had read by the mercy of dim candlelight the night before. My memory was briefly jarred. I held it up and saw nothing but jagged, unintelligible markings through my squinting eyes as sunlight diffused through the parchment. At once they reminded me of the Chinese characters Muddy always seemed to wipe on her apron.

Thomas Willis White—whom I would be remiss in speaking of without mentioning Mr. Kennedy first—wrote the letter. John Pendleton Kennedy was a popular Baltimore novelist. Whether those reading this story of my life know his name remains to be seen. In all due respect, I am not sure whether his brand of pleasing audiences via small words and formulaic themes to keep the story "moving along" in his words, will etch his name in the annals of classic authors. Nevertheless, John Kennedy is, and always has been a man of the highest integrity, a gentleman's gentleman. It was not until after I had won the prize money for *MS. Found in a Bottle* that I learned he was one of the judges and was most impressed with my writing.

I took the opportunity to contact Kennedy and we exchanged letters about the various philosophies of the written word. We met on several occasions in Baltimore. Kennedy was always dressed in an Abe Lincoln-styled top hat and he carried a watch in his vest pocket that he checked often, displaying a strange punctuality for a novelist.

He found my "unitary perspective" theory of ideal short stories intriguing. My thoughts that morals should play no part in tales gave him pause. "Morals," I informed him, "are best taught from church pulpits."

To this he responded: "Those who can actually read in our society—lawyers, doctors, and politicians—are the ones who need morals the most."

The scraping rollers made another pass, crushing the grains of thought. Did Muddy's desires cause this attack on my senses? Was it Sissy's? I struggled out of bed with the balance of a drunk. My equilibrium was dependent upon the health of my ear; a sorry mess. Drumbeats were the pulses of blood at my temples. Henry's last day flashed before me as I stumbled over to the dresser. On my way I tripped and fell into a pile of clothes that I had no clue as to how they got there. The black as pitch material told me they were mine.

As I struggled into the chair and lifted my deadwood legs one by one into a bent position, I tried to shed Muddy's suspect desires for my future and was reminded that Kennedy's thoughtfulness was never ending on my behalf. Amongst many discussions of how an unknown poet could make a living doing that which he loves, Kennedy contacted Thomas Willis White, the owner of the *Southern Literary Messenger*. Kennedy suggested that White give me permanent employment as assistant editor, where I could routinely publish my tales.

Baltimore, April 13, 1835

Dear Sir,—Poe did right in referring to me. He is very clever with his pen—classical and scholar-like. He wants experience and direction, but I have no doubt he can be made very useful to you. And, poor fellow! He is very *poor. I told him to write something for every number of your magazine, and that you might find it to your advantage to give him some permanent employ. He has a volume of very bizarre tales in the hands of —, in Philadelphia, who for a year past has been promising to publish them. This young fellow is highly imaginative, and a little given to the terrific. He is at work upon a tragedy, but I have turned him to drudging upon whatever may make money, and I have no doubt you and he will find your account in each other.*

J.P. Kennedy[30]

White had been writing me for a month or more, offering this position if I could prove myself in a review of Kennedy's latest novel *Horse Shoe Robinson*, which I did in haste due to the health problems that were plaguing me to no end. Our household desperately needed the money the position would provide and this forced me to respond to White *before* my review had ripened via many revisions.

I rent the letter in my hand when I thought about it as the heavy stone wheels made another revolution through my head. Flattening. Crushing! I tossed the confetti onto the floor and shakily grabbed my pen. Oh that it was a dagger into my heart!

The ink was nearly dry in the well and I had to poke at the corners to find some fluidity beneath its hardened ebony skin. It was then, at the end of May, with nausea in my stomach from what I felt in my skull, I finally found it within me to write Mr. White and excuse my hasty review: *In regard to my critique I seriously feel ashamed of what I have written. I fully intended to have given the work a thorough review, and examine it in detail. Ill health alone prevented me from so doing. At the time I wrote the hasty sketch I sent you I was so ill as to be hardly able to see the paper on which I wrote, and finished in a state of complete exhaustion. I have therefore, not done any thing like justice to the book, and I am vexed about the matter, for Mr K has proved himself a kind friend to me in every respect, and I am sincerely grateful to him for many acts of generosity and attention.[31]*

The subsequent months brought more uncomfortable prodding from Muddy and a chance at redemption from White. When I received his letter it sent me dancing down the two flights of stairs leading from the attic to the lower level with the lightest of feet. I sprung into the parlour where Virginia was practicing her singing of "Cape Cod Girls" in front of the mirror that sat on the railroad tie mantel over the fireplace.

I came to an abrupt halt when I saw her profile. Sissy's honey brown hair was long and brushed back. Her face was flawless and the muscles of her throat were carved alabaster. She had the most beautiful voice, unearthly, angelic. If it was of this world, it was natural as any whippoorwill's.

For a moment I watched her upper body rise and fall with each chord, her full lips oscillate. Whether it was the way Muddy's homemade cotton dress clung to her form or just my exuberant state that made me notice Sissy in a different light, I am not sure; but one thing was set in stone: Sissy, now twelve, had entered womanhood seemingly overnight. The seedling had become a daisy.

"Eddy?" She turned away from the mirror. "How long have you been standing there?"

"Uh, just a second. Great news," I said, holding up the letter. "You are looking at the new assistant editor of the *Southern Literary Messenger*!"

My aunt wandered in from the kitchen wearing her usual gray dress that was elegant, but worn, and a widow's cap, graying hair flowing from underneath. She had the look of a stalwart about her, yet a caring woman also.

"Did you hear me, Muddy, the job pays five hundred and twenty dollars a year,[32] can you believe it, this will be the most money I have made in my life, Mister White has promised to publish a number of my tales in the magazine, a great deal of them, he wants me writing more, more!" My exuberance left me talking in a run-on sentence.

The sparrow tracks at Muddy's eyes did not move as she asked, "When do you plan to leave?"

"Soon as possible, why, if I could start this very second Mister White would be all the happier."

"Leave?" Sissy questioned, a beleaguered look overtaking her.

"I am glad for you, Eddy," Muddy added with only a hint of joy.

"I plan to go to-morrow morning. I need time to pack tonight."

"Where?" This was overwhelming to Sissy and her questions were limited to one word.

"Back to Richmond, a place to which I am very familiar. I will be close to Rose once more!"

Muddy spun the wheel on her thread device, and looked down. "But where will you stay?"

My speech slowed to something more akin to proper English. "For the life of me, I have not given it much consideration. Perhaps Rose can help me find a place. Making that kind of money I should have no problem. Maybe I'll buy Moldavia, or at least its carriage house so I can burn it. This is so exhilarating!"

Later in my bedroom, under the constant glow of an oil lamp, I packed in jubilation. Through the parchment-thin walls and cracked floorboards I overheard Sissy talking to Muddy down in the kitchen.

"—and he has a mysterious manner about him but at the same time an indescribable charm."

"That's Eddy," Muddy said, "so talented and gifted, yet unassuming."

"What are we to do?"

Their tone was heavy, weighted under the obvious concerns of my leaving, which I was slow to ascertain in my excitement.

"Let's talk of other things," Muddy said, "of the magnetism of his grey eyes that can draw people to him, and yet a moment after turn them away if he so chooses to use them as a weapon. He is not as others make him out. I have learned that day-by-day. Eddy is gentle, caring, and happy most of the time despite the awful circumstances of his childhood and that pitiful excuse he had for a foster father."

"Now, now, let us not mar the name of the deceased, Mother. Mister Allan had some good traits, I am just lax to think of them."

They broke into laughter, which cut through the somberness of their voices but did not last.

Virginia lowered her voice. "And Eddy is such an understated gentleman, a teacher, a poet, always dressed in black with faultless taste and simplicity. He is calm of person and takes time to enjoy nature. Why, upon entering the shade of a tree he removes his hat and pushes back his hair to enjoy the coolness."

"I believe if he could afford the finest clothes he would dress the same, only of newer material."

"Mother! That thinking could only come from a seamstress, but I believe this to be true. Our Eddy is a man of growing importance who still takes time to pluck a wild flower or to stop and examine a butterfly lit on a trellis. And he is leaving us to-morrow. Why does he have to go?"

Muddy, the matriarch of the home, began sniffling.

I heard the patter of light feet up the steps, a door rattle into its frame, and then Sissy crying in her rear bedroom. I continued packing for some time, not under feelings of elation, but those of guilt and remorse. My hopes that Sissy would stop her sobbing and prance off on one of her whims were to no avail.

When I had finished, I climbed down the narrow attic stairs with my packages as if Santa bumping down a chimney, but I had no gifts to give the young lady below. On the landing I turned and entered Sissy's room. I sat quietly on the edge of her small mattress and began brushing tears from her cheeks.

"Why do you have to leave us like this, Eddy? How am I going to learn French?"

"I promise to visit often and to write every day. Part of it can be in French. You and your mother mean the world to me."

"It's not about the French lessons, Eddy, you know it's not about them. That is just an excuse to get you to stay." Sissy pushed herself to a sitting position, but did not face me. "We will be unable to support ourselves if Granny dies and it's on your head."

"I will be able to send you money from my new job. Lots of it."

She expressed concerns about not having a man to take care of her and I took this—I swear to you—as meaning a father figure. I held her tight, so fragile in my arms, and we fell asleep on her bed until daybreak. I was convinced Muddy told Sissy nothing of her clandestine marriage plans for us after hearing their conversation earlier, and I did not mention this as we lay together, crying more than laughing.

The next morning Muddy hugged me goodbye in the parlour after I had kissed Granny's limp cheek upstairs. Muddy looked square in my eyes and said, "Take her hand in marriage, Eddy. You can then support her while I stay here and tend to my mother."

My feet were leaden. The front door appeared so far away that I could not reach it in a day's journey. "With all due kindness for that which you have shown to me, finances is hardly a reason to join in matrimony."

"I have seen you gaze at her budding womanhood."

"That is not true," I lied.

"First cousin or distant stranger, do not feel like you must hide your natural desires. This alone will keep our family together. I have witnessed for myself the closeness between you two during the tutoring sessions. She has expressed to me ... that she loves you deeply, Eddy."

Sissy was still in her room crying and would not come out. My packages were anchors at my sides.

"I said, 'she loves you deeply.' Do you understand? Give a nod of the head before you leave us. Acknowledge only this one statement."

I felt on the edge of another migraine attack and the room began to tilt. Without saying a word, I spun out of the Clemm duplex with its mounting pressures just as I had entered it—knapsack in tow—and went to Richmond to edit the *Southern Literary Messenger*. Being a writer I preferred to explain all and hash out our differences of opinion by letter.

Love was blossoming in my heart for Sissy, but at this moment I chose my career, knowing such feelings for a first cousin were not natural.

I forgot everything when Mr. White greeted me at the front door of his office. From the reflection in the glass my grin stretched from Maryland to Michigan. "Master Poe, please come inside. I am delighted to have you under my employ."

"I am delighted to be here!"

White was an older man who wore spectacles on the tip of his bottlenose. A leather smock was tied about his waist and his hands were ink-stained from assisting the copyright in running the printing presses that labored noisily in the rear of the office. White did not fit the picture of a wealthy businessman that I had in mind, but this was none of my concern. His magazine was one of the most successful in the country outside of New York and I could not wait to get officially started in my career—to get paid for doing what I loved.

"Your new desk." He referenced a small escritoire near the front of the office covered in stacks of manuscripts so that not an inch of surface was showing. I must have been staring in disbelief, for he said, "Have faith. In a few months time you will be caught up and your editorials will be flying out of here like a trapped dove."

"Thank you, Mister White. You will not be sorry."

On my lunch break I found a two bedroom apartment a block from the *Southern Literary Messenger*. The owner charged me sixteen dollars a month, a sum I could easily afford on my salary. During my first weeks of employment I saw little of the apartment as I worked fervently to read the solicited manuscripts, which were those requested by White from local authors or sent his way by the likes of Kennedy. The stacks of unsolicited manuscripts (the "pulp piles" as White called it) grew with each visit from the mail carrier.

And it was the mail carrier who brought me more bad news at the end of my second week in Richmond. On the latest stack of unsolicited manuscripts sat a vexing letter—a letter from Muddy.

Granny, Elizabeth Cairnes Poe, had died two nights prior in her sleep.[33] Although my heart bled for her, we all knew the time was nigh. My initial thoughts for Muddy were that this would relieve her custodial burden, but in a tear-stained paragraph she told me how Granny's pension would now be extinguished and so would hopes of staying in the duplex. Muddy asked my advice about Neilson Poe of Baltimore, my prosperous cousin who had married Virginia's half-sister. She had apparently told him all for he had offered to take Sissy into his home and support her, as well as provide for her education in an attempt to subvert any love between us that he deemed improper at her age and from our cousinly bond. If after a few years of living apart, with Sissy having reached legal age, she could marry me then by his estimation. Of all the nerve! Who was Neilson to judge Sissy or me for that matter? Did his wealth magically grant him wisdom? In all my rage I did not pay much weight to the obvious work of Muddy in this situation.

This offer was an affront to my manhood as a provider for those I deemed my true family. One cannot understand the great and fond attraction I had for Muddy and Sissy unless one has suffered so much loss in life as I, so much desertion compliments of the grave and their own foster father. I was determined to hang onto what little family I had, to those few blessed souls who had encouraged my writing. To ensure as much, I knew I had to call out for Sissy's love.

Neilson's tender was no different to me than offering to take care of my own mother and daughter. Every accusatory word John Allan ever said to me came rushing to the forefront. *You will never be anything but a disgrace!* It wound me into a tight ball of emotions and my pen released them.

Aug: 29th
My dearest Aunty,

I am blinded with tears while writing this letter — I have no wish to live another hour. Amid sorrow, and the deepest anxiety your letter reached — and you well know how little I am able to bear up under the pressure of grief. My bitterest enemy would pity me could he now read my heart. My last my last my only hold on life is cruelly torn away — I have no desire to live and will not. But let my duty be done. I love, you know I love Virginia passionately devotedly. I cannot express in words the fervent devotion I feel towards my dear little cousin — my own darling. But what can [I] say? Oh think for me for I am incapable of thinking. Al[l of my] thoughts are occupied with the supposition that both you & she will prefer to go with N. Poe. I do sincerely believe that your comforts will for the present be secured — I cannot speak as regards your peace — your happiness. You have both tender hearts — and you will always have the reflection that my agony is more than I can bear — that you have driven me to the grave — for love like mine can never be gotten over. It is useless to disguise the truth that when Virginia goes with N. P. that I shall never behold her again — that is absolutely sure. Pity me, my dear Aunty, pity me. I have no one now to fly to. I am among strangers, and my wretchedness is more than I can bear. It is useless to expect advice from me — what can I say? Can I, in honour & in truth say — Virginia! do not go! —

do not go where you can be comfortable & perhaps happy — and on the other hand can I calmly resign my — life itself. If she had truly loved me would she not have rejected the offer with scorn? Oh God have mercy on me! If she goes with N. P. what are you to do, my own Aunty?

I had procured a sweet little house in a retired situation on Church Hill — newly done up and with a large garden and [ever]y convenience — at only $5 month. I have been dreaming every day & night since of the rapture I should feel in [havin]g my only friends — all I love on Earth with me there, [and] the pride I would take in making you both comfor[table] & in calling her my wife. But the dream is over [G]od have mercy on me. What have I to live for? Among strangers with not one soul to love me.

The situation has this morning been conferred upon another. Branch T. Sunders. but White has engaged to make my salary $60 a month, and we could live in comparative comfort & happiness — even the $4 a week I am now paying for board would support us all — but I shall have $15 a week & what need would we have of more? I had thought to send you on a little money every week until you could either hear from Hall or Wm. Poe, and then we could get a [little] furniture for a start for White will not be able [to a]dvance any. After that all would go well — or I would make a desperate exertion & try to borrow enough for that purpose. There is little danger of the house being taken immediately. I would send you on $5 now — for White paid me the $8 2 days since — but you appear not to have received my last letter and I am afraid to trust it to the mail, as the letters are continually robbed. I have it for you & will keep it until I hear from you when I will send it & more if I get any in the meantime. I wrote you that Wm. Poe had written to me concerning you & has offered to assist you asking me questions concerning you which I answered. He will beyond doubt aid you shortly & with an effectual aid. Trust in God.

The tone of your letter wounds me to the soul — Oh Aunty, aunty you loved me once — how can you be so cruel now? You speak of Virginia acquiring accomplishments, and entering into society — you speak in so worldly a tone. Are you sure she would be more happy. Do you think any one could love her more dearly than I? She will have far — very far better opportunities of entering into society here than with N. P. Every one here receives me with open arms.

Adieu my dear aunty. I cannot advise you. Ask Virginia. Leave it to her. Let me have, under her own hand, a letter, bidding me good bye — forever — and I may die — my heart will break — but I will say no more.

E A P.
   Kiss her for me —— a million times

For Virginia,

My love, my own sweetest Sissy, my darling little wifey, think well before you break the heart of your Cousin, Eddy.

I open this letter to enclose the 5$ — I have just received another letter from you announcing the rect. of mine. My heart bleeds for you. Dearest Aunty consider my happiness while you are thinking about your own. I am saving all I can. The only money I have yet spent is 50 cts for washing — I have 2.25 left. I will shortly send you more. Write *immediately. I shall be all anxiety & dread until I hear from you. Try and convince my dear Virga. how devotedly I love her. I wish you would get me the Republican wh: [which] noticed the Messenger & send it on immediately by mail. God bless & protect you both.*[34]

Days passed while I awaited their decision, knowing I would have to deal with Muddy's marriage notions if they accepted my offer to come to Richmond. As I waited for a response, no matter how many tales I read, I could not shake the constant sense of dread that had overcome me. I wrote Kennedy for consolation, who I now considered to be one of my confidants.

Richmond   Sep: 11ᵗʰ 1835
Dear Sir,
...
Through your influence Mr White has been induced to employ me in assisting him with the Editorial duties of his Magazine at a salary of $520 per annum. The situation is agreable to me for many reasons — but alas! It appears to me that nothing can now give me pleasure — or the slightest gratification. Excuse me, my dear Sir, if in this letter you find much incoherency. My feelings at this moment are pitiable indeed. I am suffering under a depression of spirits such as I have never felt before. I have struggled in vain against the influence of this melancholy — You will believe me when I say that I am still miserable in spite of the great improvement in my circumstances. I say you will believe me, and for this simple reason, that a man who is writing for effect does not write thus. My heart is open before you — if it be worth reading, read it. I am wretched, and know not why.

Console me — for you can. But let it be quickly — or it will be too late. Write me immediately. Convince me that it is worth one's while — that it is at all necessary to live, and you will prove yourself indeed my friend. Persuade me to do what is right. I do not mean this — I do not mean that you should consider what I now write you a jest — oh pity me! for I feel that my words are incoherent — but I will recover myself. You will not fail to see that I am suffering under a depression of spirits which will not fail to ruin me should it be long continued. Write me then, and quickly. Urge me to do what is right. Your words will have more weight with me than the words of others — for you were my friend when no one else was. Fail not — as you value your peace of mind hereafter.

...
Yours most sincerely
Edgar A. Poe[35]

September 19, 1835; Baltimore

My Dear Poe, — I am sorry to see you in such plight as your letter shows you in. — It is strange that just at the time when every body is praising you and when Fortune has begun to smile upon your hitherto wretched circumstances you should be invaded by these villainous blue devils. — It belongs, however, to your age and temper to be thus buffeted, — but be assured it only wants a little resolution to master the adversary forever. — Rise early, live generously, and make cheerful acquaintances and I have no doubt you will send these misgivings of the heart all to the Devil. —You will doubtless do well henceforth in literature and add to your comforts as well as to your reputation which, it gives me great pleasure to tell you, is every where rising in popular esteem. Can't you write some farces after the manner of the French Vaudevilles? if you can — (and I think you can —) you may turn them to excellent account by selling them to the managers in New York. — I wish you would give your thoughts to this suggestion.

More than yourself have remarked the coincidence between Hans Phaal & the Lunar Discoveries and I perceive that in New York they are republishing Hans for the sake of comparison.

Say to White that I am over head in business and can promise never a line to living man. — I wish he would send me the Richmond Whig containing the reply to the Defence of Capt Read. Tell him so.

I will write to Carey & Lea to know if they will allow you to publish The Tales of the Folio Club in their name. Of course, you will understand that if they do not print them they will not be required to be at the risk of the printing expenses. I suppose you mean that White shall take that risk upon himself and look for his indemnity to the sale. My own opinion is that White could publish them as advantageously as Carey.

Write to me frequently, and believe me very truly

Yours
John P. Kennedy[36]

Never had I found my writing to be so persuasive (and parts of it misleading) as when Virginia and Maria Clemm moved to Richmond in early October. Sissy accepted my (dare I say "forced") marriage proposal and we were engaged almost before she crossed the threshold of the apartment. A ring I had fashioned from tin was all I could afford at the moment. She did not care in the slightest when I slipped it on her finger. It could have been made from yarn and Sissy would have gushed over it.

1836 - Age 27

Over the winter Muddy was relentless in her speak of marriage. She wanted the matrimony date to happen sooner than later. The engagement ring placated her to some extent; yet after a month the guilt she wrought was never ending and foisted upon me at the most inopportune moments, like at Sunday brunch while within earshot of Sissy.

My promises of matrimony were under false pretenses to keep the only family together that I had ever known. Sissy was a lovely brook to me that offered a cool drink from the heated cares of my life, a brook that I could sit beside and watch for hours and wet my face and dip my feet, but never swim no matter how scorching my forlorn life had become given the shallow waters of her young age and lack of education. I loved her on the same level, not deeply, but it was perhaps what they call puppy love.

The demands of my new editorial position had me in the office from dusk till dawn, which I used as an excuse as to why this was not the proper time to be newly married. I relished every second of my job no matter what the hours. I was coming in contact with up and coming writers and gaining a name for myself as my tales began to be published in the *Southern Literary Messenger.*

As spring came into full bloom I procured the sweet little house on Church Hill Street — newly remodeled and with a large garden out back that Muddy was excited to get digging in.

One fine day at the end of April, or perhaps the start of May, I found Sissy rocking on the porch swing as I left for work. "Off to the races?" she asked.

Startled, I clutched my chest. "Try not to do that to an old man."

"You are not old."

"Closer to thirty than twenty."

Something was troubling her. "I feel we are growing farther apart instead of closer together," Sissy said. "Your tutoring has fallen away like Texas seceding from Mexico."

I sat down next to her and the swing began creaking beneath its rusty chains, struggling with our combined weight. "You know the demands of my job. It is a great burden to support you and your mother, but it gives me even greater satisfaction."

Sissy looked over at me with her almond eyes that had become pools of care and need. "You have only taken Christmas and New Year's off since we moved here. I want to spend more time with you. Can you skip today? We can do nothing but spend time as other engaged couples do. Pleassssse, Eddy?"

While horses clopped by on Church Hill Street and the swing groaned, I thought. Finally: "The query letters never stop piling up at the magazine. How about an afternoon?"

"*This* afternoon?"

"It's a date."

"Grand! I will have lunch waiting, come hungry."

That bright, mirthful afternoon I had no sooner put my briefcase inside our sweet little house than Sissy whisked me into the backyard, ticking her finger down a picket fence as we ran. We tramped between sprigs of upstart cornrows, splitting the middle of Muddy's garden, and made our way along two side streets and a narrow alleyway lined in crates and brick tenants on either side.

"Where on earth are you taking me?" I questioned.

"You'll see."

We were in a dead run now, cobblestone clacking under feet. Turning right at a cent shop, off the main thoroughfare, a huge meadow rose up before us. It expanded as far as could be seen into powder blue flowers.

With Sissy pulling me by the hand she located what appeared to be a trail slicing through a copse of weeds and thickets. We struggled down the trail. A hill emerged and when we crested it, a pond sat below, its sun-flecked surface a bed of jewels.

Near the pond Sissy spread out a quilt on an array of wildflowers and beat it down until flat. She had packed a basket lunch with plenty of gingerbread cookies for dessert. Honeysuckle scented the air as we ate and bullfrogs made themselves known. Two swans were gliding effortlessly across the peaceful water.

I tore off my coat and let the spring breeze infuse my cotton shirt and lungs. How free I felt. The day-to-day dregs of work at the *Southern Literary Messenger*, of sorting through the never-ending pulp pile, had slowly made me forget the wonder of the outdoors.

"What are you writing now, Eddy?"

"I never divulge the content of my next tale for it is bad luck. You know that. But I can tell you the working title is *The Collapse of the House of Usher*."

"You mean Moldavia."

"In many ways, yes," I verified.

"I would enjoy seeing Moldavia collapse like a griddlecake around the chimneys. And when Louisa poked her head out of the rubble, I would push the largest chimney with the end of my smallest finger and it would topple on her thick skull."

"*Louisa*," I uttered, noticing that the very mention of her name brought spite from my lips. It then struck me what Sissy had said and I chuckled. I finished an apple hiding in a corner of the basket and immediately loped off the head of a gingerbread man.

As Sissy was accustomed to doing, she diverted the subject away from writing to an entirely different matter, one dear to her heart. She was lying on the quilt, hands behind her head, peering into the cobalt sky; her tin ring winking. "I hear that a composer named Chopin is packing orchestra houses across Europe."

"Women swoon—"

"As they do under your stories. I hear music in your writing, Eddy."

For the first time Sissy had found a remarkable way to intertwine our loves. "That is astounding! I have always thought skillfully versed prose has a rhythm to it, a melody."

Sissy stood, spread her arms, and began spinning. Her lank hair went horizontal. "Like your *Bridal Song* poem music is everywhere. Gander the swans, graceful in their beauty. Their necks are the shape of a treble clef." She stopped twirling and began peeling out of her dress. I hid my face in embarrassment.

She cackled. "Eddy, have you never seen a young lady in a bathing suit? I am your fiancée."

When I parted my fingers I saw Sissy pulling the crumpled dress off her ankles, revealing a one-piece bathing suit with ruffles. Tiny violets speckled the material and they made my vision swirl. If there was any doubt about Sissy's womanhood, it was cast aside as I embarrassingly noticed the figure of the thirteen-year-old. I tried to view my first cousin in a family sense, but no matter how much I wanted to disbelieve, I was physically attracted to her.

"This is my personal swimming hole. I come here to sing most days. No one knows about it but us." With tomboy proficiency she skipped to the edge.

"I'm sure the water is freezing. What are you trying to—"

Sissy's tongue shot out her mouth and she did a cannonball into the shimmering pond. The swans paddled to the opposite shore, squawking in fear. Sissy splashed and whirled. She swam in a circle then did handstands in the shallow end; her gangly legs knifing from the water, slicing back down again. They were long and slender, lightning bolts on a cloudless day.

"Come on in," she cajoled. "The water is chilly, but I am already used to it." She swatted at the surface, spraying my leg and the gingerbread man's, too.

I waved her off but she was determined in her playfulness.

"Chicken! Take your shirt off, roll up your pants."

"No. Please." It was not my clothes, but my pride and dignity that I was trying to protect in keeping my shirt on.

Sissy climbed out, her suit clinging to the curves of her femininity, not an ounce of bashfulness in her. She rushed over to me and began trying to pull me into the water. "Come on, Eddy. I have heard of what a swimmer you are. You cannot be fearful of drowning."

"Stop, Virginia. I have had enough. You are getting the quilt sopping wet. Now please—"

"Ooh, he called me 'Virginia.' I must be getting to my hubby-to-be." By this time she was tickling me and tugging at my shirt as though she had sprouted octopus arms. The basket tipped and bottles clanked. Cool pond water was dripping over my thighs. Muscles that I did not know existed tightened with my every flinch.

She became draped over my shoulders. Before I could fight her off she grabbed hold of my untucked shirttail and pulled it over my head. My shirt peeled off and I was left with my fears.

Sissy screamed. Hand to mouth, she said, "The stripes ... scars across your chest![37]"

I twisted away from her in shame and tried to get my shirt back on. "They are from my miserable excuse for a foster father who sought to beat the sensibilities of the world into me, to make me forget writing. John Allan always wanted me to be the rational businessman, to stifle my dreams and individualism."

Sissy began shedding tears that disappeared into the patches of moisture already on her face. By holding my hand she consoled me. "The scars that despicable man has left on you, Eddy, run much deeper than those on your chest."

In May, finally yielding to Muddy's pressures and my own desires, I signed a marriage bond stating Virginia was at least twenty-one, though she was only thirteen. The laws of Virginia required her to be of legal age. From my lie came a young lady filled with mirth. The word "giddy" comes to mind as she danced out of the courthouse to plan the wedding that was only a few days off.

Sissy, to no one's surprise, wore a floral print dress on that day and held a bouquet of tulips and daisies in her hand. Muddy, a satisfied look across her matriarchal face, said beforehand, "I can think of no greater gentleman and man of honour to have my daughter's hand in marriage."

We were joined before a small group of friends and relatives, including Rose and Mrs. Mackenzie, in Richmond. Muddy's spring flowers decorated the pulpit.

In the vestibule I was shifting my weight to and fro in nervousness. Rose was trying to console me and all I could think to say to her was, "That is a remarkably wrinkled dress for a wedding."

"Just love me," was her response.

The minister was Reverend Amasa Convers, a Presbyterian who took leave of his normal fire-and-brimstone sermons to deliver our vows. His charge was short. Having no money to buy a diamond ring, we used Granny's, God rest her soul. I placed it on Sissy's thin finger until it abutted the tin engagement ring.

Afterwards Muddy invited everyone over to our small house for quail baked in the brick oven and all the "fixins," as Sissy called them. For dessert there was every flavor of cobbler imaginable, stacks of chocolate sheet cakes, and strawberry shortcake if any grazers should still find themself hungry after the feast.

Judge Stanard and my old friend Robert were in attendance. We had renewed our acquaintance earlier in the year when we ran into each other on the street.

"So you are a new lawyer," I said, a large part of me wishing John Allan had let me return to the University of Virginia.

"Followed in my father's footsteps. And I know you are still scaring all with your tales. Father has a subscription to the *Southern Literary Messenger*."

"Guilty as charged."

"Still swimming?"

"Swimming in debt, but my current job should get us out of it soon."

Robert pulled me aside into the parlour. "Listen, I have noticed you and your family are not in the best of sorts." He took out a money clip. "Here's fifty dollars, I owe you for keeping Reynolds away from me."

I swatted it away out of pride. "I do not accept charity."

"My friend, this is nothing of the sort. Please understand. This is merely repayment of an old debt."

"Put the money away. This is embarrassing for me, Robert, on what is to be a festive occasion." He stuffed the money back into his pocket. He had grown up to be bigger and stronger than me and I detected no stuttering in his speech. I could envision him talking before a jury. His suit was nicer than my wedding outfit. "I feel wealthy in life's gifts: love and family and friends, but unfortunately as others see you, so you are." The words of John Allan flashed in my head to this day. "We have gone on such divergent paths it is hard to believe we were once boyhood chums."

"Nothing has changed, Edgar. Your prose still has a dramatic effect on me. As it was then, so it is now."

"Know that on my wedding day I have given pause to remember your mother and her early words of encouragement."

On a table next to the sofa was a pitcher of cranberry juice Muddy had prepared. Robert poured us each a glass and lifted his in the air. "Cheers!"

"Drink of the Injun blood," I said.

That was one of the last times I saw Robert Stanard. I later found a fifty-dollar bill in the wedding card Robert gave Sissy and me.

From that day of our marriage forward people in Richmond gossiped about our new union ceaselessly. Some went so far as to view our marriage certificate and to call me a forger. It got to the point where Sissy and I took to flaunting our union in their faces at every chance. Public kissing, which was frowned upon in every nook and cranny of our society, we found to be quite fun under the disapproving noses of church ladies and politicians.

We did not take a honeymoon due to my work schedule, or at least that is what I told Muddy. For the next two years I lived with my new bride as I had lived before, with the kindness and respect of an older brother; much as I loved my own dear sister, Rose.

For two years we did not consummate our union. Sissy appeared fine with this, and I think too immature (mentally not physically) for the coupling.

1837 - Age 28

The teeth of January were especially sharp. New Year's was but three days past. I remember walking into the *Southern Literary Messenger* office one particular morning bundled in layers of clothing. When I unwrapped my long scarf and hung my hat on the rack next to the door, Mr. White was standing before me, red moving up his face as if the spectacles on his nose were an anger measuring line.

He peered over them, his leather vest besmeared with fresh ink. Rolled in his hand was the latest issue of the magazine. White pointed it in my direction. "I do not appreciate your stories of fright. What I am building here is a magazine of *literature*."

I tried to collect myself as the heat thrown off the rear printing presses invaded my clothing. "In due respect, sir, not all of my tales are horrific."

He unfolded the magazine and hurriedly flipped it open to an earmarked page. "And I quote from your tale *King Pest the First*: 'Before each of the party lay a portion of a skull, which was used as a drinking cup. Overhead was suspended a human skeleton, by means of a rope tied round one of the legs and fastened to a ring in the ceiling. The other limb, confined by no such fetter, stuck off from the body at right angles, causing the whole loose and rattling frame to dangle and twirl about at the caprice of every occasional puff of wind which found its way into the apartment. In the cranium of this hideous thing lay quantity of ignited charcoal, which threw a fitful but vivid light over the entire scene; while coffins, and other wares appertaining to the shop of an undertaker, were piled high up around the room, and against the windows, preventing any ray from escaping into the street.'[38] I most certainly call *that* horrific. How can talk of skulls and coffins be literature in any form?"

"Literature takes many forms. It is not just about relationships, contrary to popular belief. I write for singular effect on the reader. If I may?" I asked, reaching for the magazine. White handed it over and I flipped to another story of mine called the *Shadow-A Parable* I had also published in the same issue without getting his editorial approval. Listen to this, 'A dead weight hung upon us. It hung upon our limbs—upon the household furniture—upon the goblets from which we drank; and all things were depressed, and borne down thereby—all things save only the flames of the seven lamps which illumined our revel.'[39] That is unitary effect on the reader and I dare say, a fine morsel of literature."

White yanked it back and read further in the tale. "'For there was yet another tenant of our chamber in the person of young Zoilus. Dead, and at full length he lay, enshrouded; the genius and the demon of the scene. Alas! he bore no portion in our mirth, save that his countenance, distorted with the plague, and his eyes, in which Death had but half extinguished the fire of the pestilence, seemed to take such interest in our merriment as the dead may haply take in the merriment of those who are to die.'[40] The effect you are having on our readers is to scare them witless. Where is the moral of any of your stories? Show me that."

Unbuttoning my frockcoat, I said, "Writers should be entertainers, not preachers. I offer escapism from life instead of ethics and I have written numerous reviews of other stories. Many of our readers love my writing and are begging for more. Kennedy tells me the ranks are swelling." I referenced a stack of letters on the corner of my desk. "Read for yourself."

"Reading your tales is enough."

White's tone was strange for his persona and this was the first I had heard of his disappointment in my writing. Wind snapped against the windowpane in the front door. "I must ask, Mister White, what is the *true* reason for your disappointment?"

He took a deep breath and glanced at the floor. "For months you have been displaying the ungentlemanly qualities of a drunk, shaking at your desk. This is not every day, or every week, but it is becoming more frequent." I went to say something in my defense and he quickly added, "Do not deny it, for I have witnessed your actions with my own eyes from the back room."

To his surprise, I quipped, "I will not deny my fits of uncontrollable shaking at my desk when great headaches grind through me, but I have neither touched strong drink at work, nor at lunch."

White propped his foot on a stack of manuscripts that had arrived over the holidays. "Shaking from a severe headache I can understand, but I cannot understand how you lose your balance. Once I noticed you crash into the pulp pile when your vision was not impaired and nothing was in your hands. I have written my friend of your dissipation.[41] These are the undesirable qualities of a drunkard and I must ask for your resignation because of it."

The fear of losing the best paying job I had ever had, the job I loved the most, overcame me in a horrid instant. I threw my fists back into the door without turning and the window clattered in its frame. "On my parent's tomb I swear I have never had a drop of alcohol on the job! My problem with balance stems from my illness. I have nervous attacks."

"Interesting. You seem to invent illnesses by the second, young man."

"No. My headaches and earaches stem from the same incident, which I will not lower myself to discuss for it is too hurtful."

White enfolded fingers around his chin and thought for a moment. "I have searched your desk for spirits while you were gone, but found none. Of course, you could keep a bottle on your person."

I patted my dark clothing. "Search me, search me now, search me every day I walk in this door. I dearly need this job, Mister White, and have worked hard for you and your magazine."

White outstretched his hand in an obvious gesture for my key to the office. "I am sorry, Master Poe. I cannot take the chance. You can still publish your tales in the magazine, but only if no blood and gore is in the stories. I know how difficult it is for an upstart writer to find a market."

I left the *Southern Literary Messenger* that morning, yet still published my tales there; although I now felt them too good for the magazine. I was trapped without another publishing venue and in dire need to provide money for my family.

With hopes of making a name for myself in New York, we moved from Richmond to a small boarding house on the corner of Sixth Street and Waverly Place. We were forced to share a floor and a common kitchen with another man because we could not afford to live in a regular apartment. To this day I cannot recall the man's name, but I most certainly know that our stay in New York was during the financial panic of 1837, which reeked havoc on the publishing industry due to no one having money to read (the small percentage of the population who could) for pleasure.

We soon moved to 113 ½ Carmine Street where Muddy opened a boarding table to bring in income while I tried to sell my stories. Once again, to my great dismay, I could not break into the industry. Once again the Literati of New York stonewalled another Southern gentleman without a popular name or wealthy ties.

1838 - Age 29

After the futility of New York I moved my loving household once again, this time to Philadelphia. We rented from a Mrs. Jones—whose personality was as flamboyant as her name—on 202 Mulberry Street. The frequent moves were easier than they appear given our few earthly possessions. Ah, Philadelphia. I figured nothing could go wrong in the city where my first short story was published in what seemed eons ago.

I took a job there as reviewer for the *American Museum*. Given my in-depth review of a number of issues, the *American Museum* did not, in my opinion, meet the literary standards the *Southern Literary Messenger* had set in Richmond under White's ownership, but the market was much larger in Philly and so was the magazine's subscribership. I was given my first chance to have the masses of a large city read my words, and I started off by reviewing Nathaniel Hawthorne's *Twice Told Tales*. The compilation of stories by the Salem, Massachusetts author was published the previous year and was a best seller. I had read most of the tales in magazines upon their printing. This made me an admirer of the author long after Hawthorne was known for being the great great grandson of the judge who sentenced young ladies to death at the Salem witch trials.

To my vast disappointment I learned that Hawthorne was using the same publisher as Waldo Emerson who was a founding member of the Transcendentalist Club in Boston; or as Emerson called it, the "Hedge Club" after Dr. Hedge, a professor of logic at Harvard. In my estimation the Boston literary clique (the "Frogpondians"[42] I called them because they were slimy and lived in shallow, brackish waters) was no better than New York's. Their snobbish behavior was not improving over time and I railed on them to friends. *They are getting worse and worse, and pretend not to be aware that there are any literary people out of Boston. The worst and most disgusting part of the matter is, that the Bostonians are really, as a race, far inferior in point of* anything beyond mere talent, *to any other* set *upon the continent of N. A. They are decidedly the most servile imitators of the English it is possible to conceive. I always get into a passion when I think about. It would be the easiest thing in the world to use them up* en masse.[43]

The very phrase Transcendentalist Club means a club of remarkable degree and I found this self-branded moniker not surprising for a group of writers and philosophers from Harvard. The members believed in the preponderance of good in the world and had strong hopes for the future of humanity. From my life experiences this was laughable. What was most unbelievable about the club was its mantra. If one was not filled with their particular brand of the Holy Spirit, they were unable to fully comprehend the meanings of the Transcendentalist Club writings and I was certainly one of them. "Transcendentaless" was a better name in my estimation.

Turning a blind eye to Hawthorne's once removed association with Emerson, I praised him for being better than the Trancendentalists, although his publishing bond was in danger of bringing his brilliant mind into their company.

From this point forward I took whatever chance came my way to pan the Literati of New York and anyone associated with the Literati of Boston who masked themselves under the self-boasting name of the Transcendentalist Club. I had little in common with these questionable highbrows of American literature and knew I would never be accepted into their folds, even if I cared for such an appointment, which I did not.

The more I excelled as literary critic, the more these groups ostracized me in the media, which only made me work harder on my own prose and reviews that shone light into the hidden crevices of their writing and pretensions.

Near summer's end Sissy began feeling sick as a result of upper respiratory problems. After Mrs. Jones raised our rent for the second time in as many months, I secured a small two-story home in Philadelphia where we ended up living for the next four years.

After we had gotten situated in our new surroundings, I was strolling home from work one day when I spied two guttersnipes trying to keep the lid on a crate they were carrying. Their pantaloons were ragged, shirts torn and stained. Their faces were begrimed with jam and other unknown substances. One was carrying a paper sign glued to a stick: KITTINS 4 SALE—5 SENT.

Figuring this might be a cure for Sissy's ills, and feeling inner-guilt for moving my family so much, I approached the ragamuffins. "What ya have there, boys?"

"Baby cats, fine sir. Whole litter."

"What kind of cats?" I asked with suspicion.

"Not sure," the other boy said, "but they are pure bred. Ain't no mutts. The finest breed. Want one, mister?"

The lid popped off and I could tell immediately that the kittens were not pure bred and were perhaps from different litters given their various sizes. While the rest squirmed to get free, a tortoise-shell tabby gazed up at me and seesawed her sizeable whiskers.

"I'll take that one," I said, pointing.

While one boy scrambled to gather up the escaped kittens, I paid the other. The coinage may as well have been a pirate's treasure. He stared in disbelief at five whole cents! "Thanks, mister. Oh, boy. Thanks!"

As I was walking away, one of them asked, "You going to a funeral or something dressed like that?"

"When am I not?" I said over my shoulder. "When am I not?" Leaving their puzzled faces I walked up Sixteenth Street and into our house with the tabby on my shoulder, not saying a word. Muddy noticed it first when glancing up from her latest sewing expedition, but I shushed her quiet.

Sissy came prancing down the stairs—which she always did upon hearing me get home from work—in a teal cotton dress. Before she reached the bottom rung, she exclaimed, "A kitten? Oh my word!" She rushed over.

"Thought you might like this."

"Of course, Eddy!"

"You have always wanted a pet and we have never had one so I—"

Sissy took the tabby off my shoulders and it purred and nuzzled against her cheek. "So you got me a cat? He's beautiful."

"Boys who sold it to me said it was a she, but they were not the world's most trustworthy souls."

"I love him ... I mean her."

"What shall we name her?" Muddy asked. "Think of a good feline name, Virginia."

She tapped her bare feet for a moment, fingers running over calico as the animal slid across her shoulders. "She is a cat, and an agile one at that." Sissy placed it on the floor and it sprang onto the armrest next to Muddy. "She could be a furry ballerina." There was more thinking. "How about Cat-terina?"

"Perfect," I said with a smile. "Catterina[44] it will be."

1839 - Age 30

My time as critic for the *American Museum* was short-lived. The owner thought my critiques were stirring too much controversy. I was perplexed that it was undesirable to bring attention to a magazine. The *American Museum* was receiving many uncouth letters wherein subscriptions were canceled, but I pointed out that it got nearly as many letters seeking receipt of the magazine from my reviews. Still, the proprietors only seemed to notice the cancellations.

I left the magazine amicably and went across town to work for one William Burton, an ex-theatre actor, much like my parents. He employed me as assistant editor of his *Gentleman's Magazine*. My first assignment was to solicit big name writers to contribute articles. Second tier writers like N. P. Willis and Paulding responded immediately. Since I was an outcast of the Literatis of New York and Boston, I turned to Washington Irving, whom I did not consider a part of these cliques and whom I respected as a writer of first tier popularity. I appealed to Irving's greater sensibilities. Local publishers Lea and Blanchard had just agreed to publish my *Tales of the Grotesque and Arabesque* in an edition running seven hundred and fifty copies. It was a tough business arrangement, as were all my publications. The editors broke off the deal a number of times until I finally agreed to give them all the profits for the privilege of having the compilation published. They even gave me a few "free-of-charge" copies.

I desperately wanted a bodacious letter from Irving to place at the forefront of my *Tales of the Grotesque and Arabesque*, which would ensure future publications alone and healthy sales. I opened by speaking of *William Wilson*, my tale that reminisced of my early school days in England.

Philadelphia, Octo. 12. 1839.

Dear Sir

I duly received your kind letter, and entirely acquiesce in what you say — that it would be improper to force an opportunity of speaking of a detached Tale. I should be grieved, however, if you have supposed that I could make such [a] demand; my request you have fully promised to grant, in saying that you will bear me in mind, and "take the first unforced opportunity" of expressing your opinion".

I take the liberty of sending you the Octo: No: of the Gents' Magazine, containing the Tale "William Wilson". This is the tale of which I spoke in my former letter, and which is based upon a brief article of your own in the first "Gift" — that for 1836. Your article is called "An Unwritten Drama of Lord Byron". I have hoped that, having thus a right of ownership in my "William Wilson", you will be induced to read it — and I also hope that, reading it, you will find in it something to appro[v]e. This brings me to another request, which I hardly know how to urge, and for urging which I am greatly afraid you will think me importunate. I trust, however, you will make allowance for the circumstances in which I am placed, for the difficulties I have to overcome, and for the anxiety which I feel.

Mess: Lea & Blanchard are about publishing a collection of my Tales, in 2 vols, to be issued early next month. As these Tales, in their course of original publication from time to time, have received many high praises from gentlemen whose opinions are of weight; and as these encomiums have already been published in the papers of the day, (being comprised in notices of the Southern Lit: Messenger and other Magazines) Mess. L & B. think there would be nothing objectionable in their reprinting them, in the ordinary form of an advertisement appended to the various books which they may issue before mine. I do not speak altogether of editorial opinions, but of the personal opinions of some of our principal literary men, which have found their way into the papers. Among others, I may mention Mr Paulding, Mr Kennedy & Mr Willis. Now, if, to the very high encomiums which have been lavished upon some of my tales by these & others, I could be permitted to add even a word or two from yourself, in relation to the tale of "William Wilson" (which I consider my best effort) my fortune would be made.

I do not say this unadvisedly — for I am deliberately convinced that your good opinion, thus permitted to be expressed, would ensure me that public attention which would carry me on to fortune hereafter, by ensuring me fame at once.

I feel, however, that I am, in regard to yourself an utter stranger— and that I have no claim whatever upon your good offices. Yet I could not feel that I had done all which could be justly done, towards ensuring success, until I had made this request of you. I have a strong hope that you will be inclined to grant it, for you will reflect that what will be an act of little moment in respect to yourself— will be life itself to me.

My request now, therefore, is that, if you approve of "William Wilson", you will express so much in your own terms in a letter to myself and permit Mess L & B. to publish it, as I mentioned.

Submitting all to your kindness
I am
With highest respect
Edgar A Poe[45]

All Hallows Eve came and left as silently as a specter in the October night with no response from Washington Irving, whose tales such as *The Legend of Sleepy Hollow* were going a long way toward increasing the mystique of this unofficial holiday no matter how much those of Puritan descent wished otherwise. This time of year was also when my stories were in highest demand and William Burton was seeking as many as I could produce.

I had no shortage!

After a long day at his *Gentleman's Magazine*, I approached our small but quaint rented accommodations on Sixteenth Street in Philadelphia. The chimney was pluming wisps of smoke into the dusky skyline. The dormer windows and overhanging roof that covered the front porch gave the home the facial qualities of eyes and lips. A massive red oak wheezed over its roofline like shaggy auburn hair.

I crunched through a colorful array of orange-red leaves swirling around my boots. From the looks of it, Sissy had gathered most of them into a large pile at the side of the house, a task for which I did not have the time and felt guilty because of it.

Through the parlour window I saw Muddy on our ratty sofa crocheting a scarf for the fast-approaching winter months. Catterina was perched on her shoulder, tail curling around her neck, which gave Muddy the appearance she was wearing a scarf of her own.

A tap came at my leg and before I could react, my breath went from me and I plunged into the maelstrom of gyrating hues below, wondering what I had tripped over or what hole I had stumbled upon. I flailed for several moments until I heard a giggle issue from the pile of leaves.

Out arose Sissy, colors woven randomly into her locks. "Scared you. Ha! The man who frightens people for a living has been given a taste of his own medicine."

I struggled to a kneeling position and began throwing leaves. My playful wife responded in kind until a scarlet blur was about us. And she *truly* was my wife at this juncture. I had grown to love her with an uncommon bond over our years of marriage while she grew in maturity. To think of one day without her was intolerable. Sissy never lost her sense of gayety and joyful spirit no matter what the circumstances of our household. From the girl who got daisies to miraculously grow on a rooftop to the young woman who had become my best friend and companion, Sissy was the flower of my life.

With all her might she tackled me onto my back and began kissing my neck.

"What will the neighbors think?"

"Who cares? No one in Philly knows my real age."

"People talk and rumors follow," I said.

"Most people claim that only a person possessed of the devil could write such horror."

"And what do you think?"

"You are an angel to me, Eddy, but never bet the devil your head."

"That would make a great title for a story," I observed.

Sissy scooped up a bunch of leaves and tossed them into the air where they shone in the anemic sunset like a flock of cardinals. Her hands reached under my frockcoat and began tickling me. We were buried under the churning pile. I finally stopped crying for mercy and her fingers calmed.

We lay there silently under the leaves, embracing. The only sound was that of crackling and bursts of wind through the denuded red oak branches. Being near her helped me think, and thoughts of a response from Washington Irving flashed through my head. For many fall weeks I had waited in anticipation while putting the finishing touches on *The Devil in the Belfry*, *The Man that was Used Up*, and *Fairyland*. I must confess that *The Fall of the House of Usher*, a tale for which Burton paid me ten dollars, was my favorite (all similes to Louisa and Moldavia aside), but I was not sure how the horrific tale would be received. Perhaps my Philadelphia audience was grittier and more accepting than the genteel people of Richmond.

Sissy claimed patronage to *Fairyland*, but I am not sure she read it from beginning to end. It was pointless to ask anymore, and my attempts of enquiring what happened at certain parts of my stories were taken with disdain. Why did I need to trouble the biggest proponent of my existence?

As time escaped us in spades and the moon slowly began waxing overhead, we held each other, kissing in our hideaway from the world's inequities against our family and the weighty cares of money. These cares caused me to pen a woeful non-fiction textbook on shells entitled *The Conchologist's First Book*. I wondered if my struggles as an artist would ever end.

"Do you think Mister Irving will write me back?"

"A man of his stature may not give you the time, Eddy?"

"His interest in my writing would mean everything, but I am beginning to wonder if he *will* respond."

"Pay him no mind," Sissy said, anger creeping into her voice. "My hubby will not be deterred by that ... that bouncing pumpkinhead!"

I burst out laughing at another one of Sissy's offhanded comments, which I am sure revealed our hideaway to passersby. If not, our subsequent lolling on our backs like dogs in play most certainly did.

The following morning Sissy came springing into the house with a letter in her hand.

Newburg, November 6, 1839,

Dear Sir, — The magazine you were so kind as to send me, being directed to New York, instead of Tarrytown, did not reach me for some time. This, together with an unfortunate habit of procrastination, must plead my apology for the tardiness of my reply. I have read your little tale of "William Wilson " with much pleasure. It is managed in a highly pictur-esque style, and the

singular and mysterious interest is well sustained throughout. I repeat what I have said in regard to a previous production, which you did me the favor to send me, that I cannot but think a series of articles of like style and merit would be extremely well received by the public.

I could add for your private ear, that I think the last tale much the best, in regard to style. It is simpler. In your first you have been too anxious to present your picture vividly to the eye, or too distrustful of your effect, and have laid on too much coloring.

It is erring on the best side — the side of luxuriance. That tale might be improved by relieving the style from some of the epithets. There is no danger of destroying its graphic effect, which is powerful. With best wishes for your success,

I am, my dear sir, yours respectfully,
Washington Irving[46]

1841 - Age 32

Irving delivered but my fortune changed little. Few known authors seemed to have the time to submit to the magazine. When subscribership began to fall, Mr. Burton began claiming that I was grossly overpaid when I was meagerly supporting my family.[47] This infuriated me for I considered Burton my friend. In disgust I left his employ and immedi-ately announced that I was planning my own magazine called the *Penn Magazine*. Only then would I have complete publishing prowess.

For months I was out of work, but kept writing a mystery I entitled *The Murders in the Rue Morgue*. I was having great pleasure in writing this story and was struck by how it could lead to a type of investigatory genre where authorities or hired crime solvers seek a killer. In all my research I found no prior tale that offered readers the pleasure and satisfac-tion of finding clues to a murder and I planned to write more of these stories.

My attempts at getting the *Penn Magazine* off the ground failed miserably, due in part to the banking crisis that quelled the pocketbooks of investors and my own lack of funds for promotion.

I watched the moves of Burton closely during this time. Later in the year when I got wind he was selling the *Gentlemen's Magazine* to George Graham, I visited Graham and offered my editorial services under tipped hat and air of humbleness. He warmly gave me the book review editorship and I started forthright. Thence *Graham's Magazine* was formed with the five thousand subscribers of the former *Gentlemen's Magazine*.

When Graham asked me for my honest input as to why Burton's *Gentlemen's Magazine* did not flourish, I stated that in my opinion the tales in such publications were going the way of the simpleton. To be truly original—as Hawthorne demonstrated in his early career—meant being initially unpopular because the reading public would have trouble relating to the tales. I believed the largest stumbling block to a successful magazine was having steady contributions from authors known to the subscribership, a task for which I had made little progress under Burton and his uncommitted approach to publishing.

Graham was of the same mind and we agreed not to publish a single issue until we had commitments from such authors. Henry W. Longfellow was one of my first contacts.

May 19, 1841

Dear Sir,
Your favor of the 3rd inst. With the two Nos. of the Magazine reached me only a day or two ago, which will account [...] a more speedy answer was not returned.

I am much obliged to you for your kind expressions of regard, and to Mr. Graham for his very generous offer, of which I should gladly avail myself under other circumstances. But I am so much occupied at present that I could not do it with any satisfaction either to you or to myself. I must therefore respectfully decline his proposition.

You are mistaken in supposing that you are not "favorably known to me." On the contrary, all that I have read, from your pen, has inspired me with a high idea of your power; and you are destined to stand among the first romance-writers of the country, if such be your aim.

Very truly yours
H. W. Longfellow[48]

Philadelphia - June 22 1841.

Dear Sir,

Your letter of the 19th May was received. I regret to find my anticipations confirmed, and that you cannot make it convenient to accept Mr Graham's proposition. Will you now pardon me for making another?

I need not call your attention to the signs of the times in respect to Magazine literature. You will admit that the tendency of the age lies in this way—so far at least as regards the lighter lepers. The brief, the terse, the condensed, and the easily circulated will take place of the diffuse, the ponderous, and the inaccessible. Even our Reviews (lucus a non lucendo) are found too massive for the taste of the day: — I do not mean for the taste of the tasteless, but for that of the few. In the meantime the finest minds of Europe are beginning to lend their spirit to Magazines. In this country, unhappily, we have not any journal of the class, which either can afford to offer pecuniary inducement to the highest talent, or which would be, in all respects, a fitting vehicle for its thoughts. In the supply of this deficiency there would be a point gained; and in the hope of at least partially supplying it, Mr. Graham and myself propose to establish a Monthly Magazine.

The amplest funds will be embarked in the undertaking. The work will be an octavo of 96 pages. The paper will be of excellent quality — possibly finer than that upon which your "Hyperion" was printed. The type will be new (always new) clear and bold, with distinct face. The matter will be disposed in a single column. The printing will be done upon a hand-press in the best manner. There will be a broad margin. There will be no engravings, except occasional wood-cuts (by Adams) when demanded in obvious illustration of the text; and, when so required, they will be worked in with the type — not upon separate pages as in "Arcturus." The stitching will be done in the French style, permitting the book to lie fully open. Upon the cover, and throughout, the endeavour will be to preserve the greatest purity of taste consistent with decision and force. The price will be $5.

The chief feature in the literary department will be that of contributions from the most distinguished pens (of America) exclusively; or, if this plan cannot be wholly carried out, we propose, at least, to make arrangements (if possible) with yourself, Mr Irving, Mr Cooper, Mr Paulding, Mr Bryant, Mr Halleck, Mr. Paulding, Mr Willis, and one or two others. In fact, our ability to make these arrangements is a condition, without which the Magazine will not go into operation; and my object in writing you this letter is to ascertain how far I may look to yourself for aid.

In your former note you spoke of present engagements. The proposed journal will not be commenced until the 1ˢᵗ January 1842.

It would be desirable that you should agree to furnish one paper each month—prose or poetry—absolute or serial—and of such length as you might deem proper. Should illustrations be desired by you, these will be engraved at our expense, from designs at your own, superintended by yourself. We leave the matter of terms, as before, to your own decision. The sums agreed upon would be paid as you might suggest. It would be necessary that an agreement should be made for one year—during which period you should be pledged not to write for any other (American) Magazine.

With this letter I despatch one of the same tenor to each of the gentlemen before-named. If you cannot consent to an unconditional reply, will you be kind enough to say whether you will write for us upon condition that we succeed in our engagements with the others— specifying what others.

With high respect,
Edgar A Poe[49]

In due course Longfellow began to contribute to *Graham's Magazine* and so did the other literary figures of our time. With these exquisite articles being sent our way, Graham and I quickly made the magazine into the most important and respected periodical in America. *The Murders in the Rue Morgue* was published in the magazine alongside our huge names of literature, to my great satisfaction.

I was paid eight hundred dollars as my first year's salary and the magazine flourished, which allowed us to pay even more for stories by the top names. *Never Bet the Devil Your Head*, which drew its title from a Sissyism, was also published in *Graham's Magazine* and detailed my personal situation in ways that only now I feel comfortable in putting on paper.

In the story Toby is a poor boy who was beaten and turned to betting, but because he was poor, he was never taken seriously. How I often felt the same in the big cities of Boston, New York, and Philadelphia, but *Graham's Magazine* appeared to be turning my fortune.

After paying off a number of debts from my unemployment, I purchased a piano for Sissy at a Baptist church sale and had it pushed into the front room of our home one afternoon while Muddy had taken Sissy with her to get sewing materials in town. Muddy knew of my piano-purchasing venture and was a willing accomplice to my plan.

When they arrived I met them on the porch and put my hand over Sissy's eyes as I led her inside. "I have a big surprise for you."

"What are you up to, Eddy? Another cat ... a dog?"

"You'll see."

Once Muddy had followed us inside, I unclasped my fingers. Sissy's eyes lit at its presence, as if sheathed in gold or gilded in diamonds.

"Thought you might like to have an instrument around the house."

She threw her arms around me. "Oh, Eddy, it's beautiful!"

"I could not afford a new model. Try not to mind the fingernail scratches and scuffmarks from decades of usage and countless renditions of *Amazing Grace* played thereon."

"If it was purple I would love it no less." She kissed me and once her fingers had finally loosened from around my shoulders, they hardly left the ivory keys for weeks thereafter. Sissy played and sang at all hours. Seeing my wife's enjoyment gave me more satisfaction than any writing this earth could offer. Catterina also enjoyed the instrument, evidenced by her prancing up and down the keys while purring.

Later I paid a local musician in signed copies of my book, *Tales of the Grotesque and Arabesque* that Lea & Blanchard had given me as my *only* compensation, and received a good tuning of the instrument in return. He said that someday the books would be worth more than the piano and I just laughed.

The piano emboldened Sissy and her musical talents to the point where she began seeking out paying singing engagements. In her mid-teens now, she was ready to face the world with her substantial talents and to help bring in money for our home.

1842 - Age 33

The growing reputation of the magazine allowed Mr. Graham to line his coffers quite nicely. He purchased the building next to ours for added space in both copyediting and printing. Workman's desks were set in neat rows and a unique numbering system was developed for logging and tracking every article and story that came in the front door's mail slot. The place was a far cry from White's *Southern Literary Messenger.* The tidiness cleared my thoughts and as a result some of my best tales followed in quick succession, including the *Mystery of Marie Roget*, another murder tale that followed on the success of the *Murders in the Rue Morgue*.

Graham's rumblings about hiring an editor of high reputation to oversee my work as book review editor came true the first week of the year. My hopes of convincing Graham that I was the right person for this job fell on deaf ears. I remember it as though it were yesterday, that sinking feeling in my stomach at getting passed over for the job promotion. It was the day when I first met Rufus Griswold.

"Good day in the morning!" he bellowed as he stepped into the office. "Doctor Rufus Dub-a-ya Griswold at your humble service, Mister Graham." When the rotund man shook Graham's hand, his jowls followed suit. A man with shiny hair strolled in behind him who I could barely see given Griswold's girth and top hat.

"What a pleasure to have Philadelphia's premiere editor of literary compilations come and work for my little publication."

"You have the largest subscribership of any magazine in the good ole U S of A, God bless her," Griswold said. "This job is an honour and a privilege. I cannot wait to get started. In fact, if I may be so bold, sir, I plan to invite one of New England's finest writers to publish in your pages a work of great social importance."

"Well," Graham said, "you waste no time."

"Who," I questioned from my desk where I sat in threadbare clothes, "Irving or perhaps Longfellow? Know that I have already contacted them." I wanted to demonstrate my value and show that I could handle Griswold's job easily.

"Doctor Thomas Dunn English, to be exact." As Griswold spoke I noticed that he routinely tried to suck his gut up into his chest and his suspenders would bulge.

"English?" I retorted. "The physician turned writer? I have read his work and I would hardly purport him to be one of New England's finest writers." Thinking quick, I used his name for a play on words. "Thomas Dunn English may have written many tales, but he has not *done* English. Character generation is also sorely lacking in his works along with grammar."

Graham motioned toward me, and said to Griswold, "I would like you to meet your very capable, and at times opinionated, book review editor, Edgar Allan Poe."

Griswold referenced the man who had remained hidden in the rear. "And I would like you to meet Doctor Thomas Dunn English."

My Adam's apple plunged. I could say nothing in response, frozen in embarrassment from my derogatory comments (although truthful in my eyes).

English was a thin man of angular proportions. A defined jaw protruded over his collar like the rock of Gibraltar and I imagined he reached over six feet in height without the heels of his boots. His hair was parted on the side and pasted down with shiny wax. I wondered if a steel rod had been fused to his spine the way he held himself. English was somewhat popular (second-tier popular along with N. P. Willis) and it occurred to me that a story by him could help grow the magazine, but taint it from a literary perspective. "No offense," I said to English, but refused to get out of my seat. "My editorial reviews sometimes extend from the page into my conversation."

English did not approach me, nor did he utter a word. He just glared.

An air of satisfaction overtook Griswold. He let awkwardness hang in the room before finally commenting, "Well, well, so you are the *book* review editor. I'll be looking forward to editing your book reports."

The way in which he said my title made it sound as the most menial task in the world, one befitting a schoolboy. I had heard of Griswold and read many of his reviews. I wanted to sink into my seat and disappear.

Griswold took off his top hat, revealing a patch of baldness that extended to his crown. "I've been reviewing prose and the authors behind the works since you could read, Mister Poor is it?"

English smirked.

"Poe. The name is Poe," I answered as he simultaneously tried to assert his dominance over me in wealth and our new working arrangement.

"Very well," said the blowhard with a deep breath and rising chest. "When I was half your age I held a position of similar stature. These reviews of mine have extended over the years to some of the greatest writers the world has known to date. Many of them I know personally, including my friend, Thomas English."

"Your reviews only offer praise to those writers who may be undeserving but popular or wealthy."

Griswold was unflappable in his haughty composure. "Balderdash." He plucked his suspenders and fat rippled down his chest. "I am sure this will be our first and last disagreement, young Poe, and that you will extend to Mister English only courtesies from here on out. Do you agree, Mister Graham?"

"Certainly and so does Mister Poe."

Before I could respond, Graham was offering the newcomers lunch at a restaurant to which he had never hinted at taking me. He was consolatory and apologetic enough for the both of us, and a few copyeditors to spare, so I kept my mouth closed and caused no more trouble.

"Good day in the morning," Griswold said to me as he left.

"Balderdash," I mumbled in response after the door closed behind them.

We lied once again about Sissy's age and she began singing in taverns in Downtown Philly that were no bigger than watering troughs with leaky roofs. I hated Sissy being introduced to this seedy atmosphere at her age. I thought of her as my little sister as well as my wife. Candlelight emanating from lanterns of ugly stained glass did little to disguise the taverns' nature. She grew a fast reputation as the "young whippoorwill." Maybe it's because I started the moniker's dissemination by whispering it in the ears of drunken revelers at my table. Rumors were spreading that I was becoming one of them. I would never buy drinks at the table. Not having enough money for them was a large part of it. It was always those who recognized me that would order a round. A mere drink or two would have the effect of thrice that many on most men. But they would always buy them for me as Sissy sang and I would never refuse.

The small paychecks started coming in and they increased in size as Sissy moved up to larger venues: watering troughs to restaurants to barn dances to wedding receptions. Her angelic voice was becoming well known and requested at social events. We were assured of this when she received an invite to sing at a town hall gala near the end of January.

On our way inside a daguerreotype met us. Sissy and I had a reluctant imprinting taken. They always left me feeling uncomfortable, as if the daguerreotypes were capturing our mercury vapor souls on silvered plates.

"I'm not sure about this," Sissy confessed as we made our way across the hunter-green marble, fissured in white rivulets. We sat alone at a round wooden table in the front, each sitting in Chippendale chairs with velvety seats. Oil lamps mounted on a massive wrought iron chandelier at the ceiling's zenith were suffusing the room in constant iodine light. Partygoers cavorted about and exchanged pleasantries with each other. Many of the men wore their periwigs loaded with blue powder that dusted their shoulders.

"This is by far my biggest audience."

I patted her hand. "You will do fine, my darling wifey. Stop looking back at all the people."

"And what am I supposed to do when I am singing in front of them, stare at my shoes?"

"Think of it as a chance to show off. This is the City of Brotherly Love."

"I hear nothing of sisterly love. Thomas English is signing autographs on his written dung and Rufus Griswold is mulling about telling anyone who will listen how great he is, I am sure."

"What does one expect from a failed Baptist minister?" I said. "The wig goes a long way in ridding the world of his bald spot."

"Good. It will not be blinding me while singing!"

Rubbing the back of my neck, I qualified, "That is enough from me. Griswold is my co-worker, the editor of the magazine, and I must treat him accordingly."

"The only thing bigger than his stomach is his ego." Sissy was nervously tapping her fingernails on the table. "Look around. There must be a hundred people here, or more; all dignitaries or toasts of the town. There are judges in here. I expect to see the ghost of Ben Franklin traipse in next."

"His kite will never float."

"With all this hot air, it just might," Sissy commented.

The host of honour—the mayor of Philadelphia himself—made a brief speech regarding the inroads he was making for city sanitation and increased hospitals, while people took their seats. He then slyly mentioned the upcoming elections before introducing "Virginia Poe, the young whippoorwill of song."

Clapping echoed off the wainscoted walls and the pilasters that rose up to the crossed ceiling.

I felt simultaneously nervous for her and proud. She had come so far—we all had.

Sissy got up from the table and smoothed her chintz dress that Muddy had made just for the engagement.

"You look fabulous," I whispered.

She took a few strides, lifted the dress over her ankles and climbed the steps to the platform where a grand piano sat in the center of the stage. Its black skin was like polished onyx under the lights; a much different appearance than ours at home. She took her place behind it, curtsied, and sat. In the background was an arch stretching to the ceiling. It fanned out at its base into the shape of the Liberty Bell. She gave me a brief look and I clasped my hands in an offer of strength.

Notes tinkled from the piano. Sissy cleared her throat and began singing "The Flowers of the Vale," her voice tremulous at first, but quickly smoothing into unearthly melodies. I thought there was no more appropriate song for Sissy.

From my seat in the front I could see her beautiful neck at work as the melodic bars progressed, a tuned flute of muscles and flesh. The piano playing was flawless. The audience of local dignitaries sat spellbound, neither a glass clinking nor silverware clanging.

With her first song reverberating into the music hall, Sissy transitioned right into her next: "The Coal Black Rose." Her hands were gliding across the keys as if on rollers. She was beautifully dawned in her chintz dress, bone corset cinched hourglass tight.

As I gazed up in wonderment and love, I felt a cold sticky liquid run down my chest. In shock I pushed off from the table thinking I had spilled my glass of wine only to see Thomas Dunn English standing over me.

"Excuse me," he said, his first words to me. "How could I be so sloppy with my drink?"

My vest, coat, and shirt were soaked; yet I tried to remain calm for Sissy's sake. "That is quite all right," I responded in hushed voice. In my peripheral vision I noticed those at the other tables pointing and looking.

Sissy obviously noticed. Her voice rose and she pounded at the ivories as if this alone would keep the embarrassing attention away from me.

"Let me help you," English said, grabbing Sissy's napkin that still remained in her goblet. He began reaching for me and when he did, spilled his plate of spinach dip and crackers into my lap.

I sprung to my feet out of reflex but soon found heated words for English. "You fool!"

The front tables of partygoers began chuckling and then it turned into riotous laughter.

From above Sissy sang louder. Now it was out of anger. Higher and louder until the piano was drowned out, and still louder after that! Sound ceased from her mouth and what emanated was pure *emotion* with notes attached, emotion that hung in the air and refused to die.

I scraped at my dark clothing, which only increased the white-green smears that intermixed with the acrid scent of spilt whiskey. My nicest outfit was ruined.

Dr. Thomas Dunn English, satisfied that he had embarrassed me to the hilt, said, "Now the drunk smells like one," and walked off into the pointing, laughing group of Philadelphia dignitaries.

Sissy's voice grew louder and more forceful. She had worked into an aural tempest. The piano playing abruptly stopped. The laughing surrounding me was deafening. When I glanced up the cables in Sissy's neck were strumming and blood was streaking from a corner of her supple lips.

She suddenly collapsed on stage like a hollow china doll in her dress, white and fragile. I mounted the stairs in two leaps and rushed to her side. I slid to my knees, realizing that she had become a martyr for my cause.

"No, no! Somebody help!"

For what seemed like minutes the upper crust of Philadelphia just gawped at us until a doctor in the audience came to assist.

Muddy and I sat alone in the parlour of a home we had rented above Spring Garden on 234 North Seventh Street. Catterina was curled into a ball on her plentiful lap. I was slumped on the piano seat, head in hands, while our family doctor (Dr. John W. Francis) tended Sissy in the upper chamber. We had been up all night tending her. Finally Dr. Francis made us go downstairs.

Sitting there I blamed Sissy's passing out on the bone corset that likely constricted her air passages. Nothing could have been farther from the truth.

Dawn was hours away.

Each footfall from above or rattle of medical instruments sent us flinching toward the stairs. We were desperately waiting for some news as to Sissy's condition. Was she terminally ill? Was she going to make it through another night?

Hands sifting through hair, I feared the worse, unable to drive away the demons of the grave that haunted my past as the wind howled against our thin windows. Groans from somewhere vibrated the walls, and when I met Muddy's gaze, it was obvious neither of us knew whether the sounds were from Nature or Sissy.

My heart was rent in a million fragile pieces of disrepair. Sissy had taught me all I knew of love, about true unconditional love. I feared with great pangs that I was about to lose it forever along with my dearest companion. I stared long and deep at the piano timer I had bought Sissy for Christmas. I flicked its brazen pendulum, which marked time in such relentless, uncompromising fashion. I imagined it ticking off the precious seconds of Sissy's life.

Click, clock. Click, clock.

"What's taking so long?" I asked Muddy.

She gave off a sigh and a fatigued look. "I could knit a flag in less time."

"Doctor Francis should at least give us a prognosis!" How I wished I could take Sissy's place. How I despised Thomas English for what he had caused.

When I glanced back at the piano timer, its swinging member had become a glinting crescent blade slicing through the candlelit air. It expanded and grew in my sorrowful delirium and swooshed at my neck. Thoughts about the end of the Spanish Inquisition invaded my head and within seconds I knew I had a grand tale, one I would entitle *The Pit and the Pendulum*. Once again my mind had tried to escape my existence through writing, but there was no egress from this situation.

Hard-soled shoes beat an uneven tempo in the chamber, then down the steps. When I glanced up and saw the terror on Dr. Francis's face, I prayed the crescent blade would save me from the misery I was about to hear.

Click, clock.

Muddy sprang to her feet and Catterina screeched under the sofa. She grabbed the physician by the lapels. "What's wrong with my daughter?"

"I usually have the family sitting for this kind of imparting."

"Tell me," Muddy insisted, nearly shaking his monocle onto the floor. Instruments within his medicinal bag clanked.

"She burst a blood vessel in her throat while singing. Dear Virginia, I am afraid, has the beginnings of tuberculosis."

This news hit me full force. "For which, I am convinced, you have no cure," I blurted from my bench seat. He could have told us she had a cold and I would have said the same.

"Good sir?"

My outburst surprised me and I took a breath. "At this point in my life I have no faith in your profession, doctor, absolutely none. Your profession only impedes death, it does not prevent it."

Dr. Francis placed his hand on my shoulder. "Only our Creator can prevent death, which he certainly did for Virginia."

I batted his arm away.

"With care she may recover, Mister Poe."

"'May recover'?" Muddy asked to no answer.

"What could we have done differently?"

"Her corset did not help matters. That is all. But of course, you were unaware of the onset of her illness."

"But not the man wearing the masque of the red death who visited us at the gala affair," I said. "The red death!"

Click, clock.

During my work at *Graham's Magazine* I solicited articles from Hawthorne, Irving, and Longfellow and had the good fortune of receiving one from each. The thrill of contacting them staved my thoughts from Sissy. Next I turned my sights toward Europe and started at the top—Charles Dickens. To my great surprise he responded to my query and claimed to be familiar with a number of my tales. He gushed at some length about *The Devil in the Belfry* in one response.

It so happened that Dickens was going to be touring Philadelphia after visiting the Boston Frogpondians, offering his books to the American public. In March we arranged to convene at a Philadelphia coffeehouse. The Revolutionary Grounds is where I stopped each morning on my way to work at *Graham's* and it was also a frequent meeting place of mine while I tried in vain to get my *Penn Magazine* to market during the banking crisis of the prior year.

I sat there in my usual seat—which should have had a brass marker on the back that read RESERVED FOR EDGAR ALLAN POE OUR MOST MYSTERIOUS CUSTOMER—beneath one of the arched windows that flanked Main Street. I faced the door in anticipation of my distinguished guest; reflections of a dying yoke sun washing over me.

Mahogany bookcases lined the wall opposite the windows and it was from them that I had extracted *The Old Curiosity Shop*. The leather-bound book with its gilded spine and onionskin pages was open on the table before me in the hopes of impressing the venerable author upon his arrival. Twice I had put it back out of nervousness after convincing myself that the gesture made me more a reader of Dickens than a peer. Twice I had returned it and thrice I had taken the adventures of Little Nell and her grandfather down, which is where the book rested beside my cup of steaming coffee.

People were staring more than usual at me. I could almost hear their whispers. *There's the man who takes pleasure in scaring women into fainting spells and changing men into little boys. Stay away from him. There is the demon writer. The man possessed of Satan's stylus.*

Before I could change my mind again about *The Old Curiosity Shop*, I noticed a distinguished gentleman stepping down from a coach outside. He tipped the coachman in a dignified way, with a nod and a tip of his derby.

Despite the failing daylight I felt a warm rush of air usher the man inside, which seemed to match his aura. To my surprise he had a goatee that pointed to a v-cut vest beneath which a gold pocket watch hung from his vest. He was all cascading points. His head swiveled atop bolt-straight posture and his gait was one of fluid motions. He was dressed in a finely pressed herringbone suit, buttoned in the front and cuffed where it met his polished shoes. The suit had a foreign make—a *London* make—written across it. There was no question that the dapper gentleman I was viewing was Charles Dickens.

I waved him over and he immediately headed for my table, chin digging into his tab collar in the hopes of not being recognized by another. I pushed back my seat and stood. "Edgar Allan Poe. Pleased to meet you." When I shook his hand I noticed his fingernails were perfectly groomed, not a speck of dirt beneath them. Perhaps, for a moment, I had felt unworthy to meet his eyes.

"Charles Dickens of England," he said in his proper manner, as if there was some *other* Charles Dickens in another part of the world to which I might confuse him. He searched for my eyes and found them.

My outfit was neat and clean, but my shirt was threadbare in places that I hid beneath a frockcoat. Comparing my worn clothing to that of Dickens's, there was no question who was the more successful author.

We sat down and he placed his derby in a corner of the table. His hair possessed the same whiplash curls as mine, though a lighter shade of brown, and his hairline was beginning to recede, too. I wondered if it was from all the use writers make of their frontal lobes. "Would you like a drink?"

"Jolly-O," he responded, which I took to mean 'Yes,' as he surveyed the wall lined with books. "Hot drinks and books, what a perfect marriage of the world's two greatest pleasures."

"Being happily married, I must rank them in the top three," I confessed.

Dickens chuckled in a reserved way. I still could not believe I was meeting *the* Charles Dickens. I went and got him his requested Earl Grey tea with fresh lemon, a dark specter as I strode, and soon returned to the table. He was glancing up at the arched windows.

"Quick, ole chap, of what do these windows remind you? No hesitation."

"Uh, translucent tombstones," I exclaimed as I sat, and then wished I could take the morbid comment back in his presence.

"Excellent! Just checking to make sure you really are Edgar Allan Poe of whom I have corresponded. Your somber clothing, the black frockcoat, white shirt, black cravat, tied somewhat loosely, black vest and boots, did give me some indication, but I had to be sure. There are so many writers penning under pseudonyms these days, especially women."

"How else are the ladies able to get published?" I asked.

After blowing on his tea, he added, "It is a sad commentary on our profession, but I am afraid more so on the political states of Europe and New England."

He referred to all of America as "New England" throughout the afternoon, and I guess to him it was. There followed an awkward pause. In my pangs of trying to keep the conversation flowing, I blurted, "*The Old Curiosity Shop* is a work that will be recognized by the most brilliant readers of our time."

"I can tell," Dickens said, referencing the novel that was still open in front of me. In my enthusiasm I had forgotten about it completely and my reddening cheeks revealed my embarrassment at his compliment.

"Speaking of the grave, Usher's wife emerging from her tomb at the conclusion of *The Fall of the House of Usher* caused me sleeplessness for days, or I should say nights. For a week thereafter my chamber lamp had to be glowing brightly for my big toe to slip under the covers. I felt her ghost might visit me at the witching hour. In fact, I have an idea for a ghost story that is actually a Christmas story. Do you think this has a chance?"

"Only Charles Dickens could get away with scaring his readers at Christmas and get them to plead for more."

"I am reticent to believe so. I have doubts about every story until the public embraces it."

"The world's most prized author is too modest."

Dickens submerged his teabag while flashing an air of humbleness.

"And if you do publish this ghost story, which I would love to read, I am sure it will be told by Christmas firesides for decades to come."

"If the Christmas season is when Dickens will be remembered, ole chap, then Halloween will be Poe's. A holiday for the Master of the Macabre."

I smiled and took a long satisfying gulp of coffee. My hopes were merely set on being known in this age, none other. This recognition from Dickens astounded me.

He scooped his tea bag out with his spoon and wrapped its string around the bag to drain its retained flavor into the cup. He then sat the spoon and wrenched teabag at the ten-and-four position on the saucer and took his first sip. What perfect English mannerisms he possessed. I recognized this from the time I spent as a boy in Britain and later under the authoritarian command of John Allan at Moldavia.

"I take it your time in Boston was well spent," I said.

"I found it most enlightening, especially the insane house."

"Even I do not visit the crazy houses, despite claims from a few readers that I live in one ... or at least belong there."

"The State Hospital for the Insane in South Boston is where I visited. I have a great compassion for those who cannot help themselves."

"Referring to the helpless, I have read with interest *Oliver Twist* and found it quite compelling. Although your protagonists are never in need of help at the end of your novels. Help from the supernatural is a good effect."

"I'll remember that for my Christmas tale." Dickens took another sip and I heard not the slightest bit of slurp. "Forgive me for asking, but we have such a short time together. Is it true that you were orphaned as a child, and then adopted by a family of renown in Richmond?"

Word about my upbringing in a wealthy family and then being cast penniless onto the streets had apparently even found its way across the Pond. "I was never adopted," I quipped. "And I expect no sympathy regarding my circumstances. I am a self-made man, as they say in New York. And I plan to be a self-made writer."

"You are on a good course. I believe there is nothing more terrible in a person's life than what you have suffered, my literary companion, but you have risen up, just like Oliver."

I loved the way Dickens referred to the characters of his books as real people and I felt warm inside from the way he called me his 'literary companion.'

"Back to Boston. The institution of which I speak has adopted a moral treatment of the deranged. I was compelled to visit it."

"Ah, yes, I have heard of this through a doctor friend of mine who served as a resident at a few of these asylums. The new soothing system they call it, where the sanitarium no longer keeps the insane bound in shackles or locked behind iron doors. Near a country club atmosphere."

"It is a system based upon the freedom of spirit, kindness, and compassion. A very humane treatment for the sick, adopted from Europe I might add, and I believe the best approach for treatment of mental illness."

I blanched at this and unfortunately expressed my thoughts as I have a bad habit of doing at inopportune times. "In all due respect, I dare say that Europe with its workhouses and homelessness and streets filled with sewage has not had much success in helping those who cannot help themselves."

To my relief, Dickens took the comment in stride. "We are, however, speaking of the moral treatment of the insane, not the poor."

"One creates the other, does it not? The impoverished are driven to insanity, if not the welcomed arms of death, and the insane are driven to an impoverished capacity upon reaching a state where they are unemployable."

Dickens sat back, crossed his legs, and stroked his goatee. "By treating the patients in a moral way they are allowed to develop their own selves in complete freedom of physical movement."

"And what is more important in these people's treatment than safety from their own selves and the harm of others?" I asked, thinking of the treatment of Jane Stanard.

"It is not simply freedom of movement that is key to their rehabilitation," Dickens added. "Those in the State Hospital for the Insane are entertained daily by banquets, dancing, and song. They learn important skills that will make them employable."

"Employable only in the theatre, I am afraid." I took another sip of coffee, but was in no need of caffeine while sitting before Dickens.

"And if this were the worst case, Mister Poe, one of our greatest art forms would be blessed. Perhaps they could get a part at the Rantipole Theatre from your tale *The Man that was Used Up*."

"I am glad you think so highly of plays and have unearthed my writing published years ago."

"One must *unearth* your writing in a matter of speaking, for most of it tells of premature burials and the undead sealed behind walls."

How could I not grin at this? I threw a reference, the greatest form of flattery to a writer, right back at him. "My parents were people of the theatre no different than Nicholas and Smikes in *Nicholas Nickleby*."

We smiled at each other and I was aware that Dickens enjoyed the mental sparring. How in awe I was of the man across the table. To merely watch him brush lint from his herringbone suit brought wonder as if it were a magician's trickery. When Dickens brought the teacup to his face again I noticed the whorls of his hair were brushed forward and folds of skin were below his eyes.

He rubbed at them. "I am an insomniac, you know, especially when in the middle of writing a story or after reading one of your tales."

"Pardon me for saying this, but I have heard rumors you are superstitious, also."

"If believing that the best chance of getting sleep is if one is positioned exactly in the middle of the bed facing in a northerly direction, heels spread to the corners, then yes, I am superstitious."

I almost gagged on a mouthful of coffee and this brought the attention of a man at the counter who was twisting his handlebar mustache in a thoughtful way, much like people do when tugging at an earlobe or cracking their knuckles to denote a contemplative habit. I thought for a moment he recognized Dickens, but I was mistaken when the hanging doorbell noted his exit.

Upon gaining my composure, I remarked, "Your use of the blabbing crow as a character in *Barnaby Rudge* was very intriguing."

"And *I* was very intrigued at your ability to foresee how my serialized novel would end in your *Graham's* review ... although you did spoil the story for a great many readers."

I leaned back in my chair, unbelieving that one of my reviews could reach the heart of so great an author. *Graham's Magazine* had grown more important than even I had imagined in a short time. The hum of caffeinated voices and the cranking of grinders were around us, so I leaned in close. "For this I ask your humble apologies. Telling the end of the story before you published it was ill thinking on my part. You could have changed the ending to trip me up if you had wanted, Mister Dickens."

"It was already written and sitting on my credenza by the time your review was printed. Plus, I never change the ending of a tale after I have envisioned it."

"Nor I, but of course no one reviews my short stories in parts, especially in London. Apart from a publication of a story I called *Pym*, I would not have been published at all in your hometown if *Bentley's Miscellany* had not pirated four of my tales."

Dickens smiled. "In our profession, unauthorized replication is not the sincerest form of flattery. I am afraid that someday printing presses will be miniaturized so that the common man can have one on his desk. Then we will be in real trouble from the copyists."

"Yes, indeed." I cleared my throat, and said, "I take this opportunity, fine sir, to ask of your assistance in finding a London publisher for my *Tales of the Grotesque and Arabesque*."

Dickens took a long sip of tea while I waited in anticipation for an answer. He dabbed at a corner of his goatee with a napkin. "I will do my best to assist you, if you think it will help." He quickly reverted the subject back to his serial novel and I wondered about his sincerity. "So you liked the bird in *Barnaby*."

"I *loved* the babbling bird. Wish it loomed larger in the story as a more central character. I find the whole idea of a talking animal brilliant. A talking parrot I could see, but a blackbird? Good show!"

"I got the idea from my pet crow, rather my *former* pet crow. He died of natural causes just after *Barnaby* was published. Name was Grip."

"I'm sorry."

"Do not be sorry for the bird. He left clear instructions for the timely and just disposal of his earthly assets, which amounted to a brass cage and wooden mouse toy. This is more than I can say for most people who die intestate."

When I saw that Dickens had no trace of remorse and was good-natured about his pet, I found it appropriate to comment: "It probably killed Grip not to be a more central character. Sparse use of him in the story made way to his death."

With that the fine gentlemen laughed aloud and I knew I had met not only a literary counterpart, but also a friend. "Grip's demise happened at midnight, which I find to be the proper time for any sable creature of this earth to die. On the clock striking twelve, in one of my frequent states of insomnia, I was working late on a manuscript when I noticed he appeared slightly agitated. Gripper paced to and fro, 'stopped to bark, staggered, exclaimed "Halloa old girl" (his favourite expression) and died.'"[50]

"Grip had character equal to any in your stories," I said.

On the other side of the arched windows horses thundered, pulling chaises and boxy carriages to destinations unknown. Orange-yellow streaks were glinting off their lacquered sides. We each took the opportunity to sip our drinks that were eddying curlicues of steam under our noses.

"And did the crow leave specific instructions as to his burial just as for the disposal of his assets?" I questioned.

"Oh yes. I adhered strictly to this death wish seeing how he did, in fact, leave me all his earthly possessions. Grip wanted to be stuffed and mounted for all to see in his glory beyond the grave. Such a vain, but trendy bird! The stuffing of deceased pets has taken the fancy of many in Europe."

"Really? Even I find that morbid."

"A friend of mine stuffed his pet giraffe he acquired from Africa. It said, 'Goodbye-ya,' when it fell to the ground, wrapped its long neck around a planter, opened its mouth as if to part words of wisdom, and expired."

"The giraffe must have known Grip," I noted.

"Said I was friends with the owner. Grip used to perch on the giraffe's head out in the yard while we played cards. Anyway, once the tall creature died, my friend had to cut a hole in his roof and build a dome over it just to keep the stuffed animal in the house. Trends die hard," Dickens said.

"And animals apparently die harder!"

Dickens and I laughed together like school chums, getting many steaming refills on our drinks until the moon was in full bloom through the translucent tombstones and many coachman's whips had flailed into the night.

At the office, Griswold continued asserting his influence over Mr. Graham to the point where I was near the edges of my sanity. The stress of having my wife bedridden—medical costs mounting—did not help matters as Griswold frequently told me of the wealth he had gained through writing his editorials and how it was serving him in the grandest of ways, to which I replied, "It is most evident in your waistline."

He convinced Mr. Graham that my tales, although growing in popularity, were only worth four dollars a page when English was getting twelve a page for his drivel. To no surprise of my supportive family, a month after I met Dickens I left the employ of *Graham's Magazine* and what had become its namby-pamby character[51] under the editorship of Griswold.

Mr. Graham and I parted as friends, nevertheless, and I promised to submit further stories for publication. I was surprised and angered to learn (though I suppose I should have been flattered) that Graham did not immediately inform his readers I had left the magazine, choosing instead to let them think I was still working for it. Three more issues of the magazine got published before Graham announced I had left back in July.[52]

For the rest of the year, once again unemployed, I continued writing my stories and planning a new magazine called the *Stylus*, which I reasoned as a better name than the *Penn Magazine*. Nathaniel Hawthorne agreed to furnish stories and so did Thomas Grey. I continued on this path toward reaching my goal of developing a magazine subscribership that far surpassed that of the faltering (at least in a literary sense) *Graham's Magazine*. Under my care *Graham's* was built and I could do it again with my own publication, which meant my household would never want for money as we had these many years.

In the fall I was handed a new copy of Reverend Griswold's *The Poets and Poetry of America*, a self-serving review of his literary friends, most living in New England, many frogpondians. The compilation was to be America's foremost commentary on the state of the country's literary circles, though his bias against the South and its writers oozed from every page.

I poured over the book and in November published my review of it in the *Boston Miscellany*, which stated in part: *We disagree then, with Rev. Griswold in many of his critical estimates; although in general, we are proud to find his decisions our own. He has omitted from the body of his book, some one or two whom we should have been tempted to introduce. On the other hand, he has scarcely made us amends by introducing some one or two dozen whom we should have treated with contempt. We might complain too of a prepossession, evidently unperceived by himself, for the writers of New England.*[53]

Low and behold, Graham sought me out to come back to the magazine. The events of this time were not surprising to me, which I expressed to a friend. *Graham has made me a good offer to return. He is not especially pleased with Griswold—nor is any one else, with the exception of the Rev. gentleman himself, who has gotten himself into quite a hornet's nest, by his "Poets & Poetry."*[54]

1843 - Age 34

The turning of the calendar year brought forth yet another review of mine regarding *The Poets and Poetry of America* in the *Saturday Museum* magazine. Griswold's reputation was cooked. *Did any one read such nonsense? We* never *did, and shall hereafter eschew everything that bears Rufus Wilmot Griswold's name.*[55]

Out of sheer pride I turned down Graham's new offer. I had my pride and the seedlings of a new magazine if nothing else. Seeking cheaper rent given my unemployment, we relocated to a small house in Philly on North Seventh Street. Weeks later I was distraught to learn that Thomas C. Clarke, the scheduled publisher of the *Stylus*, had to withdraw his commitment because of financial difficulties and his claims that I had displayed the undesirable qualities of a drinker. He would not tell me who made these statements, but I guessed it was Griswold or English.

Dr. Francis had recently diagnosed me as having brain congestion, which I knew was carried with me all these years in worsening degrees from John Allan's fit of rage in the carriage house; his kicks to my head. Dr. Francis noted that congestion of the brain resulted in me having an acute sensitivity towards alcohol and drugs. He warned me to be wary and I responded that once again his profession had told me nothing new.

I personally showed this evaluation to Mr. Clarke, but he was in denial given my off balance behavior when under an attack. For weeks I said nothing to Sissy or Muddy about this huge setback and did what I always did in these situations—buried myself in prose.

A devilish tale of mine called *The Black Cat* was published under much interest in Philadelphia.[56] Catterina and her exploits made me think of this story. I found it odd how many men hated cats and I wondered how a sable feline could get revenge on the male gender. Thankfully my tale *The Gold-Bug* won the $100 prize in the *Dollar Newspaper*. The story was so popular it required a second printing. In the story I created a cryptography puzzle in reverse and then solved it before the readers. This slight of mental hand was not my best work, but readers loved it. *The Gold-Bug* sold over three hundred thousand copies and in August of the year was adapted into a play, yet I received no further income than my initial $100 prize money as I had to assign over all copyrights to the publisher, which was routine.

To supplement my income I began lecturing on American poetry in Baltimore, Redding, and Philadelphia. Yet another affirmation of my growing popularity was not the invites themselves, but the overflow audiences that received me. There were also the accompanying great reviews. One critic touted my speech at the Wirt Institute as being superior to all lectures ever delivered in its confines.

I became adept at quoting from my tales and when I signed autographs afterwards, found that my audiences possessed the same skills. How fulfilling it was to know that the masses were not only reading and enjoying my work, but also memorizing key turns of phrase; the highest form of flattery to an author.

My lecturing trips were quick. I sought to be gone the minimum duration from our humble abode on North Seventh Street where Sissy lay under the dominion of tuberculosis. After one of my lectures I was handed an issue of *Clarke's Saturday Museum*. The giver, a teenage boy with acne who begged me to keep writing horror tales, directed my attention to a story inside by English called *The Doom of the Drinker*.[57] I traveled by rail that afternoon and read the malicious portrait of myself in the *Museum's* pages while chewing Muddy's homemade caramels with spiteful purpose. The very words made me stop reading the galley of Dickens's *A Christmas Carol* that Dickens had sent me. The fine ghost story remained in my valise the entire journey. I was livid when I reached home. I tossed the magazine to Sissy who was propped up in bed. The article was flagged and she began reading it.

Her ashen skin matched the color of the bed liens and her thinning legs disappeared into them almost imperceptibly.

Sissy was only a quarter of the way through when she heaved the magazine against the wall in a display of strength unequaled in months. A small painting of Baltimore's Inner Harbor rattled loose and knocked against the floorboards. "I would rather use the writings of English as a liner for my chamber pot or Catterina's sawdust box than read them!"

"He must have been the one who talked with Clarke."

"It is jealousy, pure jealousy!"

I kicked the floor surround. "Libel is what it is, and I will sue English into the next century for it."

"Did your review of Griswold's compilation prompt this attack?"

Staring out the window at the brazen horizon, I responded, "Not sure. Probably. English and Griswold are best friends."

"Never trust a man named Rufus. Sounds like a disease more than a name." Sissy thought for a second. "If you spell it backwards it's pronounced suffer. And that's exactly what he is trying to make you do. Oh, Eddy, I am sorry. You deserve so much better."

I walked over and stroked her colorless cheek. "Even when sick you bring me joy as no other."

Sissy leaned over the side of the bed and began coughing with great force beneath a veil of stringy hair. I handed her a glass of water that Muddy always kept filled on the nightstand. Minutes passed before she could sustain herself to drink from it with shaky hands that spilled the liquid down her neck.

"There has never been, nor will there ever be a more tender or devoted companion than you, my love. And I am convinced you will be back out of bed and playing your piano in no time. Your sickness only fuels mine," I said. She scolded me for saying this, but it was the truth. My migraines increased with each slippage of Sissy into the grasps of the disease, the masque of the red death.

After she finished with her choking swallows, Sissy made it clear she was not done with my former boss. "Reverend Griswold considers himself the moral superior to you from his ministry days, yet acts like your friend while he and English plot your destruction under shady trees in the heat of day."

"How right you are, as much as I hate to admit it. Griswold and English view me as nothing more than a higher learning dropout who is not talented; a poor boy from the South looking to make a name in the North."

She took my hand in both of hers. "Be careful, my dear husband."

1844 - Age 35

To increase my publications and to publish tales outside my normal gothic modes of literature, I sometimes wrote under the pseudonym Ida Grey; Ida being the Norse goddess of youth and Grey being the last name of Thomas Grey, a writer I respected. I thought of using a middle name Ben for kicks, but realized the world would immediately suspect it was a pseudonym. The name was a nice slap in Griswold's face, whose offhanded references to me being "short in the tooth" and "having yet to reach literary maturity" in his reviews of my works, were increasing in frequency. I also wrote under the pseudonym Edward S. T. Grey, the moniker being a combination of a few favorite writers: Edward [Bulwer-Lytton] S.[amuel] T.[aylor Coleridge] [Thomas] Grey.

It was not until I frequented a number of reviews penned in my usual voice and tone of writing that I was uncovered as being one of the Greys, and when one name fell, the other followed like a house of cards. While most editors found humor in my names, Dr. Thomas Dunn English took it upon himself to attack me by the name in the title of his story *The Ghost of a Grey Tadpole*. As soon as I read it to Sissy, we identified the piece as a burlesque of my fiction in the *Irish Citizen*. Yet again another English story brought further ridicule to my career and made a mockery of me as a serious writer.

We had to get out of Philadelphia, if just for a few weeks. Virginia and I decided to leave Muddy and Catterina behind and to visit New York in the hopes that time away would breathe some life into my writing and Sissy. Muddy packed us a huge lunch and gave Sissy a daisy-embossed coverlet that she had made for warmth.

On the journey *Sissy coughed hardly any and had no night sweat*[58] to the point where I almost forgot about her dreadful sickness. We rented a third-floor back room in a boarding house on Greenwich Street that had brown steps and a porch with brown pillars.[59] The house was ancient and buggy[60] but the landlady was nice. *For breakfast we had excellent-flavored coffee, hot & strong – not very clear & no great deal of cream.*[61]

I had procured a few lectures at small institutions that welcomed me with open arms. They had heard great reviews of my lectures around Philly and Baltimore the prior year. Our newfound freedom impelled us to stay in New York longer than planned, and I published a number of works including *The Oblong Box* (I had seen a large piece of luggage in transit and wondered if it was secretly a coffin.) that I sold to *Godey's Lady's Book*. I sold *The Purloined Letter* for a mere twelve dollars, but it was well received by the public and my reputation continued to grow.

"The price will not pay two weeks rent for us," Sissy aptly pointed out from her bed that I had pulled next to the window to overlook Greenwich Street. The window was half open and purple curtains, of very misplaced taste, played and soughed in the gentle breeze. I had learned many times over that a renter must accept the existing accompaniments of his abode or waste precious money in trying to change them.

Sissy had taken a turn for the worse in the past days no matter how badly the sunlight tried to scorch the TB. She could not speak without coughing and I tried to calm her.

"March back there and demand more!" she hacked.

"I got the editor up from ten, and that was a heated struggle."

In her frail hands was a parchment with my handwriting on both sides to save money. The current of warm air was crinkling it. I recognized the writing as a tale of mine that I had finished the night before under candlelight, and I cringed. She raised it, with some effort. *"The Premature Burial.* I will not be hurt if you were thinking of my impending death."

"Give me that," I said, reaching for it in vain, "and never speak so. I hoped you would not find it." A distraught look overtook me. "You are going to be fine. The story is not about you. It is non-fiction."

"Do not be ashamed, Eddy. It is good to get your feelings down on paper. A mental purging."

"There are many ways in which I am not deserving of you," I said, feeling a sense of guilt at trying to make money off my dear wife's illness.

"This is great writing." She held the parchment to the sunlight and read. *"The boundaries which divide Life and Death are at best shadowy and vague. Who shall say where the one ends and where the other begins?*[62]*"*

When the last syllable fell from her pallid lips, a sudden gust of wind sent the purple curtains flapping, snapping off at the ends as though swollen Atlantic waves. The parchment released from Sissy's hand and was pinned to the far wall.

Bamp! The door behind me slammed into its frame and it sent my head spinning.

"Look, look," Sissy implored.

As I turned back toward the window I noticed the gust of wind had quelled and a raven had landed on the windowsill. The bird was dark as a moonless night and its feathers had a glossy sheen. Its chest was swollen and proud, beak daggerlike.

"Your name Grip?" I asked, thinking of Dickens's bird. "Returned from a grave of stitching and stuffing to haunt us? Or have you reanimated yourself, the undead, like the monster Prometheus?"

"Listen, it is speaking to us," Sissy whispered and then tried to repeat the bird's cawing sound. "Wha-wha-rower."

"Wha-ra-mower," I tried.

The raven sidled along the windowsill, raised its head, jutted its stiletto beak, and cried out.

"No, no, no, I think he's saying 'Wha-ra-more.'"

Sissy coughed at the end and I tried to repeat her translation. "Wha-ver-more?"

"I have it now 'Neverroar' like a lion, no wait ... 'nevermore.' That's it 'Nevermore!'"

I grinned. Oh how I loved her. From my vantagepoint the raven was a glossy shadow, proud and stoic, unaffected by the tragedies of this world and able to leave it at a flapping of its wings.

Sissy leaned toward the window, "Mister Raven, will the South rise up over the North?" The bird scratched a swatch of whitewash off the sill, and cawed, *Nevermore!*

"Will Thomas Dunn English be more well known than my gifted husband in the annals of literature?"

Nevermore!

The raven sat on the window ledge for a great length of time while we talked of music and books, until Sissy's lids grew heavy and she dozed off, so delicate and pure as I held her in my arms. I pulled the daisy embossed coverlet that Muddy had made around her neck and turned toward the window. "Mister Raven," I said in a whisper, "I ask you this one last question and no more. Will my dear Virginia rise again?"

To my surprise the sable bird flapped its wings, arched its muscular back, and took flight. I rushed to the window, spread the royal curtains wide, and stuck my head outside in demand of an answer.

It called out from the air: *Nevermore! Nevermore!*

1845 - Age 36

The raven, the stoic fowl that lit on the windowsill remained with me, unshakable in its ominous presence and three-syllable wisdom. I was compelled to write a tale using the same raven as a key character, having a much larger roll than Dickens's bird in *Barnaby Rudge*.

I dashed downstairs and began penning the poem in a maddening fit. The words flowed from me. The curled pages were wings and ink the bird's glossy coat. I wrote long into the night till many candles had glowered into tallowy rivulets down spindly table legs and were extinguished into uselessness.

When *The Raven* was completed and Sissy and Muddy had gushed over its text the following day, I rewrote it in neat penmanship and hand delivered it to the offices of *Graham's Magazine* under snapping January weather. I had the manuscript bound in sable ribbon and the outline of a raven on the front cover that Sissy had sketched.

With arms outstretched I presented the manuscript to George Graham, who was glad to see me for the first time since I left the magazine. We exchanged pleasantries and he promised to read *The Raven* for possible publication in his magazine.

A week later I was back on his doorstep. I was excited about the tale, not so much because I thought it my best prose, but from the resulting effect it had on everyone who read it.

I removed my hat and searched for Mr. Graham. It was not like him to be tardy for a meeting, especially in his own noisy office. When he finally appeared from the rear, the manuscript was in his hands and he returned it to me under a sigh. "I am sorry."

Pushing the manuscript back into his chest, I asked, "What do you mean? The others who have read the poem think it my best gothic romance, though not in the ordinary genre. I am sure your readers will find it of interest."

"The raven in the story is too one dimensional. Singular in color and speech. You yourself in the text said that nevermore is its only 'stock and store.'"

"But that is the idea as it sits on the bust of Pallas, the Greek goddess of wisdom. There is the contrast of black on the white sculpture. The purple chamber curtains represent sorrow and it is a tale I have worked backwards for solitary effect. Please, Mister Graham, I desperately need this money to help Virginia who, as you know, has been sick from tuberculosis for years."

"Again, I apologize," he said while studying the floor. "This tale is not for us. It did not meet editorial approval."

Graham shoved the manuscript back and I saw Rufus Griswold over his shoulder. He stepped, or rather rolled, out from behind reams of paper and binding machinery. On his rotund face he wore a thin smile.

The snubbing at the hands of my former employer and Griswold made me all the more determined to find a home in which *The Raven* could roost. I revised the poem a couple more times and the *American Review* enthusiastically bought all copyrights in it for ten dollars. Rent for merely two weeks as Sissy pointed out!

But first, the *Evening Mirror* published it[63] with an introduction by the popular author N. P. Willis: *We are permitted to copy, (in advance of publication,) from the second No. of the American Review, the following remarkable poem by Edgar Poe. In our opinion, it is the most effective single example of 'fugitive poetry' ever published in this country; and unsurpassed in English poetry for subtle conception, masterly ingenuity of versification, and consistent sustaining of imaginative lift.... It is one of those 'dainties bred in a book,' which we feed on. It will stick to the memory of everybody who reads it.*[64]

The Raven, in its entire publication history, brought me less than a month's rent or enough to buy a quart of lung tonic for Sissy. Ultimately, it was about the art. The poem transpired into a huge overnight success and garnered many flattering reenactments and reviews across the country. Doilies were embroidered with the dark bird and artwork of all sorts. I received many letters from women across the country who told me they fainted at each reading.

A feeling of great satisfaction enveloped me. The dark bird had flown me to a position of widespread notoriety.

Sissy said, "It is about time, darling hubby."

She was good-natured about the letters scented with perfume and sealed in red nail polish, including one from Detroit that contained a swatch of a ruffled black undergarment cut
into the outline of a raven. I showed it to Sissy and to my surprise she gave me a hug. "My
Eddy, the one who has romanced women across the country, from valley to mountainside,
in a few swoops of his pen."

"Your side is the only one to which I aspire," I said, running my fingers through her hair
as she lay in bed.

"In my opinion, this is your best tale to date."

"I am not so sure. The bird beat *The Gold-Bug*," I told her, "though all hollow."

1846 - Age 37

"Tell me again why we had to sell the piano," Virginia said.

"It will not fit in our smaller arrangement," Muddy answered from her bench seat facing
Sissy and myself. Catterina was nestled on her lap.

"And look at this train," I said, sweeping my arms around the cabin, "it would have been
impossible to load it. The instrument would have had to ride up with the conductor, him
sitting on the keys, and we all know train conductors are not musically inclined. I am
convinced he could not produce music with his rump."

Sissy tittered. How fortifying to see her smile. "Maybe if his name was Rumplestiltskin."

"Then he could spin gold out his—"

"Eddy!" Muddy exclaimed.

Sissy withdrew into herself again. "You are sure the piano was not sold because I have
been bedridden and unable to play it in months?"

"Not at all," I said. "Besides, the money will help get us into a country area where you
will be free of your illness. The fresh air and solitude will do you much good."

"And your writer's block," Muddy added.

"I prefer the term 'idea impediment.'"

The early summer of the year is when we moved to West Farms in Fordham by train. At
the station we piled off, me having two suitcases under each arm. Muddy had two by the
handles and Sissy took Catterina and the map that gave directions to the house we had
rented unseen from John Valentine.

As we nudged our way past the engine car and I scanned the unloading area for an avail-
able coach, Sissy spoke up. "From the street signs, I think that's it over there. But that's not
a house ... a cottage at best!"

She pointed to the other side of the tracks, past a weatherworn junction building, and I saw a tiny structure a ways off. The grass was knee deep around it, soughing in the wind like a horse's mane. The surrounding trees were gangly and unkempt. A branch of one was knocking against the cottage, as though beating it farther down into the weeds.

Our cottage was so close, we did not have to rent a coach to get us there. Instead we took a shortcut through the shipping yard, which caused me to stumble a number of times over the tracks with my unwieldy load.

"Are you sure? Is the map upside down?" I kept asking Sissy as we got closer, stepping between a stack of railroad ties and pea gravel. "Positive?"

"Yes, the address matches that on the rickety For Sale sign in the front yard. If the weeds were any higher, we could not see it at all."

The Fordham cottage had chipped brick and weather-scrubbed paint. Segments of crumbled mortar were evident. A section of the chimney was sheered off into a brick spire and the rest of it lay in a heap on the ground. Slate shingles littered the sides of the cottage, which was literally crumbling around itself, ruinous on its foundations. It made one wonder if the cottage had ever been completed, or if the builders simply ran off in mid-construction.

With me bumping alongside in the middle, both Clemm ladies gave me a stern look. It was hard to shrug carrying four suitcases. "Mister Valentine assured me it would be fine after a bit of fixing up. And besides, the price is right at one hundred dollars for a year's rent." I would later be forced to spend many hours outside fixing the exterior and clearing away God's overgrowth while taking breaks from writing. I did not complain. The fresh air cleared my head.

We made our way across the prairie that used to be the front lawn. Muddy tripped over the handle of a plow buried in the weeds on our way to the front door and nearly cursed.

I sat the suitcases down on the front porch and tried the key in the lock. White paint on the door had peeled into curlicues. For minutes I jiggled the key every which way. The door finally came ajar, straining on its rusty hinges. We slowly peered inside. The air was heavy and dust-ridden, as though we were opening an ancient crypt.

The floor looked trustworthy, so in we went. I sat the suitcases down and began peeling back the moth-pocked curtains. The lower half of the cottage had a tiny bedroom (with the lone fireplace downstairs), parlour, and kitchen. An ugly, moldering sofa was against one wall of the parlour and the horsehair plaster above it was chipped in sections. Wet rot had overcome a number of baseboards in the lower bedroom and water stains ringed the ceiling. The gossamer filament of a large spider web was festooned in a corner and plumed when Muddy shut the door.

"This place is supposed to nurse me back to health?" Sissy blurted just prior to breaking into a coughing fit from the dust.

When she had finally stopped, Muddy said, "Now Virginia, this will be our home for awhile and we will make the best of it. It just needs a little tending."

"I have seen nicer outhouses."

I was in the empty kitchen by now and noticed a rat hole while checking inside one of the splintered cabinets. I tried to hide it from the ladies with one leg. At times like these I missed the glass-fronted hutches of Moldavia with their arrays of china and drawers lined in velvet where polished silverware was always at the ready.

The Clemm ladies followed me.

"What are we going to eat on?" Sissy thought aloud.

"Not my good looks," Muddy said.

They quickly trailed me upstairs. There we found another bedroom, which Muddy took for her own after granting me full reign of the study across from it. It had a fireplace (the only source of heat upstairs) and a small table that I could use as a desk. She was so gracious to me.

That day we took to cleaning. Sissy polished the brass doorknobs, which left her wheezing and we had to order her to stop. Muddy wiped the windows using a vinegar and water solution. After I had shored the rickety beds, I fashioned two tables from boards I found out back. I thought brass-headed nails would be an elegant touch to fasten the legs and a few coats of green baize would offer warmth to the home. Muddy also needed a bolt of fabric to cover the sofa. A trip into the city was in order.

I set out for Downtown New York the following morning to get the supplies. I was so excited to improve my family's living arrangements that I forgot to have my usual cup of coffee, which I blamed on Muddy not having the kitchen arranged.

The streets of the city were sparsely populated that Sunday, noon bells having yet to ring on the cathedrals and steepled churches, which numbered roughly the same as in Richmond though New York was ten fold the size. Most stores had their usual Closed signs facing outward. None had a special sign that bragged HAPPILY CLOSED ON SUNDAY, which one typically saw in Richmond or parts of Baltimore. Church attendance seemed more a duty here than a source of redemption or pride.

I came upon a corner fabric shop with quilts hanging in the windows. An array of carved wooden poles was supporting the sidewalk's overhang. The apparent owner, a woman of ripe age, was standing outside beating dust from a rug. I introduced myself and impressed upon her my needs. She took an air of reluctance as I glanced around. Caddy corner was the sullen confines of the New Yankee Saloon, which by law could not operate on Sunday. The remnants of its patrons' beverages of choice littered the street.

After near pleading on my part, she agreed to let me shop for Muddy's fabric, though immediately qualified that she had just gotten back from the early Sunday service (Obligation completed!) and would not officially be open for half an hour.

Holding my breath as I slipped past the lingering plumes of dust, I walked inside. I found myself surrounded by bolts of every design and color imaginable. They were stacked to the ceiling in tight rows like stiff bodies at a mausoleum and I was in awe at the craftsmanship.

Suddenly I felt the first razorblade of pain carom through my brain, I blamed it on my lack of morning coffee, but then abrasive rollers passed through. My balance abandoned me. This was an attack, not a minor headache from lack of caffeine.

I stumbled into a wall of fabric, which kept me from falling. Grains were pelting the back of my eyes. I blinked tears and tried to breathe and clutched for support from the wooden spindles on which the bolts of fabric were mounted. The one on which I put the most weight spun towards me and I plunged to the floor.

The burst of pain in my lower back was nothing compared to the grinding between my temples. I lay there for a few seconds or perhaps minutes until I heard the storeowner's frail voice. "Si ... r, a ... re you-all righttt?"

The syllables of her language would slow, then speed up, then pause into a hum.

I comprehended nothing as I used all my power to get back on my feet and fight through the streams of material that had washed over me. When I opened my eyes I saw a kaleidoscope of colors rolling and snapping off in a mad circle. They were closing in on me, crashing down.

"May ... I ... helllllp ... yo?"

I had to get outside. My nervousness and paranoia were growing by the second.

Pushing past the old lady, I shot out the front door—stumbling over the uneven wood planks that fronted the fabric shop—and found myself in the middle of the cobblestone intersection. I spun to get my bearings and was faced with a rearing stallion, front legs wheeling in the sun. The light hurt my vision more.

Just as I was about to apologize, I heard: "You seem out of sorts," a manly voice called from atop the horse.

My lids were uselessly trying to blink away the pain. My arm was raised to block the light. "I am suffering from congestion of the mind," I responded, easing back.

"Interesting, Grey Tadpole."

I knew it was Thomas English.

Using his riding crop, he pointed to the bottles on the ground. "Apparently you are suffering from congestion of the liver, also. Always heard that the best time to quaff alcohol is Saturday night and the worst time is Sunday morning. A few hours make all the difference. Don't they, Tadpole? Just as now, for if I found you midday, I guess you would be sober. I even heard a few hours would have mattered to you before Missus Allan expired."

I was incensed with this comment, especially coming from English, and found it ironic he was perched on his high horse when he said it. "You disgust me, and I am not taken with alcohol!"

English threw his head back in laughter and reigned in his stallion. "I should expect no less a denial from a so-called writer who leaves morals from his tales and, as best I can tell, displays none in public, either."

"Poetry has no concern with duty or truth in life. Tales have only one purpose, and that is the desired effect on the reader."

"Why not make the one purpose social good—morals?"

I had staggered back onto the porch and was steadying myself against one of the posts holding up the store's overhang. "My readers want to be entertained, not preached to. Some write and tell me my stories will be remembered."

"And others tell me you are a drunk bordering on insanity who writes short stories because that is all you are capable of doing."

"One drink has the effect on me that ten would on others, English. I do not have the luxury of steady income to write a novel over the course of a year, and besides, I write poems and short stories because they are the most ideal form of writing. They can be read in one sitting without interruption of the outside world to the reader, much like viewing a painting in the whole, one that does not span two city blocks." While saying this, the pulverizing rollers made another pass and I flinched back in anguish. The little storeowner was at the screen door goggling us.

English hopped off his stallion and tied it to a crossbar outside the store, his riding clothes consisting of tall riding boots, gray breeches, a long-tailed petticoat, leather gloves, and a top hat. His heels clunked onto the uneven planks and his shadow fell across the storefront.

"Burdening the reader is not part and parcel with our business. We are entertainers in the finest sense," I said.

"And what about dutiful citizens? I trust you will sober up enough to vote in the upcoming elections?" English asked.

"Voting is nothing more than meddling in the public affairs of a democracy where capitalism reigns supreme and true artists are scorned, which is a very admirable form of government—for dogs."

"You have an active imagination, Grey Tadpole, coupled with traitorous aspects of grand proportion. And your mother's maiden name was Arnold. Hoom. I wonder if she was related to Benedict Arnold." English moved within a foot of me. I felt his putrid breath on my cheek. "Know that I will be voting for my first cousin who is running for Inspector General ... and I have no aspirations to marry him."

I stared English down, eyes unflinching while the tiny grains pelted the backs of them. "You have questioned my profession and patriotism, do not question the sanctity of my marriage."

"Your marriage to Virginia Clemm is an incestuous one at best!"

Rage overcame me and I swung as hard as I could. I wanted to hurt English, to cripple him for life. My fist hit squarely in his midsection and he doubled over like the deflated windbag that he was.

The next blow glanced off his angular chin and the follow-through caused me to lose my balance, yet I somehow latched on to a carved support. When I tried to right myself, I felt an explosion in my bad ear, then another, and another.

I crashed to the planking in anguish and raised my hand to fend off blows from English's riding crop. Visions of my return from the University of Virginia so many years ago flashed in my head and I became confused whether I was reliving the past before John Allan or had become a tortured soul of the present.

More explosions went off in my brain and it was not until the storeowner began yelling and making a scene that English mounted his horse and sped off. I lay on the planking with blood streaming from my bad ear. The elderly storeowner was crying at my side.

From that day forward the mutual and lasting hate between Thomas Dunn English and myself would not abate. And from that day forward rumors of my insanity began to circulate in droves.

Days later, after Muddy had tended to my purulent ear and the migraines had stopped, I was shaving in the upstairs study at the small table that had become my writing desk at the Fordham cottage. Trains ran every four hours and their blaring sirens did not help my brain congestion. Yet they never ceased blaring like clockwork, evidence of normalcy and routine outside my random and turbulent life.

Muddy appeared in the mirror as I shaved the last strip of lather from my face. I told her to come inside, knowing something was pressing on her mind.

"May I have a word with you, Eddy?"

"As always. How is Sissy? Forgive me for failing to check on her, I have been lost in my writing and day's old growth."

Muddy positioned herself next to the fireplace with its cold, sooty mouth. "She is no worse than yesterday, but I am afraid no better, and that is what I want to speak to you about."

"This country life is the perfect place for her. I am sure she will overcome her affliction in no time."

I folded up the razor and toweled off. When I glimpsed Muddy again, her head was hung low. For a brief second I thought her chin was going to find its resting-place on the mantel. "Virginia has been sick for years, Eddy. She has not left her bed in months. I wanted to let you know that I would not hold you accountable for leaving us."

"I would laugh if I did not think the notion so preposterous. I love Sissy, my darling wifey, and I love you. You are the only real family I have ever had. Listen to this beautiful poem she has written me." I took a piece of parchment off the desk and read:

> *"Ever with thee I wish to roam -*
> *Dearest my life is thine.*
> *Give me a cottage for my home*
> *And a rich old cypress vine,*
> *Removed from the world with its sin and care*
> *And the tattling of many tongues.*
> *Love alone shall guide us when we are there -*
> *Love shall heal my weakened lungs;*
> *And Oh; the tranquil hours we'll spend,*
> *Never wishing that others may see!*
> *Perfect ease we'll enjoy, without thinking to lend*
> *Ourselves to the world and it's glee -*
> *Ever peaceful and blissful we'll be."*[65]

Through the window Muddy watched a train puffing smoke from its stacks, trying to gain speed out of the station. Tears dotted her cheek.

"The love between you is beautiful."

"I truly cherish it."

Muddy had to get something off her mind. "I know of the many attacks on your character for marrying a woman so young, not to mention one that is your first cousin, Eddy. I have heard of your scuffle with English on your trip into the city. Word seems to follow you. You have many friends in Richmond and an equal amount of enemies here. If you feel that you can further your career elsewhere I will not hold it against you. You have shown us five lifetimes of kindness."

I pushed away my chair and pounded the desk, causing the porcelain jar of lather to bounce and its head of foam to spill over the side. "I will take a hundred blows to my character *and* person for Sissy. She is lovely even in sickness, sweet and gentle in disposition. From her illness is my strength. She deserves all the love I have within me to bestow. I will be with her until one of us expires first, and I hope it is *I*."

Muddy rushed over and hugged me in her matronly way. "You are a man beyond compare."

"I am trying my best to provide for all of us."

"And I am forever devoted to you."

The following week I journeyed back to New York City to interview a potential publisher for a story I had been working on entitled *The Literati of New York* wherein I fleshed out the problems in the Northeast publishing industry. The train ride seemed longer than usual and I missed Sissy every second.

June. 12th — 1846

My Dear Heart, My dear Virginia! our Mother will explain to you why I stay away from you this night. I trust the interview I am promised, will result in some substantial good for me, for your dear sake, and hers — Keep up your heart in all hopefulness, and trust yet a little longer — In my last great disappointment, I should have lost my courage but for you — my little darling wife you are my greatest and only stimulus now, to battle with this uncongenial, unsatisfactory and ungrateful life — I shall be with you tomorrow P.M. and be assured until I see you, I will keep in loving remembrance your last words and your fervent prayer!

Sleep well and may God grant you a peaceful summer, with your devoted Edgar[66]

While in the city I petitioned Nathaniel Hawthorne for a copy of his new collection of short stories, and the gentleman responded promptly as always.

Salem, June 17, 1846.

My Dear Sir, — I presume the publishers will have sent you a copy of "Mosses from an Old Manse" the latest (and probably the last) collection of my tales and sketches. I have read your occasional notices of my productions with great interest — not so much because your judgment was, upon the whole, favorable, as because it seemed to be given in earnest. I care for nothing
but the truth; and shall always much more readily accept a harsh truth, in regard to my writings, than a sugared falsehood.

I confess, however, that I admire you rather as a writer of tales than as a critic upon them, I might often — and often do — dissent from your opinions in the latter capacity, but could never fail to recognize your force and originality in the former.

Yours very truly,
Nath. Hawthorne[67]

My meeting with the publisher was a success and later in the year I published a series of articles in *Godey's Lady's Book* regarding the Literati. Oh how they played with their ordinary talents at extraordinary jobs that were handed to them on silver platters by wealthy and politically connected families of the North. Their lives were a poetic spin on mediocrity. It felt great to get my true feelings out about my literary contemporaries in this area, to publicly expose those guilty of tiny writing and grand estimations of themselves.

Publication of *The Literati of New York* cemented my reputation throughout the country as a literary renegade. My life had left me no other option and I would play this bloodsport for the rest of it. One of my primary targets was Thomas Dunn English whom I referred to as being prone to taking "bold literary plunges into shallow, icy waters." How I loathed the very mention of his name!

Needless to say, this little commentary of mine drew heated attention from many author cliques. Anonymous letters were penned and angry rebuttals printed in subsequent issues of *Godey's Lady's Book.* A section of the public agreed with me and applauded my honesty, but it was the writing community that chastised me for rebuking those in my own profession.

In reply to his own portrayal, English claimed I had committed forgery on writings that were not my own in the *Morning Telegraph* on June 23rd. He also stated that I was *guilty of some most ungentlemanly conduct, while in a state of intoxication ... [68]* The article was then printed verbatim in the *Evening Mirror.* I immediately fashioned a rejoinder where I denied English's claims and told the world of the libel he had caused my good name.

To prove that his statements about me were true—which Enoch L. Fancher, Esquire (my attorney) informed me was a complete defense to libel—English challenged me to sue him.

This left me in a tight position, for I had little money to provide for my family, let alone fund a lawsuit. English was well aware of this. Thankfully Mr. Fancher, Esquire, in his good graces, offered to delay most of his fees until a verdict. Having no other recourse, I sued the editors of *Evening Mirror* magazine in New York Superior Court for publishing English's libelous story. The complaint read in part: *said defendants ... contriving and wickedly and maliciously intending to inure the ... plaintiff, in his good name ... did print ... a certain false, scandalous, malicious and defamatory libel over the name of one Thomas Dunn English ... .[69]* The suit made a splash in the papers, but the wheels of justice churned slowly.

The year passed without a verdict being rendered and the money situation for my family only worsened.

1847 - Age 38

Trial was held early in the year. Mr. Francher, Esquire proved many of the claims made by English to be false and I received a favorable verdict. My character, however, was at issue in the trial. Witnesses stated that they had not heard an unkind word about me except one stated me as being *occasionally addicted to intoxication.*[70] Muddy had wanted to attend the reading but she was nursing Sissy who had taken a turn for the worse. Thank goodness she did not hear that statement by the witness. The justice, in his full periwigged regalia, announced that I was due $225 in damages. This was two years rent in the Fordham Cottage, but my family was in such financial straights that most of it went to pay Sissy's medical bills and legal fees.

The money was welcomed, but what was most important was that my name was exonerated. Yellow-bellied Thomas English skipped town and fled to Washington D.C., refusing to speak to reporters. His comments about my character were silenced for the year.

After getting off the train in Fordham I raced through a heavy blanket of snow to the cottage with news of my victory. My mind was racing. I cared not that my coat was too thin for the wintry air. The clearing of my name had happened right when I thought there would never be any justice in my life.

My path from the train station to the cottage gave me full view of Sissy's bedchamber on the lower level. Frost had formed a craggy picture frame around the window. Through it I saw that my wife's face was emaciated to the point where I hardly recognized her.

Muddy was at her side and so was Mary Louise Shew, a kindly New York nurse who had taken to offering her services to Sissy at little or no charge after finding us in such a state of sickness and poverty. She was nearly as plump as Muddy and always wore her hair pulled back in a tight bun, a silver cross about her neck. The kind woman took to writing the local papers on our behalf to drum up financial support. I never would have allowed this had I known, for I was a proud man—a self-made man. Yet the more I thought about it, I was a self-*unmade* man.

Once in the cottage I announced the good news, hoping this might raise my wife's smile from the grave. "Today the law delivered justice." I am not sure that Sissy heard me. Her closed eyelids were robin's eggs and she did not flinch at my announcement.

Muddy placed a finger to her lips and escorted me into the parlour while Mrs. Shew stayed in attendance.I had just finished my first of several poems to the nurse. "Virginia has been sleeping for over an hour. Congratulations are in order."

"I have finally cleared my name."

"What a relief, Eddy! I will cook a huge celebration feast."

I flashed a ten-dollar bill. "Then we will take this money and not return until our arms are so full we cannot carry any more food."

Mrs. Shew stood watch and we left for the nearest store. I doubt we even noticed the cold as we walked. Happiness felt like a newfound emotion in our lives. An hour later we returned with enough food to feed India. Muddy had armfuls of fresh chicken and I had two sacks of grain riding on my shoulders.

A "feast" was an understatement once inside! Muddy prepared so much food for dinner that the kitchen table I had fashioned could not contain it. Bowls of yams and bread pudding overflowed onto the deep windowsills. Rolls were coming out of the hearth as if the cottage had been transformed into a bakery. Pots of cranberry and apple juice with mulling spices were steaming into the air. Two of the largest chickens I had ever seen were turned on spits. Shoofly pies were baked for dessert. Muddy prepared more food than I had witnessed at any holiday, even at Moldavia.

We brought Sissy out to the sofa in the hopes that the atmosphere would force an appetite on her, but to our dismay she only ate a few carrot sticks and a wedge of green bean casserole.

One frigid evening at the end of January I heard a shrill moan wafting up through the floorboards. Sissy had awakened or a demon from my tales had gotten loose. The day prior, Mrs. Shew measured her sleeping for eighteen hours. Sissy's own convulsive hacking did not wake her anymore.

I cast aside my writing and came downstairs from my study. A candleholder was in my hand, a flickering column of tallow slicing through the chilled air. I took a seat on her bed. The mattress was made of bundled straw covered only by sheets.[71] We could not afford feather stuffing.

The gentle nurse was tending her and Muddy rushed in right behind me.

"Sissy, can I get you anything? What can I do to make you feel better?"

The questions were futile and I knew that, but had to ask.

A ring of sweat had formed on her pillow, a ring that was a halo to me. I brushed back her matted hair with a damp cloth and Mrs. Shew swapped out her pillow. Money from the libel suit had run out quickly and we were rationing cords of wood for the fireplace in Sissy's bedroom that shared its chimney with the one in the study upstairs.

My poor wife shivered incessantly under the unflinching grasps of tuberculosis, yet her pores would not stop oozing as if she had run a race. The weather was unloving and one could feel it through the cracks in the clapboard and around the windowsills. Candlelight was jittery as a result and so were my nerves.

"Is the pillow to low? Can I get you water?"

Our poverty forced us to let the fire embers burn down in her room at night and we had gone weeks without heating the upper level apart from the warmth that rose up the common chimney and stairwell. I peered out the window and saw that our former woodpile was nothing but a flat section of ice in the sallow light cast outside. Snow was whipping across the panes, forming crescents in angles of the window, but to me they were the wintry blades of an executioner's ax.

Having no other recourse I busted the legs off one of the green tables I had made in the kitchen and stoked up a meager fire. I feared if I did not keep Sissy fully warm this night there would be no other. So I went to work on breaking up the planks that formed the tabletop to add more warmth to the room. If I had to start busting up the walls of the cottage I would have.

Meanwhile, Muddy pulled the coverlet back and draped Virginia in the few blankets left in the house that were not already keeping Sissy warm. My frockcoat was laid as the final topping and the daisy coverlet was placed over her legs. Catterina bounded up and sat on Sissy's nonexistent bosom. The cat was obviously aware of her need to supply warmth.

"Can you feel that, Sissy? The heat is rising." After fanning the fire into licking flames with bedside linens (we had few but they were always pristine, cleaned daily by Muddy), I raced next to Sissy. No matter how much I held her, she would not stop quivering or coughing blood. I cried out to God: "Help my dear wife!"

Muddy braced against the draughty air of the side window in only a crocheted shawl for covering and a threadbare nightgown. She minded Sissy's feet and I her hands to keep her extremities warm as best we could. Mary Shew continually wiped Sissy's forehead and mouth, soaking the rags in the water basin next to the bed. More than once she drowned out the candle I had brought down with a few misplaced drops. The water quickly turned brown in the porcelain container and I was forced to exchange it with fresh snow, which then had to be melted next to the fire.

That night was exhausting and Sissy's anguish never ending. We often heard rats skittering behind the walls toward the centralized warmth of the cottage. I ensured no extremity of Sissy's was hanging off the bed for good measure against the hungry creatures.

As the fire grew, though never reaching a decent robustness, the bedchamber did not seem to get brighter. Just the opposite. It was as though darkness was seeping into the room instead of light escaping. Glancing out the lone window, I noticed it was snowing harder, the fields around our cottage were being covered in a swirling blanket of white.

I spun. "Sissy, can I get you anything? What can I do to make you feel better? Is the pillow to low? Are you too hot or cold?"

The coverlet rose as Sissy launched into a violent coughing spell that seemed to last for days. Her body made tumultuous waves beneath the coverlet and when the spell at last ended, her eyes glazed over and she fell mercifully asleep.

While Muddy dabbed blood from the corners of her daughter's mouth, Mrs. Shew suggested a horrific idea. "Perhaps bloodletting would help."

I sprung from the bed in anger, not at the nurse but rather at the medical profession that could do little to help Sissy with its antiquated and useless cures. "This disease has caused Sissy to have built in bloodletting. I do not see her getting better as a result. We live in the Dark Ages or she would be saved," I said, pacing. "Nostrum peddlers roam the countryside taking advantage of the masses awed by science. They sell blood purifiers and skin ointments to cure every ailment, yet there is no evidence of their usefulness. Only half a century ago they saw fit to perform bloodletting on George Washington. Drained eighty ounces from our first president for a constricted throat. Killed the great man. Nothing has changed. Doctors perform bloodletting on the unstable of mind like they did on the mother of my boyhood friend. Patients of our day pray to die of the disease instead of the cure. No doctor will pierce Sissy's skin!"

Over the next excruciating winter hours many trains left the nearby station and squelched into the night. The wind lamented into the hungry darkness that was swallowing the snowflakes whole. We cried so long over Sissy that it was hard to tell whether her pillowcase was sodden from night sweats or our tears.

Almost five years to the day since Virginia showed her first signs of the wretched disease while trying to mask my embarrassment through her gift of singing at the Philadelphia Town Hall, she died January 30th at the age of twenty-five.

I screamed into the ceiling, fists balled. When I looked back, I noticed that Catterina was completely covering the daisy on the coverlet.

Death, my constant companion and bitter friend since childhood—my first memory— had visited me once more. Yet another lock of hair was coiled with my mother's inside the cap of my mourning ring.

Through much kindness our landlord, John Valentine, allowed us to bury Virginia in the Valentine family plot that was laid out behind the churchyard of the Dutch Reformed Church. Mrs. Shew provided the grave clothes for sissy. Mr. Valentine knew our situation was desperate regarding money.

Valentine also let us borrow two of his horses to pull the coffin bier. I'll never get over how small the sarcophagus was. Sissy was never a large woman to begin with and the ravages of TB caused her to lose many pounds over the years.

On the greyest of February days Sissy was laid to rest in the wrought iron-fenced church-yard of the Dutch Reformed Church with a smattering of neighbor ladies (and dear Mrs. Shew) standing around the grave in shin-deep snow, mourning behind fishnet veils. Some comforted Muddy and some me as we cried for the death of our hearts and a vapid-looking sexton watched from the side. Sissy was buried with the tin ring still on her finger.

Fueled by Sissy's death, my own sickness continued through the month and Mrs. Shew checked in on me with increasing frequency as I took Sissy's place.

One terrible day I was bedridden from migraines and a broken heart. Mary Shew helped Muddy change me out of my dress clothes (for I was unable to go into town as planned). The nurse saw the scar from John Allan's whip across my chest. Muddy had never seen it before and I told her only Sissy knew.[72] At this point in my life I had forgotten all about it.

Muddy arranged for Dr. Valentine Mott to examine me. I resisted, feeling guilty for my sickness that had caused impoverishment to visit my family and being distrustful of physicians no matter how well reputed, but Muddy insisted in a way that only she can.

We traveled into the city and visited the home of Dr. Mott who practiced out of his study. It needed no wallpapering due to the medical books lining his shelves. A skeleton was in the corner and, of course, bloodletting instruments. He poked many devices in the orifices of my head that morning. Dr. Mott wrote down his calculated numbers then reviewed the scar on my chest. He rubbed ointments on my hair and then felt my cranium, took more readings, and felt some more. When he was finally finished, he announced that I was suffering from a "brain lesion."

"What could cause such a thing?" Muddy questioned.

"In my experience, ma'am, a severe head injury." I was standing in the doorway of the study in a rude attempt to make an early exit.

"Doctor," Mrs. Shew said, "your patient may have suffered some early incident to his person, though he cannot remember such."

The good doctor faced me. "When you were young did you fall off a horse or down a flight of stairs? I have seen a number of these."

"Hardly," I said, refusing to give credit to what I knew was a proper diagnosis from a physician of our day. "Not once," I added with John Allan's beating replaying in grey through my head.

"Surely you can remember the scar to your chest. This is quite a trauma, sir."

"I am at a loss. It must have happened when I was an infant." My hands plunged into my pockets and I took to watching the sidewalk traffic.

"Or the trauma made you forget," Mrs. Shew said.

"Search back, Mister Poe," Dr. Mott implored. "Maybe there was something. All indications point to a brain lesion and congestion. Your motor skill disorders are part of it. Brain lesions can even cause emotional disorders and trigger depression."

"Will that be all?" I asked, still a skeptic. "I have tales to write. You tell me of an aliment you cannot prove? Is bloodletting next?"

"*Eddy*," my aunt called out.

The doctor flipped through the pages of a thick medical book on his desk. "You also have a heart murmur, Mister Poe. Even one or two glasses of wine with these conditions will uncover a severe intolerance to alcohol and may trigger many of these symptoms. I suggest you stay well clear of strong drink."

"As always," I barked, insulted.

1848 - Age 39

The year after Sissy's death I was in the middle of reading a book from one of the Bronte sisters when I heard a knock on our cottage door. I forget whether it was Charlotte Bronte's *Jane Eyre* or Emily Bronte's *Wuthering Heights*, but I do remember that I preferred the eeriness of *Jane Eyre* to the stable boy antics in *Wuthering Heights*, though I could relate to many of them.

Muddy was at a local sewing club meeting so I came down from my study and answered the door. To my shock Dr. Thomas English was standing there in his polished riding boots. My initial reaction was to clench into a posture for fisticuffs, but he was all grins.

"I have recently returned to New York from my absence."

"You mean from running scared to Washington."

"Never got to congratulate you on your defamation victory, Poe."

"Don't bother. My win was sufficient vindication."

English glanced over my shoulder. "Apparently the prize money was not enough to buy you a decent home, nor your young wife a life insurance policy."

This deserved no response and the air grew thick with tension. I found my hands balling. "If you have nothing constructive to say, then good day to you."

"Well now, perhaps you will congratulate me on my new magazine. I wanted to hand deliver the first copy to your doorstep. You should keep it in good condition because it will be very valuable one day. I'm calling it the *John-Donkey*."

"The *John-Jackass* would be a better title in my estimation."

"Tisk-tisk. Sorry you could never get your own magazine to print."

"I will, believe me, and it will be the top magazine in the country."

With that English slapped the copy into my midsection and walked away, saying, "Enjoy the frequent commentary I will be writing on the Grey Tadpole. All satire, of course."

I left Muddy at the cottage while I traveled abroad for a few weeks lecturing in Providence, Rhode Island. My headaches were never ceasing and my vision became blurred to such a point that I was forced to stay in my hotel room during a lengthy and violent episode that I thought would never end. My brain congestion was never ceasing.

One evening I felt well enough to venture from my hotel room and I decided to take a stroll along the Benefit thoroughfare of the seafaring town. The briny air suffused my nostrils and brought clarity of thought that I had not experienced for days.

Lamps were lit on their posts, casting pools of soft quavering light before me. I stopped momentarily under one to clasp a buckle on my boot. Upon looking up I noticed the silhouette of a woman tending a rose garden behind a large house.

She was dressed in the blackest-of-black flowing dresses that was blowing in the wind, a drapery of clothes set against the indigo sky. An alabaster scarf hung from her neck and was twisting into the flaps of her garments like the chocolate-vanilla taffy I had watched vendors make at sunset while strolling the harbor. Her skin was the color of the scarf. Her hands would have disappeared into its folds as she gathered it around her had it not been for her red-painted fingertips.

I watched her tirelessly as though she were not from this planet. A handkerchief was often brought to her face and I listened for sobbing carried on the sea breeze but heard nothing. She plucked a flower then suddenly spun and looked right at me. She locked onto my eyes and I could not move. For a bizarre second I felt as though we were communicating with our minds and that she had been waiting for me to happen by the garden.

For how long I watched her from under the lamplight is unknown, but I had never seen a greater person of mystery. She moved with grace among the blood flowers, petals luminescent in the hazy moonlight. There was a *flowing* quality about her and I blamed my wild imagination for tricking me, yet I am unsure whether that was the case.

At that moment I felt a knock against my leg. A boy with a harelip had rolled a wooden hoop into my side and this broke me from my gaze with a start. I bent to his level and asked him, "You from around here, son?"

"Sure, miztar. Lived 'ere my entire days."

"Do you know who that is in the rose garden?" I glanced back and the scarf was now waving behind her, meshing into the strands of her long dark hair. In some ways I was surprised that she had not vanished into thin air.

The boy placed the hoop over his shoulders. "Believe that's Sarah Helen Whitman, the dark poet."

"A poet," I repeated. Her name was familiar. I had heard of her and liked her work, but could not place any of her writings from memory at the moment. I dug into my pocket and then pressed a copper into his palm. "Tell her Edgar Allan Poe of Fordham, New York was admiring her."

"Sure thing. Thanks, miztar!"

When I rounded Sarah Helen Whitman was gone. The scarf remained, however, snagged on a thorny branch, frothing like a crashing wave. "What do you know about her?"

"Widowed. Some'll tell ya she's a ghost raised from the sea. Poseidon of Providence! She'll fill ya full of the hackakacha if ya gets too close." With that, the boy continued rolling his hoop along Benefit Street. He ran down the street laughing and yelling, "Ooh, roo hachakacha!" over the clack of his hard-soled shoes on the cobblestones. "Ooh, roo hachakacha!

"Make sure you tell her what I said," I yelled after him. When I returned to Fordham, however, I admit I forgot about the encounter due to my illness, writing schedule, and struggles of trying to get *The Stylus* up and running to compete with the *John-Donkey*. That was my first mistake regarding Sarah Helen Whitman.

On Valentine's Day I received a sable envelope with no return address. The choice of color was certainly odd for the holiday. When I pulled the letter out, rose petals spilled across my lap. But it was not a letter, rather a poem titled *The Raven*, oddly enough, which was not a copy of mine, but instead a poem that paid tribute to it. In flattery I read the perfect rhythm and pace of the poetry. I thought of half a dozen women who may have written the verses as I made my way down the parchment, for *The Raven*—my *Raven*—continued to gain in popularity. At once I suspected the woman in Detroit who kept sending me those Raven cutouts from her undergarments. When I reached the end I noticed the poem was unsigned.

The roses across my lap and boots got me thinking, and so did the text that was written in calligraphy, dark broad strokes and daring curvatures, the same shape of the silhouette I saw blowing in the Providence rose garden. It struck me. This beautiful poem needed no signature or return address, I knew who had penned it although I had never met the writer.

I scooped up the petals and breathed their sweet fragrance. They were swatches of crimson silk. "Sarah Helen Whitman," I whispered while exhaling. "Sarah Helen Whitman. She makes me full of the hackakacha." I chuckled.

To say the least I was intrigued. I did not respond until June, which gave me time to read all of her poetry that I could find in the library. To my wonder Helen Whitman expressed many of my own sentiments in her writings and ideas relating to unity of purpose. She apparently saw no need to preach morals. All this and we had never met! I further learned that she was the widow of a Providence lawyer named John Whitman, who had left her with a comfortable estate and land. Helen, I was told by acquaintances in the publishing world, stood to inherit even more wealth when her mother died.

Emboldened, I sent her a poem titled *To Helen*, the name she published under, remembering that my first *To Helen* poem was to Mrs. Stanard. In the poem I spoke of the first time I beheld her in the rose garden and what a deep affect it had on me.

During the summer of 1848 Helen and I exchanged many letters and thoughts on writing. How brilliant and well versed she was in prose and literature. Unable to control myself, I traveled to Providence from New York in September to meet her for the first time and told Muddy the half-truth that I was going to lecture. A year and a half after Sissy's death I could still not find it within me to talk of a new female interest before Muddy.

At dusk I arrived at the Whitman home (76 Benefit Street) promptly at eight. It had a flat façade with eight uniformly spaced windows around the front door and was located on the fashionable hillside avenue that overlooked Providence's busy waterfront. As I waited for someone to answer the front door, I noticed the whaling ships that were moored at port with their huge masts and furled sails wheezing in their resting positions. The changing colors in the trees were vibrant and I felt the same, more alive than I had in years.

A third gentle knock brought a woman to the door. Helen's mother blandly introduced herself as Mrs. Power and showed me inside. She appeared no less rigid than the front of the home itself. Her eyes surveyed my worn clothing and her brow furrowed as she escorted me to the dinning room where two heated brass urns flanked a hutch of cobalt-blue china. The urns were producing a fragrant potpourri steam that was filling the room.

Mrs. Power left without so much as a word as I sat in the middle of a long oak table, lined down the center with garish candles and sprinkles of rose petals. I found the dining room a strange place to wait for Helen Whitman, but then I knew going in that nothing was going to be traditional or standard about her.

No sooner had I sat down than a Mr. Pabodie, who claimed to be a neighbor from six doors away, came strolling inside without so much as a knock. He was close to the age of Helen's mother and wore a purple vest with a white tab-collar shirt that matched his color-less hair. "Just dropping off fresh bread for you ladies," he announced.

"Thank you, William," Mrs. Power said. "You must stay and have diner with us one of these times."

"Busy is as busy does." It was then that he noticed me sitting in the dining room and I turned in the chair to introduce myself. "*The* Edgar Allan Poe? So pleased to meet you. *Imp of the Perverse* was very intriguing. Where do you come up with it?" He threw up his hands. "Wait, wait, do not tell me. It will spoil the fun. I certainly would never ask a magician how he does his tricks, although I am sure my comparison to that art form leaves you wincing. What brings you to Providence? Oh never mind. How presumptuous and rude of me. Thank you for your many stories, and do keep writing, Mister Poe."

With that Mr. Pabodie was gone, leaving me feeling as though I had had a conversation by merely speaking my name.

I remained at the table a considerable duration, waiting under a nervous feeling that I had not felt since my first date with Sarah Elmira Royster. Shadows pranced in merriment on the walls in celebration of the night's return. A number of times her mother strode past the doorway and issued what I perceived as a glare in my direction. The longer I sat, the more anticipation transformed into nervousness. I passed my hand over one of the flickering candles to remind myself that this was a situation that could get me burned inside.

"Hello, Poe," someone whispered.

The words startled me. I did not hear an approach. I jerked my hand from the candle "*Pooooe.*"

I looked at the doorway but did not see anyone. The whispers were coming from every-where at once, from the urns and the flickering candles. I spun toward the far end of the table and only saw wisps of steam. Another call of my name brought my attention to the doorway once more and when I turned back toward the far end of the table, a woman clad in layers of black was standing there. She was a gypsy in appearance. I wondered if she had magically appeared. "Helen?" I stood, but could not take my eyes off her. A stack of magazines was rolled under one arm and a scarf covered the tip of her nose and disappeared into her neckline. I searched to make out her face through the sheer folds. "Are you the lady poet to whom I have been writing?"

She placed the magazines on the table. "Are you the dark romantic who can make a woman's heart palpitate out of fright or fondness?"

I bowed. "Edgar Allan Poe."

Her painted fingertip outlined the edge of the table. "What do you think of love?" she asked without introducing herself formally or otherwise.

In a blink I had become a part of her mysterious life. "A man is nothing if he has never known love," I blurted.

"'He who has never swooned, is not he who finds strange palaces and wildly familiar faces in coals that glow; is not he who beholds floating in mid-air the sad visions that the many may not view; is not he who ponders over the perfume of some novel flower – is not he whose brain grows bewildered with the meaning of some musical cadence which has never before arrested his attention.'[73]"

"You simultaneously scorn and flatter by quoting from *The Pit and the Pendulum*. Be forewarned, however, I have read many of your works also."

She laughed behind the veil. "I am flattered and at the same time realize that Edgar Poe, the man, is much more than his tales of sensation and romanticism." She put hands to her temples and her eyelids dove shut. I watched her lips move under the silky gauze. "You strike me as one who loves the South; who thinks us Yankees are slaves to our conservative Puritan heritage and wishes we were more open and loving of life."

"How are you so sure, having just met me?"

Helen (or at least the woman I thought was Helen having yet to introduce herself) plucked a magazine from the tabletop, opened it, and squinted in the anemic light. "I quote now from *The System of Dr. Tarr and Prof. Fether*, your tale of the asylum, where the visitor remarks to Monsieur Maillard, 'They behave a little odd, eh? – they are a little *queer*, eh? – don't you think so?' But his host feigns surprise and replies, "Odd! – queer! – why, do you *really* think so? We are not very prudish, to be sure, here in the South – do pretty much as we please – enjoy life, and all that sort of thing, you know –"'[74]"

"Had no idea my words of fiction, written years ago, would be presented to me this evening."

"You are right," she said, "that is most unfair." Her mystical nature was only compounded in person. On her wrists were bejeweled silver bracelets that rivaled the size of any gladiator's. They clanked against the table as her fluid hands moved along its edge.

Mrs. Power came through a door from an adjoining room and poured fresh water into the urns. They hissed and gurgled and the smell of flowers infused the air. Beyond the open door, I saw another room where a round table sat in the faint glow. A pyramid of candles was in the center of it and strips of colorful material streamed down from the chandelier.

"May I ask what that room is used for?"

"Séances." Helen (?) said the word nonchalantly, as if talking to the dead was as common as town hall meetings. "I practice mysticism when I'm not writing. Séances are back there, in the parlour, on Sunday nights. I am the medium, delivering messages from the unliving." She leaned across the dining room table to a point where I feared her scarf would alight on one of the center candles. I swallowed hard when I noticed what looked to be a small wooden coffin slip out of the folds of her scarf. A cross was carved into its lid. "Do *you* have anyone you would like to speak to in the afterlife?"

"Where would I begin? The afterlife is filled with a multitude of loved ones who have gone before me. The thought is tempting, but I must refrain."

"*Good!*" The sharply inflected word startled me. "Then you have no deep ties to the past. Impressive." She sat back in her chair. "But there is one vision I have had about you that I must divulge."

Holding onto the table, I braced for the response. At times Helen seemed jittery and distant, then her mind would snap back. An infirmity was about her face, but I blamed it on the scarf.

"I can foresee entire series of books being written based on a central character who is a crime solver. Your *Purloined Letter* and *The Murders in the Rue Morgue* have created an actual genre of crime detection. You are the master of mysteries because of it." She propped her feet on the arm of the chair next to her and I noticed she was barefooted, toenails matching her fingernails. Perhaps this explained why I failed to hear her approach. Rings encircled her second toes. Her knees were bunched to her chest and even in her layered clothing it was impossible to hide her desirable figure. "You are different from any other writer in this respect."

"Ah, but we are the same in our foundations," I countered. "We both use the eyes of our characters as a window into their souls. Dreams in our poetry are keyholes to the inner workings of the mind."

The lady I thought to be Helen smiled. There was a silhouetted beauty about her and her eyebrows arched perfectly above the scarf. "But we are different all the same. Your un-named narrators, some insane or drug crazed, are brilliant! It is as if you have personally known the experiences."

"I will never tell."

"What a thin line exists between the lucid and the irrational. You demonstrate it perfectly. Sleep is a vortex in your tales, swirling a person into deep places of their minds where consciousness is scared to tread."

I pointed to the coffin hanging from her neck. "And you obviously enjoy my use of the premature burial as a life-in-death theme."

"We have a shared fascination with death, Mister Poe, and I would have it no other way."

She got up to leave without uttering a word. She kept walking. She was nearly to the door. She just kept walking! Anxious, I blurted, "When can I see you again?"

"Same time and place tomorrow evening. Oh, and by the way, my name is Sarah Helen Whitman."

On my first visit to Providence we spent three successive evenings together in the dining room, flickering candles a blur down the center of the table. For three successive evenings I watched Sarah Helen Whitman's painted toes wiggle next to me while she touched my hand or moved about the room restlessly, a swirl of material amongst the fragrant urns. Helen spoke of ancient philosophers and poets as if she knew them. She spoke of the druids as if she had started the pagan religion and of history as if it happened last week. At a few instances she broke off into Latin and I surprised her when I matched her conversation in the antediluvian language.

There were times when the shadow of a raven would flutter on the wall in the moments before she would appear. On one night the raven was seemingly caught in a netting of scarf—trapped! The symbolism was not lost on me, yet upon Helen's entrance she would act as though she knew nothing of the event.

Where Sissy was lacking in a love of literature and philosophy, Sara Helen Whitman had an over abundance. Where Sissy was light and airy, Helen was heavy in thought and grand ideas of life and the afterlife. Where Sissy missed the point of my tales, Helen sharpened them with the deftness of an ax grinder. How she fascinated me at every turn of phrase and led me down paths of emotion and feeling that I had dared not tread before.

Sara Helen Whitman was a true woman of dark mystery.

I could not get enough of her thoughts when I arrived back in Fordham. They invaded every pore of my being. I began writing her daily from the cottage and immediately scheduled another trip to Providence at my first chance, which happened to be early fall.

That night a chilly evening surrounded me as I approached 76 Benefit Street and the grayest of rains could be seen falling under the street lamps. I drew my greatcoat tight, tired from my long journey and the pervading darkness. For reasons of which I did not inquire, Helen would never agree to a meeting in the day. Conjuring images of Rose, she told me how she preferred to stay up late and sleep past noon. Who cared as long as I got to see her again!

A carriage was parked outside the home and was but a few yards from the front door due to the structure's close proximity to the street. The driver sat motionless on his box seat, one leather glove wrapped around the staff of an umbrella and the other around the reins of the two horses that were giving off sunbursts of alabaster from their muzzles. Iron lamps glowed near his waist on hooks and rain was hissing against the hot glass as it lit.

The carriage door was open, but I oddly found no one inside. I shivered up to the home.

Before I could clank the brass knocker, Helen came whisking outside in a hooded cloak. She grabbed me by the arm and pulled me toward the street. We stepped on the carriage stone that rose well above the curb and launched ourselves into the carriage. I had not seen a chiseled step-up since Moldavia.

"Where are you taking me?" I asked as we piled into the bench seat.

"The place of our common bond!"

"Where? Tell me!"

"Quoth the maven, 'Nevermore.'"

Helen tapped the roof to signal the driver. A whip cracked and the horses reared. They came stamping back to earth and swept into the clotting gloom of Benefit Street. The carriage door knocked shut on its own.

From the corner of my eye I glimpsed Helen's mother watching from the parlour, her gaze colder than the rain speckling our windows and melting her face into an awful specter. I wondered if Nature was revealing Mrs. Power's true self. At the moment, however, I was thankful for the relative warmth of the carriage and shelter from the driving rain.

Minutes later the rumble of cobblestone vanished from beneath us, replaced by the pinging of a gravel road. The compacted buildings of Providence expanded into open plains and farmland. The moment reminded me of a phrase Elmira used to say: "We have caught the carriage, *now* what do we do?"

Helen would not speak no matter what I asked, but she shot me a wink on occasion as her hand stroked mine. She wore no scarf on this evening and as the lamps oscillated on either side of the driver, I glimpsed her entire face for the first time. It was more beautiful than I imagined—flawless porcelain. Her somber face paint was immaculate.

With the horses running abreast, we flew past churches and barns making our way into the country. The road grew narrow and transitioned from gravel to dirt, topped in the colors of fall reflecting in the carriage lamplight. Best I could tell we were driving south.

Thunderheads roiled in the brooding sky. Out the oval back window a swirl of leaves was kicking up behind us only to be beaten into submission by the raindrops. I heard the whip lash out again and the driver snarl.

From a pocket of her cloak Helen produced a hanky and brought it to her nose. I had detected no sniffles, but suspected she had a cold given the abrupt fall weather—Yankee fall weather that in all my days I would never get used to.

But Helen did not blow her nose, taking a deep breath from the hanky instead. My heart stuttered when I inhaled the metallic scent of *ether*. I tried my best to reason or explain it away, but there is no mistaking the gaseous vapor that had become fashionable for practitioners to prescribe for various ailments. It struck me as I sat there that Helen's vice explained the frequent pressings of the scarf to her face on the first three evenings we spent together. I realized she was neither crying in the rose garden the first night I saw her nor sick.

Her eyes rolled into her head while holding the ether inside. She put the sodden rag back into her pocket and exhaled. I said nothing in detraction as we drove. We were now in a hollow of overhanging trees that clawed and scraped at the sides of the carriage. It appeared to stretch for miles. The driver's calls and horses' stamping possessed an echoy quality. Thunder was heard but there were no flashes of light in the murky tunnel where darkness reigned supreme.

Upon emerging we slowed up an incline in the road and my anticipation became fright. For a moment I envisioned we were in Europe heading for an ancient and haunted castle as we skirted foothills and stony outcroppings. A pulse of lightning revealed that below my side of the carriage the earth was carved away into the sea. Waves were crashing into the rocks below in a wild frenzy. Helen gave more taps on the ceiling and the driver started looping us back, back toward the city!

I thought this bizarre, but we were soon on the same pathway that led to the heart of Providence and once again shooting through the hollow of overhanging trees. At times the lingering ether vapor would strike me and a tinge of nausea made itself known before fleeting.

After sloshing through deepening puddles and rattling across cobblestone once again, the carriage came to an abrupt halt in the city, yet I heard no commands of stoppage by the driver.

The carriage was rocking on its springs at the rusty gate of a colonial cemetery behind the Cathedral of St. John on North Main Street. The horses protested the radiance of the dead. A carpet of mist was shifting among the tombstones, which made them appear to move as though rigged to levers and pulleys in a theatrical production. I knew, however, this was no dress rehearsal between us. I was brimming with passion at every passage of her hand against my flesh.

"Here we are," Helen said as I helped her out of the carriage. "A detour through the countryside is always nice to clear one's head."

The driver hopped down and offered his umbrella, but Helen waved him off because the rain was attenuating. We walked arm-in-arm to the wrought iron gate and I swung it open after a squeaking protest. The air was salty and when I glanced down our feet had disappeared in the mist.

Inside the graveyard the rain lightly chattered as it hit the stonework of carved wreaths and angelic figures. Water dripped from outstretched arms and hewn faces. On our way into the heart of the cemetery Helen noticed something and gripped my arm. "Look, bells tied to a pull chord that extends down into a fresh grave and ultimately into the coffin below just as you wrote about in *The Premature Burial*."

"The irony is that if a person is alive under there, no one is usually around to hear them ring for help. And if they were, the ringing of bells might be mistaken for a visit by the traveling sharpener or butcher."

"You are cruel, but so right," she exclaimed, taking another breath from her hankie. "From your tale I take it you have a mistrust of doctors."

"That is an understatement. If a person is alive, they should not be buried and loved ones mistakenly wrought into sorrow. Can you imagine the horror of waking up in a crypt? I believe there is a fine art to mourning and reliving ones past that should not be misdiagnosed at the whim of an incompetent. Death clearly is an art form I try to capture in my writing."

"You do so beautifully." Out of nowhere she began quoting from *The Pit and the Pendulum* as the Atlantic crashed somewhere in the distance. "'I will not attempt to define, or even to describe; yet all was not lost. In the deepest slumber – no! In delirium – no! ... . In death – no! even in the grave all is not lost. Else there is no immortality for man.'[75] Beautiful! Gorgeous! I recite the passage to those who attend my séances. How do you do it? I have read *The Pit and the Pendulum* many times. Your brilliance shines in keeping the swinging blade of the pendulum on the tip of the auditory senses of the reader." Helen drew close and whispered into my ear. "I remember terms such as 'cessation,' 'crescent,' 'blackness,' and 'abyss.'"

The way she repeated my text back to me, the way her warm breath felt on the folds of my ear, made me tingle inside. "I am truly flattered. What's dead can be made alive, just as Mary Shelley wrote."

A bell jingled into the night and Helen flung to look at the pull chord leading down into the grave. Her heart fluttered and terror invaded her skin in bright hues. She swiped away the grey liquid coursing down her furrowed brow. When she looked to me, I began laughing and the end of my shoe retracted from the bell chord.

"You should have seen your face!"

"So much for impressing the master of the macabre with my bravery." We walked further, skirting tombstones around which the luster of fallen leaves had dulled in the weather. On this moonless night under watch of the cathedral, Helen suddenly pulled me down onto the edge of a mausoleum that was carved from limestone and topped by a Moline cross. We heard a squishing noise rise out of the fog. "What if it's the monster from *The Masque of the Red Death* rising from his grave?" She then began quoting: "'[T]all and gaunt, and shrouded from head to foot in the habiliments of the grave. The mask which concealed the visage was made so nearly to resemble the countenance of a stiffened corpse that the closest scrutiny must have had difficulty in detecting the cheat. And yet all this might have been endured, if not approved, by the mad revelers around. But the mummer had gone so far as to assume the type of the Red Death. His vesture was dabbled in *blood*—and his broad brow, with all the features of the face, was besprinkled with the scarlet horror.'[76]"

"You will have to do better than that, Helen. My own stories do not frighten me."

"All writers pale under your gothic style. You speak of confined spaces in the walls and beneath dusty floors, in closets, pits, cellars, and tombs. You are intimate with man's greatest fears."

"I know the death experience as no other. As you can also tell, a close circumscription of space is necessary for the insulated incident in my stories. Once you have the protagonist trapped—confined—you can do what you want to them *and* the reader."

Helen threw back her hood, tousled her flowing jet hair, and breathed in the damp air. "I feel most alive around death. I come here often to think when I am writing. My home can be confining sometimes."

This last statement triggered the visage of her mother glaring out the parlour window. I almost inquired as to her seeming dislike of me, but the snorting and neighing of horses in the distance while the driver wrestled at the reins broke me from implicating my thoughts. The animals were still uncomfortable in their surroundings, but I was feeling more at ease every moment.

Thunder boomed over the ocean as fat raindrops began exploding around us.

I put my shaking arm around her hourglass figure for the first time. Helen snuggled close. How wondrous she felt.

"Our souls speak the same language, Edgar."

Waves crashed somewhere and the sea raged. A great passion betook me as its own. I fell to my knees right in front of the mausoleum and Sarah Helen Whitman, rivulets streaking my face. "Be mine, Helen, not only in the blessed union of this life, but in the afterlife as well."

The unplanned proposal surprised even me. As I waited silently for a response, my finger never felt so weighty under the mourning ring that contained locks of hair from my mother, Granny, Ma, and Sissy. It was as if my finger had swelled and the ring would now have to be cut off or the finger severed.

"Edgar, this so sudden. For all I know you are still in love with your first wife."

"That is not true. At the time of Virginia's death, when she was only twenty-five, I believed remarriage was nothing more than disloyalty to the dead, but I have changed my thinking ... *you* have changed my thinking."

Helen sat there for a moment, the breeze struggling to lift her sodden hair. I heard the cemetery gate beating against the latch that I forgot to engage on our way inside. I felt mud soaking into the knees of my pants, but I did not get up from my genuflecting position.

"I am afraid I must refuse at the moment."

Hope leeched from my heart. "Forgive me for being so blunt, dear Helen, but does your mother have something to do with this?"

"To be honest, she thinks you are after my ... *our* money. If it were not for me being diagnosed with a feeble heart, and we did not live in an age where the husband automatically got the estate of his wife upon her death, things may be different. She has always steered me toward upper society as evidenced by my late husband's profession."

I repositioned my knees in the muck. "Oh Helen, I chose a life of poverty for artistic freedom and to become the writer that I am. My motto is: *tenui musam meditamur avena.*"

"We cultivate literature on a little oatmeal."

At the moment I had forgotten she was fluent in Latin. "Believe me when I say I am not in love with your money, but your soul! You said yourself our souls speak as one. Virginia was too young and unsophisticated in her thinking." I wiped rain from my face. *"Helen, I love now—now—for the first and only time."*[77]

She took my hands in hers. Her locks were slicked coal. "But I have chronic heart problems. My death will inevitably disappoint you."

This excuse sprung me to my feet with the mud puckering as I extracted my knees. "What a huge mistake to use death as a tool against me! I will follow you to the grave if I must, for I have no fear of death, my constant friend since childhood. Perhaps I will be more elusive in death than life and I would have it no other way."

Helen's crimson lips spread. "You must pledge not to drink anymore. I have heard rumors."

"They are untrue, I can assure you. When I am taken with only one glass of wine I display the symptoms of inebriation." My wits came about me for a brief second and I remembered something. "And what of *your* vice in the gaseous form?"

"The ether is for my medical condition of an infirm heart, and nothing more," she responded aloofly.

We both agreed that neither of us had a problem, yet I did not hear words of acceptance from Helen that evening and the ensuing months became the most frightening story of my life.

In the morning I checked out of my hotel room and re-visited the cemetery:—at 6 P.M. I left the city in the Stonington train for N. Y.[78] Our footprints were embossed in the drying earth and my kneeprints on either side of where Helen's feet had rested. This verified for me that the encounter was not a dream and I kicked the coffin bell from a broken heart on the way out.

Later, when I arrived in Fordham, I told Muddy nothing of what had transpired. I wrote Helen immediately but received no response. I was in a deeply troubled state for days thereafter, demons haunting me that Mrs. Power had stolen the letter. When Muddy asked, I blamed it on a Griswold review. It was not until the end of September that I got a response letter from Helen. It went into further detail as to why an engagement was too sudden.[79]

On Sunday night a terrible rainstorm arose—a sister to the one that had blown through Providence—while I crafted a response. The cottage roof sprung leaks in three places, including an annoying one right above my writing desk that I caught in my lathering cup, which I had to dump out every half hour. Carriages around Fordham were being swept into ditches from flash floods and others stuck up to their axles in mud. I finished my response by candlelight, but the storm kept me from going into the city to mail it until Tuesday.

Sunday Night—Oct. 1—48.

I have pressed your letter again and again to my lips, sweetest Helen—bathing it in tears of joy, or of a "divine despair". But I— who so lately, in your presence, vaunted the "power of words"—of what avail are mere words to me now? Could I believe in the efficiency of prayers to the God of Heaven, I would indeed kneel— humbly kneel—at this the most earnest epoch of my life—kneel in entreaty for words—but for words that should disclose to you— that might enable me to lay bare to you my whole heart. All thoughts —all passions seem now merged in that one consuming desire—the mere wish to make you comprehend— to make you see that for which there is no human voice—the unutterable fervor of my love for you:—for so well do I know your poet-nature, oh Helen, Helen! that I feel sure if you could but look down now into the depths of my soul with your pure spiritual eyes you could not refuse to speak to me what, alas! you still resolutely have unspoken—you would love me if only for the greatness of my love. Is it not something in this cold, dreary world, to be loved?—Oh, if I could but burn into your spirit the deep—the true meaning which I attach to those three syllables underlined!—but, alas: the effort is all in vain and "I live and die unheard".

When I spoke to you of what I felt, saying that I loved now for the first time, I did not hope you would believe or even understand me; nor can I hope to convince you now—but if, throughout some long, dark summer night, I could but have held you close, close to my heart and whispered to you the strange secrets of its passionate history, then indeed you would have seen that I have been far from attempting to deceive you in this respect. I could have shown you that it was not and could never have been in the power of any other than yourself to move me as I am now moved—to oppress me with this ineffable emotion—to surround and bathe me in this electric light, illumining and enkindling my whole nature—filling my soul with glory, with wonder, and with awe. During our walk in the cemetery I said to you, while the bitter, bitter tears sprang into my eyes—"Helen, I love now—now—for the first and only time." I said this, I repeat, in no hope that you could believe me, but because I could not help feeling how unequal were the heart-riches we might offer each to each:—I, for the first time, giving my all at once, and forever, even while the words of your poem were yet ringing in my ears:—

Oh then, beloved, I think on thee
And on that life so strangely fair
Ere yet one cloud of Memory
Had gathered in Hope's golden air.
I think on thee and thy lone grave
On the green hill-side far away—
I see the wilding flowers that wave
Around thee as the night-winds sway;
And still, though only clouds remain
On Life's horizon, cold and drear,
The dream of Youth returns again
With the sweet promise of the year.

Ah Helen, these lines are indeed beautiful, beautiful—but their very beauty was cruelty to me. Why—why did you show them to me? There seemed, too, so very especial a purpose in what you did.

I cannot better explain to you what I felt than by saying that your unknown heart seemed to pass into my bosom—there to dwell forever—while mine, I thought, was translated into your own. From that hour I loved you. Yes, I now feel that it was then—on that evening of sweet dreams—that the very first dawn of human love burst upon the icy Night of my spirit. Since that period I have never seen nor heard your name without a shiver half of delight, half of anxiety.

The merest whisper that concerned you awoke in me a shuddering sixth sense, vaguely compounded of fear, ecstatic happiness, and a wild, inexplicable sentiment that resembled nothing so nearly as the consciousness of guilt.—Judge, then, with what wondering, unbelieving joy I received in your well-known MS., the Valentine which first gave me to see that you knew me to exist. The idea of what men call Fate lost then for the first time, in my eyes, its character of futility. I felt that nothing hereafter was to be doubted, and lost myself, for many weeks, in one continuous, delicious dream, where all was a vivid yet indistinct bliss.—Immediately after reading the Valentine, I wished to contrive some mode of acknowledging—without wounding you by seeming directly to acknowledge—my sense—oh, my keen—my profound—my exulting—my ecstatic sense of the honor you had conferred on me. To accomplish, as I wished it, precisely what I wished, seemed impossible, however; and I was on the point of abandoning the idea, when my eyes fell upon a volume of my own poems; and then the lines I had written, in my passionate boyhood, to the first, purely ideal love of

my soul— to the Helen Stannard of whom I told you—flashed upon my recollection. I turned
to them. They expressed all—all that I would have said to you—so fully—so accurately and
so exclusively, that a thrill of intense superstition ran at once throughout my frame. Read
the verses and then take into consideration the peculiar need I had, at the moment, for just
so seemingly unattainable a mode of communicating with you as they afforded. Think of the
absolute appositeness with which they fulfilled that need—expressing not only all that I
would have said of your person, but all that of which I most wished to assure you, in the
lines commencing "On desperate seas long wont to roam." Think, too, of the rare agreement of name—Helen and not the far more usual Ellen [—] think of all these coincidences,
and you will no longer wonder that, to one accustomed as I am to the Calculus of Probabili-
ties, they wore an air of positive miracle. There was but one difficulty.—I did not wish to
copy the lines in my own MS—nor did I wish you to trace them to my volume of poems. I
hoped to leave at least something of doubt on your mind as to how, why, and especially
whence they came. And now, when, on accidentally turning the leaf, I found even this difficulty obviated, by the poem happening to be the last in the book, thus having no letter-press
on its reverse—I yielded at once to an overwhelming sense of Fatality. From that hour I
have never been able to shake from my soul the belief that my Destiny, for good or for evil,
either here or hereafter, is in some measure interwoven with your own.—Of course, I did
not expect on your part any acknowledgment of the printed lines "To Helen"; and yet,
without confessing it even to myself, I experienced an undefinable sorrow in your silence.

And now, in the most simple words at my command, let me paint to you the impression
made upon me by your personal presence.—As you entered the room, pale, timid, hesitat-
ing, and evidently oppressed at heart; as your eyes rested appealingly, for one brief moment, upon mine, I felt, for the first time in my life, and tremblingly acknowledged, the
existence of spiritual influences altogether out of the reach of the reason. I saw that you
were Helen—my Helen—the Helen of a thousand dreams—she whose visionary lips had so
often lingered upon my own in the divine trance of passion—she whom the great Giver of
all Good had preordained to be mine—mine only—if not now, alas! then at least hereafter
and forever, in the Heavens.—You spoke falteringly and seemed scarcely conscious of what
you said. I heard no words—only the soft voice, more familiar to me than my own, and more
melodious than the songs of the angels. Your hand rested within mine, and my whole soul
shook with a tremulous ecstasy. And then but for very shame—but for the fear of grieving or
oppressing you—I would have fallen at your feet in as pure—in as real a worship as was
ever offered to Idol or to God. And when, afterwards, on those two successive evenings of
all-Heavenly delight, you passed to and fro about the room—now sitting by my side, now
far away, now standing with your hand resting on the back of my chair, while the
praeternatural thrill of your touch vibrated even through the senseless wood into my heart—
while you moved thus restlessly about the room—as if a deep Sorrow or a more profound
Joy haunted your bosom—my brain reeled beneath the intoxicating spell of your presence,
and it was with no merely human senses that I either saw or heard you. It was my soul only
that distinguished you there. I grew faint with the luxury of your voice and blind with the
voluptuous lustre of your eyes.

Let me quote to you a passage from your letter:—"You will, perhaps, attempt to convince
me that my person is agreeable to you— that my countenance interests you:—but in this
respect I am so variable that I should inevitably disappoint you if you hoped to find in me
to-morrow the same aspect which won you to-day. And, again, although my reverence for

your intellect and my admiration of your genius make me feel like a child in your presence, *you are not, perhaps, aware that I am many years older than yourself. I fear you do not* *know me, and that if you had known it you would not have felt for me as you do."—To all* *this what shall I—what can I say—except that the heavenly candor with which you speak* *oppresses my heart with so rich a burden of love that my eyes overflow with sweet tears.* *You are mistaken, Helen, very far mistaken about this matter of age. I am older than you;* *and if illness and sorrow have made you seem older than you are—is not all this the best of* *reason for my loving you the more? Cannot my patient cares—my watchful, earnest atten-* *tion—cannot the magic which lies in such devotion as I feel for you, win back for you* *much—oh, very much of the freshness of your youth? But grant that what you urge were* *even true. Do you not feel in your inmost heart of hearts that the "soul-love" of which the* *world speaks so often and so idly is, in this instance at least, but the veriest, the most* *absolute of realities? Do you not—I ask it of your reason, darling, not less than of your* *heart—do you not perceive that it is my diviner nature—my spiritual being— which burns* *and pants to commingle with your own? Has the soul age, Helen? Can Immortality regard* *Time? Can that which began never and shall never end, consider a few wretched years of* *its incarnate life? Ah, I could weep—I could almost be angry with you for the unwarranted* *wrong you offer to the purity—to the sacred reality of my affection.—And how am I to* *answer what you say of your personal appearance? Have I not seen you, Helen, have I not* *heard the more than melody of your voice? Has not my heart ceased to throb beneath the* *magic of your smile? Have I not held your hand in mine and looked steadily into your soul* *through the crystal Heaven of your eyes? Have I not done all these things?—or do I dream?—* *or am I mad? Were you indeed all that your fancy, enfeebled and perverted by illness,* *tempts you to suppose that you are, still, life of my life! I would but love you—but worship* *you the more:—it would be so glorious a happiness to be able to prove to you what I feel!* *But as it is, what can I—what am I to say? Who ever spoke of you without emotion—without* *praise? Who ever saw you and did not love?*

But now a deadly terror oppresses me; for I too clearly see that these objections—so *groundless—so futile when urged to one whose nature must be so well known to you as* *mine is—can scarcely be meant earnestly; and I tremble lest they but serve to mask others,* *more real, and which you hesitate—perhaps in pity—to confide to me. Alas! I too distinctly* *perceive, also, that in no instance you have ever permitted yourself to say that you love me.* *You are aware, sweet Helen, that on my part there are insuperable reasons forbidding me to* *urge upon you my love. Were I not poor—had not my late errors and reckless excesses justly* *lowered me in the esteem of the good—were I wealthy, or could I offer you worldly hon-* *ors— ah then—then—how proud would I be to persevere—to sue—to plead—to kneel—to* *pray—to beseech you for your love—in the deepest humility—at your feet—at your feet,* *Helen, and with floods of passionate tears.*

And now let me copy here one other passage from your letter: —"I find that I cannot now tell you all that I promised. I can only say to you [that had I youth and health and beauty, I *would live for you and die with you. Now, were I to allow myself to love you, I could only* *enjoy a bright, brief hour of rapture and die—perhaps [illegible]."—The last five words* *have been [illegible] Ah, beloved, beloved Helen the darling of my heart—my first and my* *real love]!—may God forever shield you from the agony which these your words occasion* *me! How selfish—how despicably selfish seems now all—all that I have written! Have I not,* *indeed, been demanding at your hands a love which might endanger your life? You will never, never know—you can never picture to yourself the hopeless, rayless despair with which I now trace these words. Alas Helen! my soul!—what is it that I have been saying to you?—to what madness have I been urging you?—I who am nothing to you—you who have a dear mother and sister to be blessed by your life and love. But ah, darling! if I seem selfish, yet believe that I truly, truly love you, and that it is the most spiritual of love that I speak, even if I speak it from the depths of the most passionate of hearts. Think —oh, think for me, Helen, and for yourself! Is there no hope?—is there none? May not this terrible [disease] be conquered? Frequently it has been overcome. And more frequently are we deceived in respect to its actual existence. Long-continued nervous disorder—especially when exasperated by ether or [excision]—will give rise to all the symptoms of heart-dis[ease an]d so deceive the most skillful physicians—as even in [my o]wn case they were deceived. But admit that this fearful evil has indeed assailed you. Do you not all the more really need the devotionate care which only one who loves you as I do, could or would bestow? On my bosom could I not still the throbbings of your own? Do not mistake me, Helen! Look, with your searching—your seraphic eyes, into the soul of my soul, and see if you can discover there one taint of an ignoble nature! At your feet—if you so willed it—I would cast from me, forever, all merely human desire, and clothe myself in the glory of a pure, calm, and unexacting affection. I would comfort you—soothe you—tranquillize you. My love—my faith—should instil into your bosom a praeternatural calm. You would rest from care— from all worldly agitation. You would get better, and finally well. And if not, Helen,—if not—if you died—then at least would I clasp your dear hand in death, and willingly—oh, joyfully—joyfully—joyfully—go down with you into the night of the Grave.*

Write soon—soon—oh, soon!—but not much. Do not weary or agitate yourself for my sake. Say to me those coveted words which would turn Earth into Heaven. If Hope is forbidden, I will not murmur if you comfort me with Love.—The papers of which you [speak] I will procure and forward immediately. They will cost me nothing, fear Helen, an[d] I therefore re-enclose you what you so thoughtfully s[ent.] Think that, in doing so, my lips are pressed ferv[ently] and lingeringly upon your own. And now, in closing this long, long letter, let me speak last of that which lies nearest my heart— of that precious gift which I would not exchange for the surest hope of Paradise. It seems to me too sacred that I should even whisper to you, the dear giver, what it is. My soul, this night, shall come to you in dreams and speak to you those fervid thanks which my pen is all powerless to utter.

Edgar

P. S. Tuesday Morning.—I beg you to believe, dear Helen, that I replied to your letter immediately upon its receipt; but a most unusual storm, up to this moment, precludes all access to the City.[80]

My dire circumstances, which were mostly financial, kept me at the Fordham cottage for weeks after I returned from Providence. I spent many afternoons repairing the place after the terrible rainstorm under eight days of awful suspense in waiting for a response. On October 10th I thankfully received a letter from Helen that was a rejoinder to mine.[81] My heart was enraptured as I read the curves of her penmanship and breathed in her faint scent on the parchment. Midway through the letter, however, the pages fell from my hand as she told me that someone had disparaged me as lacking in morals. She would not divulge whom.

It took me over a week to calm down and respond in a manner befitting a gentleman.

Wed- Oct 18—48

In pressing my last letter between your dear hands, there passed into your spirit a sense of the Love that glowed within those pages:—you say this, and I feel that indeed it must have been so:—but. in receiving the paper upon which your eyes now rest, did no shadow steal over you, from the sorrow within,—oh God! how I now curse the impotence of the pen—the inexorable distance between us! I am pining to speak to you, Helen,—to you in person—to be near you while I speak—gently to press your hand in mine—to look into your soul through your eyes—and thus to be sure that my voice passes into your heart. Only thus could I hope to make you understand what I feel; and even thus I should not hope to make you do so; for it is only Love, which can comprehend Love—and alas! you do not love me.—Bear with me! have patience with me!—for indeed my heart is broken; and, let me struggle as I will, I cannot write to you the calm, cold language of a world which I loathe—of a world in which I have no interest—of a world which is not mine. I repeat to you that my heart is broken—that I have no farther object in life—that I have absolutely no wish but to die. These are hackneyed phrases; but they will not now impress you as such—for you must and do know the passionate agony with which I write them. "You do not love me":—in this brief sentence lies all I can conceive of despair. I have no resource—no hope:—Pride itself fails me now. You do not love me; or you could not have imposed upon me the torture of eight days' silence—of eight days' terrible suspense. You do not love me—or, responding to my prayers, you would have cried to me—"Edgar, I do." Ah, Helen, the emotion which now consumes me teaches me too well the nature of the impulses of Love! Of what avail to me, in my deadly grief, are your enthusiastic words of mere admiration? Alas;—alas!—I have been loved, and a relentless Memory contrasts what you say with the unheeded, unvalued language of others.—But ah,—again, and most especially—you do not love me, or you would have felt too thorough a sympathy with the sensitiveness of my nature, to have so wounded me as you have done with this terrible passage of your letter:—"How often I have heard men and even women say of you—'He has great intellectual power, but no prin-ciple—no moral sense.' " Is it possible that such expressions as these could have been repeated to me—to me—by one whom I loved—ah, whom I love—by one at whose feet I knelt—I still kneel—in deeper worship than ever man offered to God?—And you proceed to ask me why such opinions exist. You will feel remorse for the question, Helen, when I say to you that, until the moment when those horrible words first met my eye, I would not have believed it possible that any such opinions could have existed at all:—but that they do exist breaks my heart in separating us forever. I love you too truly ever to have offered you my hand—ever to have sought your love—had I known my name to be so stained as your expressions imply.—Oh God! what shall I say to you Helen, dear Helen?—let me call you now by that sweet name, if I may never so call you again. —It is altogether in vain that I tax my Memory or my Conscience. There is no oath which seems to me so sacred as that sworn by the all-divine love I bear you.—By this love, then, and by the God who reigns in Heaven, I swear to you that my soul is incapable of dishonor—that, with the exception of occasional follies and excesses which I bitterly lament, but to which I have been driven by intolerable sorrow, and which are hourly committed by others without attracting any notice what-

ever—I can call to mind no act of my life which would bring a blush to my cheek—or to yours. If I have erred at all, in this regard, it has been on the side of what the world would call a Quixotic sense of the honorable—of the chivalrous. The indulgence of this sense has been the true voluptuousness of my life. It was for this species of luxury that, in early youth, I deliberately threw away from me a large fortune, rather than endure a trivial wrong. It was for this that, at a later period, I did violence to my own heart, and married, for another's happiness, where I knew that no possibility of my own existed.—Ah, how profound is my love for you, since it forces me into these egotisms for which you will inevitably despise me! Nevertheless, I must now speak to you the truth or nothing. It was in mere indulgence, then, of the sense to which I refer, that, at one dark epoch of my late life, for the sake of one who, deceiving and betraying, still loved me much, I sacrificed what seemed in the eyes of men my honor, rather than abandon what was honor in hers and in my own.—But, alas! for nearly three years I have been ill, poor, living out of the world; and thus, as I now painfully see, have afforded opportunity to my enemies—and especially to one, the most malignant and pertinacious of all fiends—the woman whose loathsome love I could do nothing but repel with scorn—to slander me, in private society, without my knowledge and thus with impunity. Although much, however, may (and I now see must) have been said to my discredit, during my retirement, those few who, knowing me well, have been steadfastly my friends, permitted nothing to reach my ears—unless in one instance, where the malignity of the accuser hurried her beyond her usual caution, and thus the accusation was of such character that I could appeal to a court of justice for redress. The tools employed in this instance were Mr Hiram Fuller and Mr T. D. English. I replies to the charge fully, in a public newspaper—afterwards suing the "Mirror" (in which the scandal appeared) obtaining a verdict and recovering such an amount of damages as, for the time, completely to break up that journal.—And you ask me why men so misjudge me—why I have enemies. If your knowledge of my character and of my career does not afford you an answer to the query, at least it does not become me to suggest the answer. Let it suffice that I have had the audacity to remain poor that I might preserve my independence—that, nevertheless, in letters, to a certain extent and in certain regards, I have been "successful"—that I have been a critic—and unscrupulously honest and no doubt in many cases a bitter one—that I have uniformly attacked—where I attacked at all—those who stood highest in power and influence—and that, whether in literature or in society, I have seldom refrained from expressing, either directly or indirectly, the pure contempt with which the pretensions of ignorance, arrogance, or imbecility inspire me.—And you who know all this—you ask me why I have enemies. Ah, Helen, I have a hundred friends for every individual enemy—but has it never occurred to you that you do not live among my friends?

Had you read my criticisms generally, you would see, too, how and why it is that the Channings—the Emerson and Hudson coterie—the Longfellow clique, one and all— the cabal of the "N. American Review"—you would see why all these, whom you know best, know me least and are my enemies. Do you not remember with how deep a sigh I said to you in Providence— "My heart is heavy, Helen, for I see that your friends are not my own."?— But the cruel sentence in your letter would not—could not so deeply have wounded me, had my soul been first strengthened by those assurances of your love which I so wildly—so vainly—and, I now feel, so presumptuously entreated. That our souls are one, every line which you have ever written asserts—but our hearts do not beat in unison. Tell me, darling! to your heart has any angel ever whispered that the very noblest lines in all human poetry are these—hackneyed though they be?

I know not—I ask not if guilt's in thy heart:—I but know that I love thee whatever thou art. When I first read your letter I could do nothing but shed tears, while I repeated, again and again, those glorious, those all-comprehensive verses, till I could scarcely hear my own voice for the passionate throbbings of my heart.

Forgive me, best and only beloved Helen, if there be bitterness in my tone. Towards you there is no room in my soul for any other sentiment than devotion:—it is Fate only which I accuse:— it is my own unhappy nature which wins me the true love of no woman whom by any possibility I could love.

I heard something, a day or two ago, which, had your last letter never reached me, might not irreparably have disturbed the relations between us, but which, as it is, withers forever all the dear hopes upspringing in my bosom.—A few words will explain to you what I mean. Not long after the receipt of your Valentine I learned, for the first time, that you were free— unmarried. I will not pretend to express to you what is absolutely inexpressible—that wild— long-enduring thrill of joy which pervaded my whole being on hearing that it was not impossible I might one day call you by the sacred title, wife: —but there was one alloy to this happiness:—I dreaded to find you in worldly circumstances superior to my own. Let me speak freely to you now, Helen, for perhaps I may never thus be permitted to speak to you again—Let me speak openly—fearlessly—trusting to the generosity of your own spirit for a true interpretation of my own. I repeat, then, that I dreaded to find you in worldly circum- stances superior to mine. So great was my fear that you were rich, or at least possessed some property which might cause you to seem rich in the eyes of one so poor as I had always permitted myself to be—that, on the day I refer to, I had not the courage to ask my informant any questions concerning you.—I feel that you will have difficulty in compre- hending me; but the horror with which, during my sojourn in the world, I have seen affec- tion made a subject of barter, had, long since,—long before my marriage—inspired me with the resolution that, under no circumstances, would I marry where "interest," as the world terms it, could be suspected as, on my part, the object of the marriage. As far as this point concerned yourself, however, I was relieved, the next day, by an assurance that you were wholly dependent upon your mother. May I—dare I add—can you believe me when I say that this assurance was rendered doubly grateful to me by the additional one that you were in ill health and had suffered more from domestic sorrow than falls usually to the lot of woman?—and even if your faith in my nature is not too greatly tasked by such an assertion, can you forbear thinking me unkind, selfish or ungenerous? You cannot:—but oh! the sweet dreams which absorbed me at once:—dear dreams of a devotional care for you that should end only with life—of a tender, cherishing, patient solicitude which should bring you back, at length, to health and to happiness—a care—a solicitude—which should find its glorious reward in winning me, after long years, that which I could feel to be your love! Without well understanding why, I had been led to fancy you ambitious:—perhaps the fancy arose from your lines:

Not a bird that roams the forest Shall our lofty eyrie share!—but my very soul glowed with ambition for your sake, although I have always contemned it for my own. It was then only—then when I thought of you—that I dwelt exultingly upon what I felt that I could accomplish in Letters and in Literary Influence—in the widest and noblest field of human ambition. "I will erect", I said, "a prouder throne than any on which mere monarch ever sat; and on this throne she—she shall be my queen". When I saw you, however —when I touched your gentle hand—when I heard your soft voice, and perceived how greatly I had misinterpreted your womanly nature —these triumphant visions melted sweetly away in the sunshine of a love ineffable; and I suffered my imagination to stray with you, and with the few who love us both, to the banks of some quiet river, in some lovely valley of our land. Here, not too far secluded from the world, we exercised a taste controlled by no convention-alities, but the sworn slave of a Natural Art, in the building for ourselves a cottage which no human being could ever pass without an ejaculation of wonder at its strange, wierd, and incomprehensible yet most simple beauty. Oh, the sweet and gorgeous, but not often rare flowers in which we half buried it!—the grandeur of the little-distant magnolias and tulip-trees which stood guarding it—the luxurious velvet of its lawn—the lustre of the rivulet that ran by the very door—the tasteful yet quiet comfort of the interior—the music—the books—the unostentatious pictures—and, above all, the love—the love that threw an unfading glory over the whole!—Ah Helen! my heart is, indeed, breaking and I must now put an end to these divine dreams. Alas all is now a dream; for I have lately heard that of you which, (taken in connexion with your letter and with that of which your letter does not assure me) puts it forever out of my power to ask you —again to ask you—to become my wife. That many persons, in your presence, have declared me wanting in honor, appeals irresistibly to an instinct of my nature—an instinct which I feel to be honor, let the dishonorable say what they may, and forbids me, under such circumstances, to insult you with my love:—but that you are quite independent in your worldly position (as I have just heard)— in a word that you are comparatively rich while I am poor, opens between us a gulf—a gulf, alas! which the sorrow and the slander of the World have rendered forever impassable—by me.

Your first letter was received by me, at Fordham, on the evening of Saturday, Sep. 30. I was in Providence, or its neighborhood, during the Monday you mention. In the morning I re-visited the cemetery:—at 6 P.M. I left the city in the Stonington train for N. Y. I cannot explain to you—since I cannot myself comprehend— the feeling which urged me not to see you again before going—not to bid you a second time farewell. I had a sad foreboding at heart. In the seclusion of the cemetery you sat by my side—on the very spot where my arm first tremblingly encircled your waist.

Edgar[82]

The first week of November I promised to meet with Helen in Providence to discuss the walls being erected between us by my foes. I was sure news of our relationship had entered the Griswold and English camps, and they were contributing misinformation and detrac-tions at every chance.

My second *To Helen* poem was published and I knew, since it was for Helen herself, that she would be pleased. I visited her once again at her home. For the first time I met her sister at the door, who bore a striking resemblance to her mother instead of Helen. Perhaps it was the same glare.

Helen and I went for a stroll outside, the scent of cider invading the chilly Providence air. The venture into the city was at my choosing as I disregarded the onset of another bought of sickness. The house that was once so inviting to me was fast becoming a place of contention and foreboding attitudes. I knew my conversations would be betrayed there.

Outside I cut right to heart of the matter. "Helen, beautiful Helen, *why* have I not received your acceptance of my marriage proposal? This is greatly troubling me."

"I have not rejected it."

"No acceptance is only slightly better than a rejection. Only a few words from you could bring me such overflowing joy."

"My dearest, Poe. Know that I feel deeply for you as no other. It is just that I am hearing so many rumors about you ... about your drinking."

"I have explained this."

"How old are you?" she questioned, which I thought odd under the circumstances.

"Thirty-nine, if you must know."

"See there, I am six years older than you and two decades older than Virginia when she expired."

"Six years is nothing," I said. "That cannot be the reason for your refusal, nor can it be the terrible untruths people have told you and that you have received by anonymous letter."

Helen took a look of frustration and sucked into her hankie. She then blinked away the ether haze floating in her eyes. A gentleman selling roasted walnuts called out to us but we ignored him.

"Helen."

"I guess ... I assume ... it is just a combination of all these things, coupled with my own infirmities."

"This important decision you must come to on your own, without my interference and I will give you the clearance you need. I have more lecturing to attend to in town and I will write before I leave," which I did on November 7th.

Dearest Helen—

I have no engagements, but am very ill—so much so that I must go home, if possible—but if you say "stay", I will try & do so. If you cannot see me—write me one word to say that you do love me and that, under all circumstances, you will be mine. Remember that these coveted words you have never yet spoken—and, nevertheless, I have not reproached you. It was not in my power to be here on Saturday as I proposed, or I would undoubtedly have kept my promise. If you can see me, even for a few moments do so—but if not write— or send some message which will comfort me.

Edgar[83]

By this letter Helen convinced me to stay another week (with her paying my hotel bill) and we spent much time together while she tended to my paranoid attack of anxiety regarding my enemies and their plots against me. She tried a number of mysterious potions she had concocted and herbal remedies, but they helped my brain congestion little.

During a brief stoppage of my nerves (and I say "brief" because I knew there would never be a cure to my ills), I returned to Fordham by steamboat, which belched white mist along the Atlantic coastline until it reached the New York harbor. I had to get back and tend to Muddy's own infirmities. On the journey, the constant noise from the steam engine returned my headache, but thankfully not the migraines, so I was able to write Helen over a strong cup of coffee, whitecaps braking outside the portal window.

Steamboat Nov 14 1848

My own dearest Helen, so kind so true, so generous—so unmoved by all that would have moved one who had been less than angel:—beloved of my heart of my imagination of my intellect—life of my life—soul of my soul—dear, dearest Helen, how shall I ever thank you as I ought.

I am calm & tranquil & but for a strange shadow of coming evil which haunts me I should be happy. That I am not supremely happy, even when I feel your dear love at my heart, terrifies me. What can this mean?

Perhaps however it is only the necessary reaction after such terrible excitements.

It is 5 o'clock & the boat is just being made fast to the wharf. I shall start in the train that leaves New York at 7 for Fordham. I write this to show you that I have not dared to break my promise to you.

And now dear dearest Helen be true to me[... .][84]

On the following Monday, as I tended Muddy at the Fordham cottage, I was placing the final revisions on *Ulalume* when I received a short note from Helen dated November 17, 1848, promising a letter longer than the tomes I had been writing to convince her to marry me.

Wednesday Morning—the 22 d.
My dearest Helen—

Last Monday I received your note, dated Friday, and promising that on Tuesday I should get a long letter from you. It has not yet reached me, but I presume will be at the P.O. when I send this in. In the meantime, I write these few words to thank you, from the depths of my heart, for the dear expressions of your note—expressions of tenderness so wholly undeserved by me—and to assure you of my safety and health. The terrible excitement under which I suffered, has subsided, and I am as calm as I well could be, remembering what has past. Still the Shadow of Evil haunts me, and, although tranquil, I am unhappy. I dread the Future.—and you alone can reassure me. I have so much to say to you, but must wait until I hear from you. My mother was delighted with your wish to be remembered and begs me to express the pleasure it gave her.

Forever your own
Edgar

Remember me to Mr Pabodie.[85]

My next scheduled trip to Providence was set for the early part of December, but I did not make it until the middle of the month. This delay was not because of my declining health, rather due to certain speaking engagements. I thought it telling that Helen, given all her wealth, could not travel to meet Muddy at the fall harvest meal.

It would have been sparse at best for us had it not been for the kindness of Mrs. Shew. The potatoes and corn that Muddy had grown in her garden behind the cottage were bad. I suspected moisture from the torrential rainstorms. Mrs. Shew prepared us a plump grouse along with a selection of garlic bread, vegetables, and apple juice from their plentiful table. She even sent over jars of cranberry preserves and a pecan pie for dessert.

The following morning, my stomach still brimming in the unfamiliar feeling, I wrote Helen and assured her of my physical firmness. I was besieged with worry regarding the anonymous letters that were appearing at her doorstep from my detractors and the constant jabs at my character from her mother and sister. I truly believe the betrayals in her own home tortured her more than the letters. I vowed on November 24th to *rest neither by night nor day until I bring those who have slandered me into the light of day—until I expose them, and their motives, to the public eye.*[86]

Muddy asked whom I was writing and I could not hide my passion for the dark poet any longer. I revealed all, including my proposal in the cemetery. I had been struggling with how to tell Muddy—*whether* to tell her—for so long. My dedicated aunt expressed only joy for my newfound love and not the slightest bit of jealousy regarding Virginia. God rest her soul! I explained to Muddy that my love for Sissy would never be replaced, that my feelings for Helen Whitman were a different kind (at a higher intellectual plain, though I kept this knowledge to myself), and they were. She hugged me in her matriarchal way and let me know she only wanted my happiness.

I wrote Helen of this and she immediately began inserting notes to Muddy in her letters. The establishment of this relationship was only positive and evidence of Helen's intentions to continue our relationship into the future. Muddy vowed to treat Helen worlds better than her mother was treating me.

The letters continued. As two writers in love are prone to do, we sent each other our poetry for review and comment while separated. I remember reviewing one poem in particular of hers titled *To Arcturus.* It was a truly beautiful piece that focused on the stars of our hemisphere. From my days of toil at *Graham's Magazine* and Burton's *Gentleman's Magazine* I could not help myself from pointing out various redundancies in her text. It was done only to help the writing of the woman I loved and admired. *There is an obvious tautology in 'pale candescent.' To be candescent is to become white with heat. Why not read—'To blend with shine its incandescent fire?' Forgive me, sweet Helen, for these very stupid & captious criticisms. Take vengeance on my next poem.—When* Ulalume *appears, cut it out & enclose it:—newspapers seldom reach me.*[87]

In subsequent letters I wrote to Helen about how our blessed union in love and business could establish *The Stylus* as a publication of unquestionable aristocracy in literary intellect. Oh that we could be at the helm of this sleek and narrow ship that would slice through the brackish waters of the Literati of New York! I did not, however, disclose my plans in any detail, as I feared what Helen's evil-eyed mother might do with them.

The close of one of my letters noted *signs of the times.*[88] Rufus Griswold had copied my *Raven* in his *Hartford Weekly Gazette*[89] (his latest editorial endeavor) and gave, what could be considered by the lucid among us, mostly favorable editorial comments. Nary did I see the use of his favorite word: "balderdash." I pictured the shake of his jowls as he wrote in his haughty manner and got a chuckle.

On Wednesday, December 20th I planned to finally be back in my love's arms in the early afternoon. It took me most of the night to travel from New York after my final lecture. By the time I wandered sleepily into Providence, I had to get some shuteye before seeing Helen. I felt my letters were pressing enough and did not plan on requesting an answer to my marriage proposal in person. I checked into my hotel and took a long nap.

We were to meet at an ice skating pond just past the covered bridge leading out of town. Children were playing when I got there; some blading across the ice, others decorating a freshly cut Christmas tree that had been slid into the center of the pond with streamers and popcorn garland. A couple freckle-faced boys were having a snowball fight off to the side.

I watched in anticipation for Helen. It was not like her to be late. Her mother was probably detaining her. I traced lines in the snow with my boot heel, and then spelled Helen, then began etching lines of prose in white. Where on God's white earth *was* she?

That's when I felt what I thought to be a punch in the upper back, but then saw a burst of snow dance over my shoulders. I wheeled, expecting to see one of the freckle-faced boys pointing in glee.

Helen was standing on top of an incline dressed in black clothing from head to toe apart from a crimson scarf wrapped about her neck. "Ha!"

"I see you are dressed festively for the holidays," I called out, for the scarf alone was the most color I had seen on her.

"I am almost blinded by it." With that she tossed another snowball and I ducked. She came running down the hill after me and flung herself into my open arms. She hit with such force that I went sprawling onto my back. My hat rolled onto the ice. When I looked up Helen was on top of me, pinning my arms to the compacting snow. The children were howling with laughter.

"Slap the raven," one called.

"Give it to 'im, lady," cried another.

"I have missed you so much. Marry me, Edgar Allan Poe!"

The phase took me by surprise as much, I am sure, as my proposal did her in the cemetery. "How?"

"Well most people go to a church and—"

"I mean, when?"

"To-morrow!" she exclaimed.

"To- ... to- ... to-morrow?"

"Alright, the day after that!"

"In two days? We need time to plan, to get a minister."

"I'm tired of thinking this through. December twenty-fourth. Christmas Eve!" She let go of one of my arms and poked my chest with her leather glove. "And I will not wait a second longer to marry you, Edgar Allan Poe."

"Fine. Yes! Ho-ho-ho. Christmas Eve it is."

We rolled and flailed off in the snow for the world to see.

We spent the ensuing day and evening shopping in the heart of Providence. Helen offered to pay for the entire ceremony. I never felt poorer in my life, but it was the only option. We visited the Cathedral of St. John on North Main Street, which we thought fitting because of my proposal in its rear cemetery. The Reverend Crocker agreed to marry us after an hour counseling session where he did nothing but grill us on our beliefs. He knew of Helen's séances and had read some of my writing that he tactfully referred to as lacking in acknowledgment of a divine power. He claimed he was still unable to make it through *The Fall of the House of Usher* after dark. Finally, Reverend Crocker gave us his blessing, albeit a reluctant one.

Later that day I met Helen at her home and we planned to head to the bakery to order a wedding cake and then to pick a bouquet of blood flowers for Helen to carry down the aisle.

"I *must* wear black," she announced in the foyer while lacing up her boots on the stairs leading to the upper level of the home. "I want to be the first woman in America to wear *all* black at her wedding!"

"It is very gothic," I responded, thinking it over. I heard the rustling of papers somewhere above, but paid no attention. "Just as long as people do not think you are in mourning for marrying me."

"Oh, Edgar you are too hard on yourself. What better way for the dark poets of America to be joined in a blessed union of souls and to—"

Before Helen could finish her sentence Mrs. Power came bounding down the stairs like a shadowy juggernaut, Helen's sister following her. They brushed Helen aside and in a few steps Mrs. Power had pushed me against the door. The doorknob stabbed into my backbone and spirals of pain twisted out from its epicenter. A legal-size parchment was pressing against my chest. "Not a chance," she said, "you charlatan."

"Beg your pardon?"

The eyes of Helen's mother were hot as burning embers of coal. I had never seen a woman so livid. "I learned of my daughter's acceptance of your ... your supposed *marriage* proposal and I will not stand for it!" Her foot stamped repeatedly into the floorboards and I imagined her heel was making a deep imprint, but did not dare take my attention off her.

"Mother, please!" Helen shouted.

"I cannot deny it, Missus Power, I shan't deny it. In two days our wedd—"

"Don't even say it. I cannot stand the dubayou word!" She yanked the parchment in front of my face. "My daughter will not come within a hundred yards of that church until you sign this."

The knob was now imprinted so deeply in the small of my back that a house key could have opened a door to my spine. Wincing, I forced my way off it and felt a thud of pain, then relief. I scanned the document now in my hands over Helen's calls of: "What *is* that, mother?" There was no question it was a legal document, embossed with the seal of a Providence law firm.

"It's called a Prenuptial Agreement," Mrs. Power said. "They are extremely rare, especially for a woman to have a man sign, but in this case it's most warranted."

Helen rushed to my side. "What does it say?"

I believed Helen's surprised reaction and read the parchment with some difficulty given its legalese of wheretofores and hereins and wherewithals. "Best I can tell, if you die before me, I would receive nothing from your estate." A giggle sounded out from her sister.

"As you know, Edgar," Mrs. Power said, "under our laws when a wife dies her entire estate automatically goes to the husband and nothing is left to her family. Whether you sign this will prove if you are marrying Helen because she is in poor health or out of true love."

"You are mistaken about my intents," I told her.

"And *you* will not be getting rich off my daughter. The gold rush may be happening in California, but it is not happening in Providence."

"He does not need to sign a contract to prove his love to me!"

"Sign the agreement or you will not have my consent to marriage." The final stomp of Mrs. Power cracked the floorboards. From her apron she extracted a stylus.

I snatched it from her, paused for a moment in deep thought, and signed at the bottom. My hardened stare did not leave her.

The signature was given over Helen's adamant protests. "You do not have to sign that agreement! I will marry you regardless."

"I realize that, but I have to sign it to prove my unconditional love for you and to show that I am not motivated by money in our union. From this day forth this document will evidence proof of that fact to the world."

The twenty-third of December brought its own challenges. I was not about to sit around at the house where Helen's contract-toting mother sat in wait like a coiled snake. Maybe she would have a new agreement requiring me to only walk on one side of the street or breathe in a certain way. My suggestion was that Helen and I spend the day meeting with friends in Providence or watching the ice skaters. *Anything* to get us away from 76 Benefit Street! There was nothing beneficial about the place for me.

I planned to request that Helen put the home up for sale immediately after our marriage so that we could live far away from Providence. Speaking of our marriage, it was only a day away and excitement was about me despite all the detractors who wished our union ill. The homes along Benefit Street were decorated in garland and mistletoe for the season. Red candles adorned the windows and boughs of holly were tacked to the front doors. Straps of bells jangled from horse bridles in the crisp air, which cleared my head as I walked to pick up Helen. The scent of pine needles was about, and chimneys were boasting from the pies and cookies being baked inside the festive homes. Snow blanketed the lawns and to a lesser extent the sidewalks. I realized in the midst of it all, now that the arrangements were finished and legal documents signed, that my second wedding was but a formality and the second Helen of my dreams would soon be living with me and Muddy in New York. The proceeds from her house would afford us new living quarters that were thrice the size of the Fordham cottage.

I had realized this before I left the Earl House Hotel and stopped off at the lobby bar for a celebratory glass of spirits. I gave strict orders to the bartender to keep the glass small.

Since I had not had a panic attack for over a week, I had reason to believe that the drink would have no more effect on me than the average man.

Turning off the sidewalk toward the home, pushing my way through a knot of carolers, I felt little effects of the spirits other than hearty warmth. I knocked on the door of my bride's home and was a tad surprised when I did not find Helen there to greet me. Instead, I heard a call from inside to enter. I tried the door handle and it was unlocked (as if anyone locks their door in this part of Providence). I went inside.

To my shock a large group of people was seated around the long dining room table. Mr. Pabodie was standing near the foyer in his trademark purple vest and shirt that matched the white of his hair, wrapped box in hand. He claimed to have arrived just before me to drop off a wedding present on his way to Boston where he planned to visit relatives for the holidays. Helen was at the far end of the table and her heavy eyeliner was smudged from wiping tears. Her sister and mother were consoling her.

I watched the scene as though viewing a picture book setting. For moments I felt detached from it all, then came crashing back to reality when I heard the shrill voice of Mrs. Powers. "Explain this, Edgar!" She clutched a letter in her hand. "Tell us all, before God and country, why my daughter is getting letters imploring her not to marry the likes of you a day before her wedding."

I stood agape in the foyer, a puddle forming about my boots from the melting snow. I tried to speak but it was as if I had dirty coppers in my mouth. My words were garbled at first. "Wara ... whr ... the matter, Helen?"

Instead of responding, Helen brought from under the table a wad of handkerchiefs and took a deep whiff.

"I'll tell you what's the matter," her sister chimed, "Helen went to the city library early this morning to get a book on French table decorating for the reception—"

"—and she had it open on her desk, and went to get another," Mrs. Power said. "Upon her return she found a note slipped into its pages."

I detected a certain satisfaction in her telling the story.

Her sister chimed out again. "The note warned Helen against an imprudent marriage and—"

"—vouched that you have already violated your promise to her not to become intoxicated."

I stood in a daze listening to the chain-linked statements.

Helen's mother tossed the crumpled note onto the table. "Do you expect us to believe you instead of this concerned author who is obviously looking out for Helen's own good? I see no reason for the anonymous writer to lie when they stand to profit nothing from the venture."

"Nothing but revenge," I offered.

Mr. Pabodie motioned to leave with a tip of his hat.

I blocked his exit. "Please stay. I want to have a witness to this episode no matter how painful it may be for you to suffer through it, fine sir." I turned back to address Helen's mother when a sharp pain stabbed through my head. My vision blurred and quavered. When I glanced up, the heads of Helen's mother and sister moved together to form one horrid face that flickered in a nightmare visage. I held on to the doorway surround for support as the effects of the spirits compounded themselves in a violent maelstrom.

"Look at him now," Mrs. Power shouted, or was it Helen's sister? "He is displaying drunken symptoms at this moment. I am glad Mister Pabodie is staying as a witness to Poe's vice."

"Dear Helen, I can assure you I have had only one glass of wine to drink at my hotel for Christmas cheer and am in full keeping of my conditional promise to you. I am *not* intoxicated."

Instead of listening to my explanation, Helen took from her chair, struggled into the adjoining living room, and fell onto a sofa in the séance room.

From instinct I rushed toward her and entreated her to speak but one word to me, yet she kept sniffing at the foul, drug-soaked material in her hands with each word from my mouth. The small coffin lay sideways on her neck. Tears were streaking her face only to be blotted out by the wad. A metallic-smelling haze wafted over her, cloying in the air. The ether was beginning to have an effect of me.

"My dearest!"

At last, almost inaudibly, she responded, "What can I say?"

"Say that you love me, Helen."

She looked up at me with her smudged, rheumy eyes, and said, "I love you," then inhaled a final breath from the handkerchiefs and passed out.

I felt the stomping of her mother across the hardwoods behind me. "There is nothing more you can do here. You have admitted you are filled with alcohol. Get out of my house, Edgar."

"This is not your house," I reminded her, standing and meeting her face-to-face. "Helen owns this place, lest you forget."

"And you never will, you moneygrubber!"

"Nothing could be farther from the truth."

"I see no qualities of value in you, Edgar."

"And I see that the Imp of the Perverse wears a dress!"

Mrs. Powers reached back. Her veiny hand fumbled for one of the center candles on the dining room table. I backpedaled toward the front door.

"Leave you stinking drunk! Leave this house. My daughter will never marry you!"

The garish candle thudded against the wall next to my head as I darted back into the foyer. It fell in a smashed clump on the floor. The oncoming migraine made it difficult for me to retain my balance as I ran. "I love you, Helen!"

"You are not good enough for her and never will be. Drunkard!"

I ran out the front door, stating: "Mr. Pabodie, you hear how I am insulted!"

1849 - Age 40

On January 19th I spent the most miserable birthday of my existence. I had not heard from Helen and likewise, she had not gotten word from me. Middle age and foolish pride were rampant on my fortieth birthday.

Muddy made a pot of coffee and baked a cake for me (black forest, my favorite), but I could hardly make it through a slice. I was in a daze of depression and regret.

"I am tired of seeing you sulk around this house. Why don't you write her, Eddy? It will do you good. Keeping matters capped up inside helps no one but the bottlers."

I looked at her with mopey eyes, chocolate shavings nestled in my mustache.

"You heard me. If Helen comes back to you, you can tell the world illness postponed your wedding. It is very plausible. I will be at your side for the entire ceremony for support."

"Once again, Aunty, your wisdom is beyond reproach."

"I may not have loved for many years, but I do remember something about the emotion." She made a waving movement with her hands. "Now eat up. We need to get weight back on you."

Fordham Jany. 25th / 49

Dear Madam,

In commencing this letter, need I say to you, after what has passed between us, that no amount of provocation on your part, or on the part of your friends, shall induce me to speak ill of you even in my own defence? If to shield myself from calumny however undeserved, or however unendurable, I find a need of resorting to explanations that might condemn or pain you, most solemnly do I assure you, that I will patiently endure such calumny, rather than avail myself of any such means of refuting it—You will see then, that so far I am at your mercy—but in making you such assurances, have I not a right to ask of you some forbearance in return? My object in now writing you is to place before you an extract from a letter recently addressed to myself—"I will not repeat all her vile & slanderous words—you have doubtless heard them—but one thing she says that I cannot deny though I do not believe it—viz—that you had been publisher to her once, & that on the Sat. preceding the Sabbath on which you were to have been published for the second time, she went herself to the Rev Mr Crocker's, & after stating her reasons for so doing, requested him to stop all further proceedings—

...

—some person equally your enemy & mine has been its author—but what I beg of you is, to write me at once a few lines in explanation—you know of course that by reference either to Mr Pabodie (who at my request forbore to speak to the minister about publishing the first banns on the day I left) or, to the Rev. Mr Crocker himself, I can disprove the facts stated in the most satisfactory manner—but there can be no need of disproving what I feel confident was never asserted by you—Your simple disavowal is all that I wish—You will of course write me immediately on receipt of this—only in the event of my not hearing from you within a few days, will I proceed to take more definite steps—Heaven knows that I would shrink from wounding or grieving you! I blame no one but your Mother—Mr Pabodie will tell you the words which passed between us, while from the effects of those terrible stimulants you lay prostrate without even the power to bid me farewell—Alas! I bitterly lament my own weaknesses, & nothing is farther from my heart than to blame you for yours—May Heaven shield you from all ill! So far I have assigned no reason for my declining to fulfil our engagement—I had none but the suspicious & grossly insulting parsimony of the arrangements into which you suffered yourself to be forced by your Mother—Let my letters & acts speak for themselves—It has been my intention to say simply, that our marriage was postponed on account of your ill health—Have you really said or done anything which can preclude our placing the rupture on such footing? If not, I shall persist in the statement & thus this unhappy matter will die quietly away—

E. A. Poe[90]

Sarah Helen Whitman never responded. She never, ever responded. The words "I love you" were the last she spoke to me.

The disgracing of our names in the papers after the breakup—which to no surprise was heavily slanted toward me being a drunk as the inherent problem—my lost love, onset of middle age, and second anniversary of Sissy's death caused me to be ill most of the winter. Blessed Muddy and Mrs. Shew tended to me like angels in the lower bedroom of the cottage.

How I feared dying in the same bed as Virginia! I missed her now more than ever.

Muddy was sick, too, but tried to keep it from me so that I would not be upset. On top of it all, we were desperately poor.

By springtime, however, my shattered heart had mended enough for me to begin writing again and to do light chores around the cottage. I was penning a story called *Eureka* that I considered some of my best work. The tale had a spiritual quality that I drew on to get me through my depression and illness. By the end of June I began a lecture tour to raise money and support for *The Stylus*. Now more than ever I wanted to show the world that I could get the literary publication of our times into circulation.

I went to New York City to give my first lectures. By the end of the week I had a relapse of nerves and could barely stand. I admit that I had a glass or so of strong drink one evening and when I stumbled into the street in anguish, crying out for Virginia, was hauled off to jail to sleep it off.

New York, July 7.

My dear, dear Mother,—

I have been so ill—have had the cholera, or spasms quiet as bad, and can now hardly hold the pen[...]
The very instant you get this, come to me. The joy of seeing you will almost compensate for our sorrows. We can but die together. It is no use to reason with me now; I must die. I have no desire to live since I have done "Eureka." I could accomplish nothing more. For your sake it would be sweet to live, but we must die together.
You have been all in all to me, darling, ever beloved mother, and dearest, truest friend.
I was never really insane, except on occasions where my heart was touched[...]
I have been taken to prison once since I came here for spreeing drunk; but then I was not. It was about Virginia.

With all my devotion,
Eddy[91]

After getting paid for lecturing in New York, I took the train to Philadelphia where I planned to make frequent stops at the Revolutionary Grounds to mend my tortured soul. For once the coffee did little to fix my dementia. One afternoon, beset with paranoia the likes I have never imagined, I appeared at the doorstep of one Dr. John Sartain who maintained an office downtown and was a publisher of his own magazine. We knew of each other from this common interest.

"My dear Poe, what a grand surprise. Forgive me, but you are a quivering mess."

I pushed into his office and begged him for protection from a band of conspirators disguised as Loungers. I now know they were imaginary, but in my swirling mind the Literati of New York had most definitely followed me to Philly on the train and were waiting for me, lounging in shadowy doorways and alleys. *They* lived in the Shadowlands and these detractors of mine were everywhere.

He grabbed me by the shoulders and shook me. "Get a hold of yourself, good sir. To whom are you referring?"

"Doctor Rufus Dubaya Griswold for one."

"Many in the publishing industry are afraid of Doctor Griswold, but he is no reason to be in a fright." Dr. Sartain let go of my frockcoat and smoothed it. "[A] notorious blackmailer ... I myself had to pay him money to prevent abusive notices of *Sartain's Magazine*"

"And I have lost my valise. My valise I tell you! They stole my work and are going to publish it under their names. I just know it!"

"Please have a seat, sir. We will find your valise. Where did you last have it?"

When I spied a razor and cup of lather on the shelf behind Dr. Sartain's desk, I attempted to shave off my mustache so the Loungers would not recognize me, but the doctor, afraid of my motives with the razor, cut off my mustache with scissors instead.[92] The good and well-meaning doctor then tried to counsel me to no avail.

I luckily came to my wits after I had stormed out of the office. Blocks removed from the office I impossibly located my hotel. I wrote Muddy of my Philly problems after I had traveled to Richmond the following day and felt a sense of safety from the Loungers.

Richmond, Saturday Night.

Oh, my darling Mother, it is now more than three weeks since I saw you, and in all that time your poor Eddy has scarcely drawn a breath except of incense agony. Perhaps you are sick or gone from Fordham in despair, or dead. If you are but alive, and if I but see you again, all the rest is nothing. I love you better than ten thousand lives—so much so that it is cruel in you to let me leave you; nothing but sorrow ever comes of it.

Oh, Mother, I am so ill while I write—but I resolved that come what would, I would not sleep again without easing your dear heart as far as I could.

My valise was lost for ten days. At last I found it at the depot in Philadelphia, but (you will scarcely credit it) they had opened it and stolen both lectures. Oh, Mother, think of the blow to me this evening, when on examining the valise, these lectures were gone. All my object here is over unless I can recover them or re-write one of them.

...

I got here with two dollars over—of which I inclose you one. Oh God, my Mother, shall we ever again meet? If possible, oh come! My clothes are so horrible, and I am so ill. Oh, if you could come to me, my mother. Write instantly—oh do not fail. God forever bless you.

Eddy[93]

In Richmond I visited Rose and found it refreshing to be near my last remaining sibling. She was lighthearted and unaware of the hurt in my life. I believe that is the way my sister chose to live her life, much like Sissy. It was great to be free of oppression regarding my character. Oh that I could live one hour without self-inspection.

I spent a number of days in Richmond and Mrs. Mackenzie bought me new clothes, but I could not bring myself to so much as look at Moldavia across the street. There were too many bad memories at the manse for me to gaze upon it.

One afternoon I was feeling near my old self, walking down the street, and came upon George's Eatery. To my surprise it was unchanged apart from a new coat of paint. I pressed my face to the window and peered inside. George was still minding the counter, temples graying, earlobes elongating, face wrinkled from age and countless smiles given while serving cups of coffee and bowls of raspberry cobbler to his customers. He was probably still telling the joke about the color he preferred his servants when a person ordered their coffee black.

The marble-topped tables were the same, and as I stood there I envisioned Elmira Royster sitting at the window seat just as she had when we first met in high school, overdressed in the latest Southern Belle style and talking with a sensuous drawl. My wanted vision suddenly transformed her into a grown woman. I wondered what road life had taken her down, how she had matured.

"P-oe!" I heard my name spoken in the unmistakable, two-syllable dialect of Elmira. *No one has ever called me Poe like that but her*, I thought.

Now I was hearing her speak! I wished my teenage years to return so badly that I was convinced I was not only seeing things, but hearing them. I pushed away from the glass, leaving ten splayed fingerprints. I loosened my collar and took a breath of the humid air. When I gawped back into the glass, the visage of a mature Sarah Elmira Royster was still there. And when I spun, the visage was standing right next to me!

"Mercy me, any man who loves coffee enough to stare at it like that is a woman's man indeed."

"Elmira?"

She turned to the side and ran her fingers along her waist that angled into her hoop skirt. "In the flesh. Is there any other?"

I stood there as though my boots were stuck in mud. Before I could move Elmira threw her arms around me. I gingerly put my hands on her back, on the palpable visage. Then I remembered Mr. Shelton. To caress another's wife in public could get a man shot full of lead in Richmond. As we embraced, I also thought how I missed those innocent days and our first kiss under the weeping willow tree.

"We have a lot of catching up to do," Elmira said, pulling back from me.

I could not believe my eyes. I tried to speak a coherent sentence but failed miserably. I was a writer, not a speaker no matter how many lectures I had given over the last years in my renown.

At the corner she flagged down an open-topped coupe and we hopped inside, each sitting across from the other on the bench seats. The horses were coaxed into action and the movement of air across my face (that I assume still had a surprised look on it) was refreshing and calming.

"It really is Sarah Elmira Royster," I exclaimed.

"Sarah Elmira Royster Shelton, remember?"

"How could I forget?" Betrayal overtook me and I searched for a wedding ring on her finger but did not see one.

Elmira raised her parasol to ward off the sun. The scent of lilacs was still about her. "Let me first apologize for the way my father treated you those many years ago. He had no right, but it was too late. I *had* to marry Alexander."

"As if there were any justice in this world," I sighed in disbelief. "You did not have a gun pointed to your head."

"Just as bad ... or worse. You have no idea what it was like living under my father's dominion. There was so much pressure! I was just a young lady."

"And I was heartbroken. You were my first love, Elmira."

"As you were mine." She brushed back her flaxen hair and smiled. Her teeth were still perfect and inviting. The coupe stopped at the next busy intersection and I noticed those on the street staring: a groom currying the mane of a black gelding, bearded men picking at their whiskers while getting their boots shined.

I slumped in my seat. "What's Alexander going to think if we are seen together?"

"Who cares?"

I felt my hands incline upward and the lace of one of her gloves weave through my fingers. "All of Richmond cares," I said, stealing back my hand. "I have enough trouble in the papers."

"I am widowed." Instead of Elmira's eyes casting down in remorse, they grew large with opportunity.

"Forgive me for prying."

"No, Poe, forgive me for not being woman enough to scorn my father and his high-society friends those many years ago." Before I could react she landed next to me on the seat in such a close fashion that our legs were touching and the parasol covered both of us.

For the next hour we wheeled about Richmond as if joined at the hip. Every time the driver would ask if we wanted off, Elmira told him to keep going in no uncertain terms. His tip depended on it. For the next hour I took in the genteel Southern mannerisms of my teenage sweetheart like swallows of cool water on a hot day. We talked and touched and talked some more.

I stayed over two months in Richmond, lecturing to the most appreciative of audiences. There were other engagements in New England I could have taken, but I chose to stay in the Southland, near Elmira, to renew our courtship. Most evenings were spent at her home at 2407 East Grace Street. She even helped me rewrite one of the two lectures I had brought (and got stolen) in my valise. I dictated them, and when she could keep her hands off me, she penned.

The socialites of Richmond welcomed me and often invited me out on the town to various engagements. I had become their most popular literary son, but rarely attended the social events because of lack of money and a proper dress coat. When I did attend a much less formal gathering in a home, I was inevitably asked to recite *The Raven* at some point in the night. I gave my rendition of it in Richmond one particular evening while Rose was napping somewhere in the house of a friend.

Once, in discussing "The Raven," Poe observed that he had never heard it correctly delivered by even the best readers—that is, not as he desired that it should be read. That evening, a number of visitors being present, he was requested to recite the poem, and complied. His impressive delivery held the company spell-bound, but in the midst of it, I, happening to glance toward the open window above the level roof of the green-house, beheld a group of sable faces the whites of whose eyes shone in strong relief against the surrounding darkness. These were a number of our family servants, who having heard much talk about "Mr. Poe, the poet," and having but an imperfect idea of what a poet was, had requested permission of my brother to witness the recital. As the speaker became more impassioned and excited, more conspicuous grew the circle of white eyes, until when at length he turned suddenly toward the window, and, extending his arm, cried, with awful vehemence:

Get thee hack into the tempest, and the night's Plutonian shore!

there was a sudden disappearance of the sable visages, a scuttling of feet, and the gallery audience was gone. Ludicrous as was the incident, the final touch was given when at that moment Miss Poe, who was an extraordinary character in her way, sleepily entered the room, and with a dull and drowsy deliberation seated herself on her brother's knee. He had subsided from his excitement into a gloomy despair, and now, fixing his eyes upon his sister, he concluded:

And the raven, never flitting, still is sitting, still is sitting,
On the pallid bust of Pallas, just above my chamber door;
And its eyes have all the seeming of a demon that is dreaming

The effect was irresistible; and as the final "nevermore" was solemnly uttered the half-

suppressed titter of two very young persons in a corner was responded to by a general laugh. Poe remarked quietly that on his next delivery of a public lecture he would "take Rose along, to act the part of the raven, in which she seemed born to excel."[94]

Between lectures I published *Sonnet—To My Mother* that expressed my unfailing devotion to Maria Clemm. I also wrote Elmira and eased her fears about my rumored drinking.

We agreed to meet for lunch at a quaint restaurant that had a second story eating area overlooking a courtyard. Our table was next to the iron railing that skirted the overhang. Potted ferns hung from an awning that jutted overhead. I pulled out Elmira's chair and she angled into the seat. How the ladies of our day sit or even stand in the contraptions they call dresses I have not a clue.

One look at the menu prices caused me indigestion. Elmira must have noticed me blanch. "This is *my* treat, Poe. Money is not an issue since Alexander left me his estate."

I smiled. She obviously had heard of the poverty that Muddy and I had been wallowing in for years. The waiter came and placed a basket of steaming biscuits and strawberry preserves on our table. Elmira ordered mint julep and I ordered iced tea.

Elmira clasped her hands. "Edgar Allan Poe in the flesh after all these years."

"Sarah Elmira Royster ... Shelton." I was always forgetting to tack it on. "I still cringe when I say Alexander's surname to this day."

She batted her long eyelashes. "Ya'll have nothing to worry about, believe me. Although, the way people return from the grave in your tales, I am not so sure." Below us were two ladies at a fountain twirling frilly parasols, which from above were red-white spinning candies.

"It's Christmas in July."

"I see you still have your sense of humor, Poe, and good looks." My face colored at this. "And you are still telling your tales. I have read every one of them. That is the way I have kept up with you over the years. Alexander would break into a fit when he caught me. To save myself grief I began reading magazines at the library. It helped me feel that you had never left. By the way—speaking of Christmas—I still have your greatcoat that you left at my father's home that fateful evening."

"Really?" This confession proved to me her love of long ago more than anything she had said. "As if I had a chance to snatch it while your father's servants tossed me out on my ear," I smiled.

"I saved the coat before he threw it into the fire with the letters. He did not know which was yours in the closet or he would have burned that, too."

I shook my head as the waiter came with our drinks. Elmira ordered a Caesar's salad for lunch that she claimed to always order at this restaurant. I realized I had not read the menu apart from the prices. I chose the turkey sandwich that came with a side of potato salad out of haste. The meal was the first item on the list.

When the waiter left, Elmira raised her mint julep glass in a toast. "To old loves made anew!" As our glasses clinked, she lowered her head without taking a sip. "I apologize, Poe. I should not have ordered strong drink in your presence."

Under some disdain I told her, "I do *not* have a drinking problem. The slightest drop of alcohol's betraying moisture drives me into madness and makes me doubt my abilities. And for a purveyor of the written word, confidence is everything."

"I find it difficult to imagine the author of so many great works of gothic literature, which send chills to places in my body I forgot I had, is for one moment shaken in confidence."

"If you believe nothing else, Elmira, believe that I do not have a drinking problem."

She nodded, but some disbelief was evident under her golden curls gleaming in the sun. She took a moment to reflect and sip after removing the sprig of mint. A refreshingly cool breeze plunged under the awning, twisting the potted ferns. Elmira sat her glass down and threw up her hands. "Here we are, both widowed in midlife."

"Tragic, but amazing," I said.

"Liberating in my case." Elmira moved in close. "I never loved Alexander. You should know that. Always you." She touched the back of my hand. "I pretended it was you when we were in the bedroom."

Just as my face had returned to its normal pale color, it flashed pink again.

"Once more, forgive me for forsaking my heart, Poe. I will never do it again if I gain your favor. Never."

Just as I was about to delve deeper into her feelings, the waiter came with our food. Nerves caused me to take a large bite of my sandwich, which left me unable to speak.

"I have kept in touch with Rose over the years, mostly to keep track of your whereabouts. Know that I feel a great deal of compassion for the man who was orphaned as a boy, reared in affluence by an abusive foster father and, perhaps worse, by a foster father that discouraged your writing. Rose told me he left you penniless on the streets. Then later, when your writing got the recognition it deserved, your jealous counterparts maliciously libeled you. No wonder you have a pervasive sense of wrong and injustice. Mercy."

"If it is pity you are in love with, then spare me," I retorted.

Elmira looked with beseeching eyes. "It is I who must be spared by your love."

For what seemed a long time we said nothing as I champed at my sandwich and Elmira plucked away at her salad, which she referred to as "darling precious." I gave an apology for eating so quickly, claiming I would get fat from it.

"Beg your pardon, but you are far from the strapping young man I once knew so long ago. The world has done this to you, my poor love. The world has caused your illness more so than any disease. For you see, I know much of the tell-tale heart."

After this, I could not stand it any longer. I was burning inside. Passionate flames had been stoked within me from embers that I realized had never been extinguished. I pushed back my chair, placed my linen napkin on the table, bent down on one knee, and in my impetuous nature at these matters took her gloved hands in mine. "Dearest Elmira, we have been given a once in a lifetime chance. God has smiled upon us in middle life, not the converse. What young loves are ever reunited after being widowed? Marry me, and our hearts will be forever young."

Her eyes grew large and she momentarily struggled to catch her breath. Those eating around us stopped their activities and watched. Most of them knew who I was.

"Elmira?"

"I am not refusing, Poe, but there is something we have not discussed for I did not feel it was the right time to bring up the subject. If I accept your marriage proposal and remarry, I will have to relinquish a large portion of my inheritance left to me by Alexander as stipulated in his will. The money and land will go to his remaining family."

"More contracts," I said under my breath. "I do not care about *money* as you can tell by the way I have lived my life. Do not mistrust your own eyes. As I told you, Helen Whitman's mother required me to sign a prenuptial agreement and I will do the same for you."

Elmira clutched at her neck. "Mercy, I would never think of such a thing. Besides, such would keep no less money from going to Alexander's family."

"And if you have any concerns about my drinking, I will join the Sons of Temperance. The Shockoe Hill Division, No. Fifty-Four is right in town. The society requires its members to completely abstain from alcohol. Say yes, Elmira. This is the second time in my life I have asked for your hand in marriage and my heart will break if I have to ask a third!"

She took a deep breath, exhaled, and smiled with those teeth. "I would give all the money in the world for you, Poe. A substantial amount of my fortune is a small price to pay. Yes! I will marry you with pleasure, Edgar Allan Poe!" A round of wild clapping arose from the overhang and was carried off by the breeze through verdant ferns.

I spent time lecturing in Norfolk and returned to Richmond the middle of September. I now considered Richmond my home, not only because of Elmira's station, but also from the overwhelming acceptance the people of the city were extending me. I was a celebrity and referred to by the children in town as The Raven. While I was gone Elmira took a vacation in the country. I broached the subject of Muddy and living arrangements upon her return for there was no taint at her place as there was for me at Helen Whitman's, cringing as to how my fiancée might react. To my blessed surprise, Elmira was so accepting of having Muddy come live with us after our marriage that she wrote my aunt out of the blue to make her acquaintance. I was overjoyed at this selfless extension of love and friendship by Elmira. I felt unworthy of her in many ways and told Muddy of this.

Richmond Va Tuesday—Sep 18—49.

My own darling Muddy,

On arriving here last night from Norfolk I received both your letters, ... I cannot tell you the joy they gave me — to learn at least that you are well & hopeful. May God forever bless you, my dear dear Muddy — Elmira has just got home from the country. I spent last evening with her. I think she loves me more devotedly than any one I ever knew & I cannot help loving her in return. Nothing is yet definitely settled and it will not do to hurry matters. I [lec] tured at Norfolk on Monday & cleared enough to settle my bill here at the Madison House with $2 over. I had a highly fashionable audience, but Norfolk is a small place & there were 2 exhibitions the same night. Next Monday I lecture again here & expect to have a large audience. On Tuesday I start for Phila [Philadelphia] to attend to Mrs Loud's Poems — & possibly on Thursday I may start for N. York. If I do I will ... send for you. It will be better for me not to go to Fordham — don't you think so? Write immediately in reply & direct to Phila. For fear I should not get the letter, sign no name & address it to E. S. T. Grey Esqre.

If possible I will get married before I start—but there is no telling... . My poor poor Muddy I am still unable to send you even one dollar—but keep up heart — I hope that our troubles are nearly over... .

God bless & protect you my own darling Muddy. I showed your letter to Elmira and she says "it is such a darling precious letter that she loves you for it already"

Your own Eddy.

Don't forget to write immediately to Phila. so that your letter will be there when I arrive.

The papers here are praising me to death — and I have been received everywhere with enthusiasm. Be sure & preserve all the printed scraps I have sent you & keep up my file of the Lit. World.[95]

My dizzying tour sent me back to Philadelphia where I read a number of works at a sitting for Mrs. Loud.[96] I also apologized to Dr. Sartain for my behavior earlier and he wished me the best. After my short trip to Philadelphia, I returned to Richmond two days later and on September 27th took the Baltimore Boat, which is commonly known as the steamship Pocahontas. I took a stroll past Amity Street where I saw our old duplex. It was late in the season, granted, but I saw no signs that Sissy's daisies were still growing in a crook of the roof.

This only made me think of Elmira. Oh how I missed her! I kept dried lilacs in my valise to remind me of her sweet perfume. We would soon be united in Richmond. Muddy was also on my mind; dear Mother. The one who treated me as her child and put my needs over her own.

September 29th is a date I will never forget. It was the day I planned to travel back to New York (via the Philadelphia train) for a literary engagement and to visit Muddy.

I had a bout of migraines in Baltimore (early afternoon I believe) and completely missed the Philadelphia train. The next one did not leave for three hours so I decided to edit one of my manuscripts at a restaurant a block from the train station. I was downing a cup of coffee, restraining myself from having more than one due to a shortage of funds (*Tenui musam meditamur avena*!), when I noticed someone outside pointing at me through the window. Figuring one of my readers had recognized me, and knowing I had to catch the train within the hour, I slouched in my seat and cringed when I heard the door to the restaurant creak open.

"Edgar Poe! Is that you, old boy?"

I tried to hide behind my manuscript, but the deep voice sought me out. "I said, 'Is that you?'"

When I peered over the top of the parchment I saw a face that took me a moment to place. Then it struck me. "Martin Reynolds?" who gets ebony lovin'.

"Martin Reynolds, ruffian of William Burke's School. That's me!"

Neither his freckles nor his fiery hair had diminished over the years. He slid in across from me. "Can you still swim like a fish?"

"To be honest, I have not been swimming for years. I miss it though."

"I have read all your stories, some twice. Proud to tell people I tried to beat you up."

"Your form of flattery is not surprising. Glad you finally learned how to read, Reynolds."

"Cut me some slack, Poe. You are the one who turned out popular, not me. Moved to

Baltimore years ago and just never made as good a living as I thought I would in the shipping yards. Always wanted to make a lot of money."

"Then stay away from writing," I warned.

The lump of a man slapped the table, which apparently meant he had an idea. "Let's let bygones be bygones. I'm meeting a few shipmates for our annual fall supper before lobster season. I was on my way when I noticed you. Join us. Dinner is on me, and you look like you could use a good filling up."

"Thanks, but I'm catching a train to Philly."

"To Philly? I know that route. Another leaves in two hours. Have a bite with us and you will be on your way. It will be a real kick to have you there. Bet I can convert the entire room to avid Poe readers. These men travel the high seas. Who knows where they will take your tales?"

Reynolds extended his hand, which had an anchor tattooed between the thumb and index fingers, and I reluctantly shook it. "A fine meal and more readers will do me good. But I will catch the next train no matter how long you boys eat."

The chained sign hanging overhead read BALTIMORE FISHERY. The establishment was fronted by a row of tables with Atlantic fish of every kind lined up on blocks of ice. Seafaring men puffed on corncob pipes and told spectacular tales as they waited to sell their catch.

Reynolds showed me inside and we headed down a flight of stairs to a reserved section of the restaurant that looked out on the pier. Two long tables were joined end-to-end and surrounded by surly deckhands. A cloud of grey hovered over them as they smoked and laughed and drank, clinking mugs in their gaiety and punching each other in the arm. Their revelry sent needles of pain shooting behind my eyes.

I took my seat next to Reynolds and we tore into the plates of salmon and steaming crab cakes being passed. My head was throbbing, but the hunger pangs won out. While I slid corn on the cob onto my plate, I realized I had never seen such a multitude of anchor tattoos in one place and had no idea there could be so many variations of the mooring device.

Reynolds wasted no time in ordering a new round of beer. At first I refused, but then gave in to his never-ending requests for me "to have one on him." The mug was frosty and large. A few sips later and I was determined to get to the bottom of the mug and the others that followed as we ate piles of food.

When I had finished, I found myself madly drunk. Night had fallen by this time and I had no idea how long I had been in the fishery. All my swirling mind could think about was making the train to Philly, so I spluttered my thanks to Reynolds and excused myself by shouting, which was the only way of communication in the room apart from hand gestures (and there were plenty of those being flung at the table).

I stumbled out the back door that led onto the pier and tried to catch my breath. The sea air was cool and refreshing. The pier was dimly lit. I slumped on the planks running behind the Baltimore Fishery. My head spun under the insipid light as I saw nets being extracted from a small vessel. Distant spots danced on the waters and I heard the din of ships' horns. My heart was beating out of my chest and the congestion of my head was making me nauseous.

Time escaped me as I sat there in my stupor.

Suddenly burly hands landed on my shoulders and before my delayed reactions, I felt the blows of fists and boot heals against my ribcage and head. It was useless to run, if I even could in my condition. Curling in a ball to protect myself, I remembered John Allan and nothing else. I remembered.

Time was missing when I awoke. The smell of rotting fish was everywhere and I lay amongst the bags of garbage the fishery had put out for the night. My hand grasped at air for my valise. It was nowhere to be found; neither was my wallet. Also missing was a copy of *David Copperfield* that Elmira had lent me. My clothes were ripped and my hat was missing along with the manuscripts and what little money I had.

My arms and legs were hurting but in working order. In the midst of pain and confusion I was able to crawl far enough away from the fish carcasses to catch a breath of sea breeze. I found a welcoming corner of a building and lay crumpled in it the entire night, a wad of anguish.

Daylight broke harshly and I somehow found my way back to the train station. I am sure that no one recognized me given the caked blood on my face and hair. Digging in my pants pocket I found my ticket that was purchased the day before and I gave it to the conductor who returned my torn stub along with his suspect gaze. I planned to see Dr. Sartain the moment I exited the train in Philly.

I slowly climbed aboard, sure the Loungers were after me, sure *they* were watching. My limp body piled into a rear seat of the compartment. The pulverizing and grinding in my head was relentless on the journey to Philadelphia. The pain was so constant that when I arrived I could only think of getting on the train to New York and ultimately to Muddy's care.

Confusion owned me on the last day of September.

Upon exiting in Philadelphia I hopped the tracks and got on the train bound for New York without checking the log, for I knew the running of the locomotives so well from this junction.

I sat again in the rear corner seat of the train, shivering and sweating all at once. From the corner of my eye I watched to see if any Loungers had followed me. The train started moving in a short while. I heard the conductor yell out from the front of the cabin, "Cee Train to Baltimore! Onward bound!"

The city's name did not register at first. When it did and I realized I had gotten on the wrong train and was heading back to Baltimore, I tried to run to the front, asking to get off. My appearance must have looked hideous and my voice sounded like a jumbled slur. Ladies were sliding away from the aisle to escape my teetering walk. Others were shielding their children.

"Into your seat, drunk!" the conductor said, pushing me down.

"'Posed to be on rain to Rew Yowrk. *They* are rafter me ... on dis rain."

"Clam up, or I'll have you arrested the second we stop."

"Please help me."

In my delirium I returned to Baltimore and hopelessly went to the fishery to look for Reynolds and my valise. For days I wandered the streets without money, unable to think how to escape my situation. I had become a deranged character from one of my tales!

I pleaded with countless people who merely dismissed me as a vagabond. A number of times I stumbled in a direction where I understood there to be a hospital only to find an abandoned warehouse or office building. Street names changed on me while I gazed at them and restaurants changed ownership as I approached them.

Yet how could I find help when I had to avoid the Loungers as I huddled next to pilings under the pier and in back alleyways with searching eyes? Children that noticed me were pointing in my direction, shouting: "There's the Raven! Look at the frightened Raven! Caw, caw, caw!" Amongst all this chaos I had to find my valise because *they* had taken it again—yet again—to steal my writing, my manuscripts, to publish them under their name; every chance the Loungers had to destroy me, and I had to find it, *find it, FIND IT*!

The crushing wheels churned relentlessly on a cross-country trip in my head to Insanityville. The pounding. *Pounding!* The gristmill in my mind!

For three sordid days and nights I saw *them* everywhere: standing outside taverns, sitting at coffeehouse windows, riding steeds through town, stringing nets on fishing boats. I saw Griswold's head sitting atop a spittoon, laughing at me, his jowls spilling over the brass sides. "Good day in the morning!" he was saying between hearty laughs. "If you had money, you could find your valise, Mister Poor."

Words from my past kept repeating and fought each other for control. *—Poetry in America has its place on outhouse walls, but not among respectable society. —And remember, never stop writing. It is the most honorable profession of the arts. —The only matter you work hard at is writing your nonsense and disgracing my name. —If the Christmas season is when Dickens will be remembered, ole chap, then Halloween will be Poe's. A holiday for the Master of the Macabre. —And others tell me you are a drunk bordering on insanity who writes short stories because that is all you are capable of doing.*

On the third of October, on Election Day, I was snatched up in my heightened state by a band of pollsters on their way to vote at Gunner's Hall. They poured large amounts of alcohol down me and forced me to vote for their candidate. When I told them I despised voting because politics were run by the rich and voting was not truly representative of the people, one gang member held a Derringer to my side and another a dagger.

The first time I was sent into the booths I wore the clothes I had on. After that they changed me into different outfits and sent me back inside to vote again for their candidate. In some instances I wore a hat and others a long scarf. They told me this practice was called "cooping" and began to laugh. They threatened to kill me if I refused.

For a good part of the day I was in a half-conscious drunken state, being dragged to booths to vote for a group of politicians that I called out against in my writings. I had never felt more powerless or degraded. When the pollsters were through, they tossed me rolling down the side of a hill in a tattered and ribbonless straw hat. On inspection I was wearing a sack-coat of thin alpaca, ripped in many places, and beltless pantaloons of a mixed pattern of caseinate that were so baggy I could hardly keep them about my waist.

I lay their semiconscious while stone wheels ground the grains of reason in my head until they were dried pulp.

Later in the day someone found me and admitted me—not to the sanitarium as I had suspected—but to Washington Medical College[97] on the corner of Broadway and Hampstead in Baltimore. Lanterns glowed overhead as they wheeled me to a room in one of the hospital's two towers. My arms and legs were strapped to the stretcher.

"Reynolds!" I cried. *"Reynolds!"*

A junior doctor, ("Dr. Moran" the nurse was calling him) fresh from medical school, was trying to impress his superior. "He's got the brain fever I tell you, the brain fever!"

"Much to early for that diagnosis. There are many possibilities including congestion of the brain and intemperance."

The stretcher wheels trundled across the chipped hallway tile and into a vacant room. A nurse busied herself lighting the lanterns on either side of the bed that were fashioned into decorative crescents.

Dr. Snodgrass, the superior, assisted the young doctor in getting me into the bed. I was too weak to struggle.

"The Loungers are in here, too," I told them, bunching the pillow into my midsection and wrenching myself into the fetal position. "Lock the door! Keep them away from me." I did not dare tell the doctors my name for that would only bring Griswold and English on the prowl, the Literati of New York would dawn their chaps and boots and guns and hunt me.

"Delusions!" yelled Snodgrass. "More than brain fever. Strap him down again and get me some cool rags."

"Reynolds!" I screamed.

I heard the abrading of leather and the clasps of buckles. My hands and feet were shackled to the bed. Church bells rang at six that evening and I told all present that there was a "Devil in the Belfry! A crimson horned Beelzebub!"

"We will do all we can to help you, sir," Dr. Moran offered.

"Then give me a pistol so I may put it to my head."

I screamed for them not to leave me in that shackled condition because the Loungers would have their way with me, and the pendulums on the wall—the hissing crescents—would slice into me. But they did not listen. They did *not* listen.

Three days later, on Saturday, I felt safe enough to tell the doctors my name. They said they had guessed as much. Dr. Snodgrass stood at my bedside, the metallic instruments hanging about his neck clattering over me. "You have settled a great deal, Mister Poe. Your cousin the lawyer, Neilson was his name, stopped in yesterday with a fresh change of clothes for you when you feel up to getting around.[98]"

This news brought more suspicion. "Why did you not grant him access?"

"You were in a heightened state and therefore we did not let him see you. He said he will be back to-morrow morning."

I spent that Saturday night tossing and turning, spitting at the rotund face of Griswold when it appeared in various low and seedy places of the room. He thought it jest to peek out from under my bed when I was almost asleep. I hated the man.

"Reynolds, how could you have done this to me? Answer me, Reynolds!"

Near five in the morning on Sunday, October 7th, I was in such an anguished state that the nurses called Dr. Moran. "Come quickly, doctor," one of the nurses said as he entered the room, "for I believe our great American poet is near death."

"Hold him down nurses, secure him!"

"Lord, help my poor soul!"[99]

Poe Postmortem

Colonel J. Alden Weston to *The Baltimore Sun*

On a cold dismal October day, so different from the ordinary genial weather of that climate, I had just left my home when my attention was attracted to an approaching hearse, followed by hackney carriages, all of the plainest type. As I passed the little cortage some inscrutable impulse induced me to ask the driver of the hearse, "Whose funeral is this?" And to my intense surprise received for answer, "Mr. Poe, the poet." This being my first intimation of his death, which occurred at the hospital the previous day (Sunday) and was not generally known until after the funeral.

Immediately on this reply I turned about to the graveyard, a few blocks distant. On arrival there five or six gentlemen, including the officiating minister, descended from the carriages and followed the coffin to the grave, while I, as a simple onlooker, remained somewhat in the rear.

The burial ceremony, which did not occupy more than three minutes, was so cold-blooded and unchristianlike as to provoke on my part a sense of anger difficult to suppress. The only relative present was a cousin (a noted Baltimore lawyer), the remaining witnesses being from the hospital and the press.

After these had left I went to the grave and watched the earth being thrown upon the coffin until entirely covered. Then, I passed on with a sad heart and the one consolation that I was the last person to see the coffin containing all that was mortal of Edgar Allan Poe.

In justice to the people of Baltimore I must say that if the funeral had been postponed for a single day, until the death was generally known, a far more imposing escort to the tomb and one more worthy of the many admirers of the poet in the city would have taken place, and attended from Virginia and elsewhere.

Colonel J. Alden Weston,[100]

Eugene L. Didier to *Appleton's Journal*

To the Editor of Appleton's Journal.

My attention has directed to communication, signed G. A. Berry, in the number of the Journal dated Februray 24th, in which an attempt has been made to criticise the Latin inscription on the stone which was intended to be placed over the grave of Poe. This inscription was furnished by the gentleman who had the stone cut (he is a near relative of the poet), and was correctly quoted in my article on "The Grave of Poe" as follows: "HIC TANDEMI FELICIS CONDUNTUR RELIQUIAE EDGARI ALLAN POE." For the benefit of Mr. Berry, and others not familiar with the construction of the Latin language, I publish the following correct translation of the epitaph: "Here are gathered the remains of Edgar Allan Poe, happy at last."

Not "Cutting" irony nor "bitter sarcasm," as suggested by Mr. Berry, but beautiful and appropriate is this inscription. Poe's life of "endless toil and endeavor," want, disappointment, and suffering, made him "long for rest," and his rest he found only in the grave. A few words from Poe's exquisite poem to "Annie" would serve as a suitable epitaph for the world-weary poet: "My tantalized spirit/Here blandly reposes."

I take advantage of this opportunity to say it was Mrs. (not Miss) Elmira Shelton to whom Poe was engaged at the time of his death.

Eugene L. Didier[101]

Colonel John C. Legg, Sr. to *The Baltimore Sun*
Letter of Colonel John C. Legg, Sr., former Commissioner of Police in Baltimore:

No stone was immediately provided for young Poe, but I placed a marker bearing the number eight over the grave. The Poe stone was laying in a marble yard near the Baltimore and Ohio Railroad tracks when a freight train jumped the track and demolished the stone and several others in the yard.[102]

Maria Clemm to Neilson Poe
New York, October 9, 1849

I have heard this moment of the death of my dear son Edgar—I cannot believe it, and have written to you, to try and ascertain the fact and particulars—he has been at the South for the last three months, and was on his way home—the paper states he died in Baltimore yesterday—If it is true God have mercy on me, for he was the last I had to cling to and love, will you write the instant you receive this and relieve this dreadful uncertainty—My mind is prepared to hear all—conceal nothing from me.[103]

<u>Neilson Poe to Maria Clemm</u>

Baltimore, Oct. 11, 1849

My Dear Madam,

I would to God I could console you with the information that your dear son Edgar A. Poe is still among the living. The newspapers, in announcing his death, have only told a truth, which we may weep over and deplore, but cannot change. He died on Sunday morning, about 5 o'clock, at the Washington Medical College, where he had been since the Wednesday preceding. At what time he arrived in this city, where he spent the time he was here or under what circumstances, I have been unable to ascertain.

It appears that, on Wednesday, he was seen and recognized at one of the places of election in old town, and that his condition was such as to render it necessary to send him to the College, where he was tenderly nursed until the time of his death. As soon as I heard that he was at the College, I went over, but his physicians did not think it advisable that I should see him, as he was very excitable. The next day I called and sent him changes of linen and was gratified to learn that he was much better. And I was never so much shocked, in my life, as when, on Sunday morning, notice was sent to me that he was dead. Mr. Herring and myself immediately took the necessary steps for his funeral, which took place on Monday afternoon at four o'clock. He lies alongside his ancestors in the Presbyterian burial ground on Green Street.

I assure you, my dear madam, that, if I had known where a letter would reach you, I would have communicated the melancholy tidings in time to enable you to attend his funeral — but I was wholly unaware of how to address you. The body was followed to the grave by Mr. Herring, Dr. Snodgrass, Mr. Z. Collins Lee, and myself. The service was performed by the Reverend William T. D. Clemm, a son of James T. Clemm – your distant relative. Mr. Herring and myself have sought, in vain, for the trunk and clothes of Edgar. There is reason to believe that he was robbed of them, whilst in such a condition as to render him insensible of his loss.

I shall not attempt the useless task of consoling you under such a bereavement. Edgar has seen so much of sorrow – had so little reason to be satisfied with life – that, to him, the change can scarcely be said to be a misfortune. If it leaves you lonely in this world of trouble, may I be allowed the friendly privilege of expressing the hope that, in the contemplation of all the world to which he has gone and to which we are all hastening, you will find consolations enduring and all sufficient. I shall be glad, at all times, to hear from you, *and to alleviate, in every way in my power, the sorrows to which this dispensation may expose you. I only wish my ability was equal to my disposition.*

My wife unites with me in expressions of sympathy.

Truly your friend and servant,

Neilson Poe[104]

Sarah Elmira Shelton to Maria Clemm
Richmond, October 11th, 1849
My Dear Mrs. Clemm,

Oh, how shall I address you, my dear, and deeply afflicted friend under such heart-rending circumstances! I have no doubt, ere this, you have heard of the death of our dear Edgar! Yes, he was the dearest object on earth to me: and, well assured am I, that he was the pride of your heart.

I have not been able to get any of the particulars of his sickness and death, except an abstract from the Baltimore Sun, which said that he died on Sunday, the 7th of this month, with congestion of the brain, after an illness of 7 days.

He came up to my house on the evening of the 26th of September to take leave of me. He was very sad, and complained of being quite sick. I felt his pulse and found he had considerable fever, and did not think it probable he would be able to start the next morning (Thursday) as he anticipated. I felt so wretched about him all of that night, that I went up early next morning to inquire after him, when, much to my regret, he had left in the boat for Baltimore.

He expected certainly to have been with his "dear Muddy" on the Sunday following, when he promised to write to me. And after the expiration of a week, and no letter, I became very uneasy, and continued in an agonizing state of mind, fearing he was ill, but never dreamed of his death, until it met my eye in glancing casually over a Richmond paper of last Tuesday.

Oh, my dearest friend, I cannot begin to tell you what my feelings were, as the horrible truth forced itself upon me! It was the most severe trial I have ever had. And God alone knows how I can bear it. My heart is overwhelmed. Yes, ready to burst!

How can I, dear Muddy, speak comfort to your bleeding heart? I cannot say to you weep not, mourn not, but I do say, do both, for he is worthy to be lamented. Oh, my dear Edgar, shall I never behold your dear face and hear your sweet voice saying, "Dearest Muddy!" and "Dearest Elmira?" How can I bear the separation?

The pleasure I had anticipated on his return with you, dear friend, to Richmond was too great ever to be realized, and should teach me the folly of expecting bliss on earth. If it will be any consolation to you, my dear friend, to know that there is one who feels for you all that human can feel, then be assured that person is Elmira.

Willingly would I fly to you, if I could add to your comfort, or take from your sorrows. I wrote you a few weeks ago. I hope you received the letter. It was through the request of my dearest Eddy that I did so and when I told him I had written to you, his joy and delight were inexpressible.

I hope you will write to me as soon as possible and let me hear from you, as I shall be anxious about you incessantly until I do. Farewell, my stricken Friend, and may an All-Wise and Merciful God sustain and comfort us under this heart-breaking dispensation, is the fervent and hourly prayer of your afflicted and sympathizing friend.

Elmira Shelton[105]

Partial Letter of Dr. John J. Moran to Maria Clemm

Having left orders with the nurses to that effect, I was summoned to his bedside so soon as consciousness supervened, and questioned him in reference to his family—place of residence—relatives &c. But his answers were incoherent and unsatisfactory. He told me, however, he had a wife in Richmond (which, I have since learned was not the fact) that he did not know when he left that city or what had become of his trunk of clothing. Wishing to rally and sustain his now fast sinking hopes I told him I hoped, that in a few days he would be able to enjoy the society of his friends here, and I would be most happy to contribute in every possible way to his ease and comfort. At this he broke out with much energy, and said the best thing his best friend could do would be to blow out his brains with a pistol—that when he beheld his degradation he was ready to sink into the earth. Shortly after giving expression to these words Mr. Poe seemed to dose and I left him for a short time. When I returned I found him in a violent delirium, resisting the efforts of two nurses to keep him in bed. This state continued until Saturday evening (he was admitted on Wednesday) when he commenced calling for one "Reynolds", which he did through the night up to three on Sunday morning. At this time a very decided change began to affect him. Having become enfeebled from exertion he became quiet and seemed to rest for a short time, then gently moving his head he said "Lord help my poor Soul" and expired![106]

"Ludwig" to New York Tribune

Edgar Allan Poe is dead. He died in Baltimore on Sunday, October 7th. This announcement will startle many, but few will be grieved by it. The poet was known, personally or by reputation, in all this country; he had readers in England and in several of the states of Continental Europe; but he had few or no friends; and the regrets for his death will be suggested principally by the consideration that in him literary art has lost one of its most brilliant but erratic stars.

…

He was at all times a dreamer-dwelling in ideal realms-in heaven or hell-peopled with the creatures and the accidents of his brain. He walked-the streets, in madness or melancholy, with lips moving in indistinct curses, or with eyes upturned in passionate prayer (never for himself, for he felt, or professed to feel, that he was already damned, but) for their happiness who at the moment were objects of his idolatry; or with his glances introverted to a heart gnawed with anguish, and with a face shrouded in gloom, he would brave the wildest storms, and all night, with drenched garments and arms beating the winds and rains, would speak as if the spirits that at such times only could be evoked by him from the Aidenn, close by whose portals his disturbed soul sought to forget the ills to which his constitution subjected him—close by the Aidenn where were those he loved-the Aidenn which he might never see, but in fitful glimpses, as its gates opened to receive the less fiery and more happy natures whose destiny to sin did not involve the doom of death.

He seemed, except when some fitful pursuit subjugated his will and engrossed his facul-
ties, always to bear the memory of some controlling sorrow. The remarkable poem of 'The
Raven' was probably much more nearly than has been supposed, even by those who were
very intimate with him, a reflection and an echo of his own history. He was that bird's

> *... unhappy master whom unmerciful Disaster*
> *Followed fast and followed faster till his songs one burden*
> *bore—Till the dirges of his Hope that melancholy burden bore*
> **Of 'Never-never more.'**

Every genuine author in a greater or less degree leaves in his works, whatever their
design, traces of his personal character: elements of his immortal being, in which the indi-
vidual survives the person. While we read the pages of the 'Fall of the House of Usher,' or
of 'Mesmeric Revelations,' we see in the solemn and stately gloom which invests one, and in
the subtle metaphysical analysis of both, indications of the idiosyncrasies of what was most
remarkable and peculiar in the author's intellectual nature. But we see here only the better
phases of his nature, only the symbols of his juster action, for his harsh experience had
deprived him of all faith in man or woman. He had made up his mind upon the numberless
complexities of the social world, and the whole system with him was an imposture. This
conviction gave a direction to his shrewd and naturally unamiable character. Still, though
he regarded society as composed altogether of villains, the sharpness of his intellect was
not of that kind which enabled him to cope with villany, while it continually caused him by
overshots to fail of the success of honesty. He was in many respects like Francis Vivian in
Bulwer's novel of 'The Caxtons.' Passion, in him, comprehended -many of the worst emo-
tions which militate against human happiness. You could not contradict him, but you raised
quick choler; you could not speak of wealth, but his cheek paled with gnawing envy. The
astonishing natural advantages of this poor boy—his beauty, his readiness, the daring spirit
that breathed around him like a fiery atmosphere—had raised his constitutional self-confi-
dence into an arrogance that turned his very claims to admiration into prejudices against
him. Irascible, envious—bad enough, but not the worst, for these salient angles were all
varnished over with a cold, repellant cynicism, his passions vented themselves in sneers.
There seemed to him no moral susceptibility; and, what was more remarkable in a proud
nature, little or nothing of the true point of honor. He had, to a morbid excess, that, desire
to rise which is vulgarly called ambition, but no wish for the esteem or the love of his
species; only the hard wish to succeed-not shine, not serve -succeed, that he might have the
right to despise a world which galled his self-conceit.

We have suggested the influence of his aims and vicissitudes upon his literature. It was
more conspicuous in his later than in his earlier writings. Nearly all that he wrote in the last
two or three years-including much of his best poetry-was in some sense biographical; in
draperies of his imagination, those who had taken the trouble to trace his steps, could
perceive, but slightly concealed, the figure of himself.

Sincerely,
Ludwig[107]

Partial Letter of Dr. Rufus Griswold to Sarah Helen Whitman

I wrote, as you suppose, the notice of Poe in the Tribune, but very hastily. I was not his friend, nor was he mine.[108]

Sarah Helen Whitman response to Dr. Rufus Griswold, *Edgar Poe and His Critics*

Dr. Griswold's Memoir of Edgar Poe has been extensively read and circulated. Its perverted facts and baseless assumptions have been adopted into every subsequent memoir and notice of the poet, and have been translated into many languages. For ten years this great wrong to the dead has passed unchallenged and unrebuked.

It is not our purpose to present specially to review Dr. Griswold's numerous misrepresentations, and misstatements. Some of the more injurious of these anecdotes were disproved, during the life of Dr. Griswold, in the New York Tribune, and other leading journals, without eliciting from him any public statement in explanation or apology.

We have the authority for stating that many of the disgraceful anecdotes, so industriously collected by Dr. Griswold, are utterly fabulous, while others are perversions of the truth, more injurious in their effects than unmitigated fiction.

We propose simply to point out some unformed critical estimates which have obtained currency among readers who have had but a partial acquaintance with Mr. Poe's more imaginative writings, and to record our own impressions of the character and genius of the poet, as derived from personal observation and from the testimony of those who knew him.

The peculiar character of Poe's intellect seemed without a prototype in literature. He had more than De Quincey's power of analysis, with a constructive unity and completeness of which the great English essayist has given no indication. His pre-eminence in constructive and analytical skill was beginning to be universally admitted, and the fame and prestige of his genius were rapidly increasing.

A recent and not too lenient critic tells us that "it was his sensitiveness to artistic imperfections, rather than any malignity of feeling, that made his criticisms so severe, and procured him a host of enemies among persons towards whom he entertained no personal ill-will."

It is not to be questioned that Poe was a consummate master of language, that he had sounded all the secrets of rhythm, that he understood and availed himself of all its resources. Yet this consummate art was in him united with a rare simplicity. He was the most genuine of enthusiasts. His genius would follow no leadings but those of his own imperial intellect. With all his vast mental resources he could never write an occasional poem, or adapt himself to the taste of a popular audience. His graver narratives and fantasies are often related with an earnest simplicity, solemnity, and apparent fidelity, attributable, not so much to a deliberate artistic purpose, as to that power of vivid and intense conception that made his dreams realities, and his life a dream.

His works are, as if unconsciously, filled with an overwhelming sense of the power and majesty of Deity. They are even dark with reverential awe. His proud intellectual assumption of the supremacy of the individual soul was but an expression of its imperious longings for immortality and its recoil from the haunting phantasms of death and annihilation. The theme of all his more imaginative writings is, as we have said, a love that survives the dissolution of the mortal body and oversweeps the grave. His mental and temperamental idiosyncrasies fitted him to come readily into rapport with psychic and spiritual influences. Many of his strange narratives had a degree of truth in them which he was unwilling to avow. In one of his stories, he makes the narrator say, "I cannot even now regard these experiences as a dream, yet it is difficult to say how otherwise they should be termed. Let us suppose only that the soul of man, today, is on the brink of stupendous psychic discoveries."

Having recorded our earnest protest against the misapprehension of his critics and the misstatements of his biographers, we leave the subject for the present, in the belief that a more

impartial memoir of the poet will yet be given to the world, and the story of his sad strange life,

when contemplated from a new point of view, will be found to present, at least, a silver lining.

Sarah Helen Whitman,
Providence poet and former fiancée of Poe[109]

Author's Note

I began researching the life of Edgar Allan Poe by pouring over his countless letters and articles by those who knew him. In no time I became convinced that not only was Poe one of America's greatest authors, but that he lived a most fascinating life—a life filled with love, sorrow, and the infinite struggles of an artist who refused to adapt his writing or join the literary clicks of the day for popularity's sake. As a result, he died in abject poverty. Is not our purest form of writing that done without the taint of money? If so, the prose of Poe is snowy white.

During the outlining process of *Coffee with Poe*, I set out to write a story using actual letters as a framework for Poe's fictional first person narrative. I wanted to unfold the events of his amazing life so readers could live it rather than learn about it. Hopefully I have succeeded, and in all respects have remained true to Poe despite me taking a few liberties with the story. *Coffee with Poe* is a work of fiction after all, but I have tried to remain factually accurate where history allowed.

The main characters were the actual people in Poe's life, apart from one Martin Reynolds. Dr. John Moran stated in his letter to Maria Clemm that Poe kept calling out to a "Reynolds" in his final hours. Some Poe scholars have found inconsistencies in Dr. Moran's versions of Poe's last days and have therefore discredited all that he accounted. Some claim "Reynolds" was an old chum from West Point or a boyhood friend that used alcohol to kick off the reunion and the horrible chain of events that ensued in Baltimore, leading to Poe's ultimate demise. I chose the latter. The inconsistencies in Dr. Moran's statements regarding Poe's last days in the Baltimore hospital are uncontroverted, but I can only wonder what benefit he would gain by lying about Poe's cries for "Reynolds." If Dr. Moran sought to lie about Poe's final days wouldn't it make more sense to have Poe calling out to "Virginia" or "Maria" or "Elmira" to whom he was engaged to be married in a few days? It is not known if Dr. Moran knew of Virginia Clemm or Elmira Royster Sheldon, but he certainly was aware of Maria Clemm to whom he wrote. The question remains: Why would Dr. Moran fabricate "Reynolds" if he was looking to make a name for himself in retelling the story of Poe's death?

There were many other acquaintances in Poe's life that could not be experienced due to page constraints, a number of which were romantic interests in a flirtatious sort of way, though it is believed the relationships stopped short of physical intimacy. "Annie" Richmond, a bored and intelligent married woman, was one of them as well as "Fanny" Osgood. He courted both through published poetry. Understandably the Literati of New York got in a tizzy over these public exchanges because they all happened while Virginia lay sick in bed with tuberculosis. Virginia, however, was fine with the tongue-in-cheek responses of Poe because he recycled a number of poems written for other people. Poe loved jerking the public around, whether it was scaring the daylights out of them or publishing tongue-in-cheek stories like *The Balloon-Hoax* and *Why the Little Frenchman Wears His Hand in a Sling*. Despite his bitter circumstances, Poe was a practical joker to his core and if he could get the rumormongers in a fluster, all the better.

Mrs. Elizabeth Ellet, a more popular writer than Franny Osgood, jumped on the bandwagon of public flirtation by confessing her repressed love for Poe in the *Broadway Journal*, which brought the written spite of Mrs. Osgood. I imagine Poe sat back and enjoyed the catfights of these women in the literary journals, but it soon turned sinister when Mrs. Ellet visited Virginia in her weakened state and alleged that the relationship between Mrs. Osgood and Poe was not innocent. Soon thereafter Virginia began receiving anonymous letters from "poison pens" and Poe immediately rebuffed Mrs. Ellet. He later stated that Virginia declared on her deathbed "that Mrs. E had been her murderer."[110]

The burning questions some people have regarding Poe are unfortunately not about how he refined the modern horror genre and invented the mystery genre, but rather: Was he a drug addict or an alcoholic?

Did Poe have a drug habit? The experts are doubtful. People through history have failed to separate Poe the writer from the fictional narrators of his tales that were taken with drugs, the "opium eaters" as he called them. There were two drugs of choice in Poe's day, opium and laudanum (a cocktail of cocaine and alcohol). Poe wrote Annie Richmond about his use of the later drug, which may have been for medicinal purposes, but he also claimed to have tried to kill himself by overdosing on it.[111] As you can tell from the letters you have just read, Poe had a flair for the dramatic. Because this statement was made only to Annie Richmond, a woman to which he was trying to seek pity, it may have been a lie wrapped in drama. Even if it is true that Poe tried to end his life on laudanum, this alone does not offer proof he was an addict or even a frequent user of drugs. Of the numerous doctors that examined Poe over the years, and in different cities, none detected a drug problem. Even Dr. Thomas Dunn English, Poe's spiteful enemy, stated after his death: "Had Poe the opium habit when I knew him, I should, both as a physician and a man of observation, have discovered it in his frequent visits to my rooms, my visits to his house, and our meetings elsewhere. I saw no signs of it."[112]

Did Poe drink? Certainly yes, but Poe was likely not a "heavy" drinker as we think of the term today. In Poe's time, a few drinks a week would have earmarked a person as being prone to excess. While at the University of Virginia, William Wertenbaker remembered of Poe's college days: "I often saw him in the Lecture room and in the library, but never in the slightest degree under the influence of intoxicating liquors. Among the Professors he had the reputation of being a sober, quiet and orderly young man."[113] There are accounts of Poe partaking in port, wine, and whisky, but it was not until after his fight with John Allan on the evening of March 18, 1827, that Poe began displaying the attributes of a public drunkard and his health fell into decline. Until that event, Poe was an extremely fit young man, able to swim over seven miles up the James River. He participated in sports while at the University of Virginia and excelled.

Poe's body later showed evidence of an altercation, although it was apparently too painful for him to discuss. He only showed the scars to Virginia. Mrs. Shew, the nurse who attended Virginia at the Fordham cottage, and later Poe, recalled a scar to his chest and head: "I have seen the scar of the wound in the left shoulder, when helping Mrs. Clemm change his dress or clothes while ill. She said only Virginia knew about it. She did not. I asked him if he had been hurt —, in the region of the heart and he told me yes, and the rest as I wrote to you. His head was also hurt ..."[114]

My theory is that in his fight with John Allan, Poe likely suffered a closed-head injury that caused a cranial lesion or scar tissue on the brain, which only worsened in its effects over the following years. Today the medical buzz term is "acquired brain injury." ABI can effect such physical skills as speech and coordination, balance, strength, equilibrium, eye-hand coordination, spatial orientation, and may cause seizures; all symptoms that could be mistaken for intoxication. Multiple doctors diagnosed Poe with "congestion of the brain," which was their best explanation at the time. On Feb 21, 1831 he wrote John Allan, saying, "my ear discharges blood and matter continuall[y] and my headache is distracting — I hardly know what I am writing — I will write no more — Please send me a little money ...."[115] A brain lesion also explains his severe migraines and bouts of manic depression, which caused some to think him insane. ABI also impairs psychological skills and can cause paranoia, which increased as Poe aged.

We know today that ABI may cause hypersensitivity to alcohol, which explains the claims that he displayed drunken symptoms after only one drink or no drinks at all. N. P. Willis, editor of the *Evening Mirror*, confirmed, "We have heard, from one who knew him well what should be stated in all mention of his lamentable irregularities,—that with a single glass of wine his whole nature was reversed; the demon became uppermost ..."[116] In April of 1841, Poe wrote to Dr. J. Evans Snodgrass defending himself against Burton's accusations that he was a drunk, "... I am temperate even to rigor.... At no period of my life was I ever what men call intemperate.... My sensitive temperament could not stand an excitement which was an everyday matter to my companions. In short, it sometimes happened that I was completely intoxicated. For some days after each excess I was invariably confined to bed. But it is now quite four years since I have abandoned every kind of alcoholic drink — four years, with the exception of a single deviation ... when I was induced to resort to the occasional use of cider, with the hope of relieving a nervous attack."[117] Poe's admission of "a single deviation" speaks in favor of his honesty. He was accused of public drunkenness a number of times, yet no one saw him drinking beforehand nor detected the smell of alcohol on his breath. On July 7, 1849, he wrote Maria Clemm from Philadelphia informing, "I have been taken to prison once since I came here for spreeing drunk; but then I was not. It was about Virginia."[118]

Sadly, the world will never know for certain.

Andrew Barger
June 12, 2003

Abbreviations

EAP   Edgar Allan Poe

EAPSB   Edgar Allan Poe Society of Baltimore

(Endnotes)

[1] *Richmond Enquirer*, December 10, 1811.

[2] "To Helen," *Tamerlane and Other Poems*, Calvin S. Thomas, 1827.

[3] Thomas Jefferson to Joseph Coolidge, Jr., April 12, 1825, University of Virginia, Electronic Text Center.

[4] EAP to John Allan, September 21, 1826, EAPSB.

[5] EAP to John Allan, January 3, 1831, EAPSB.

[6] Ibid.

[7] EAP to John Allan, January 3, 1831, EAPSB.

[8] Ibid. at 1.

[9] Ibid. at 1-2.

[10] EAP to John Allan, May 25, 1826, EAPSB.

[11] Ibid.

[12] Ibid.

[13] EAP to John Allan, September 21, 1826, EAPSB.

[14] Ibid.

[15] EAP to John Allan, January 3, 1831, EAPSB.

[16] Ibid.

[17] Ibid.

[18] EAP to John Allan, March 19, 1827, EAPSB.

[19] John Allan to EAP, March 20, 1827, EAPSB.

[20] EAP to John Allan, February 4, 1829, EAPSB.

[21] EAP to John Allan, January 3, 1831, EAPSB.

[22] Al Aaraf, Tamerlane, and Minor Poems, *Hatch & Dunning*, 1829.

[23] Thomas W. Gibson, quoted in "Edgar Allan Poe: Life, Letters, and Opinions"; John H. Ingram, Balentine Press, Inc., Vol I, 1880.

[24] EAP to John Allan, January 3, 1831, EAPSB.

[25] Ibid.

[26] EAP to John Allan, February 21, 1831, EAPSB.

[27] "Metsengerstein": *The Saturday Courier*, January 14, 1832.

[28] EAP to John Allan, April 12, 1833, EAPSB.

[29] Letter of Thomas Ellis, *The Poe Log*, 137, G. K. Hall & Co., 1987.

[30] John P. Kennedy to Thomas W. White, April 13, 1835: quoted in "Edgar Allan Poe: Life, Letters, and Opinions"; John H. Ingram, Balentine Press, Inc., Vol I, 1880, 117.

[31] EAP to Thomas W. White, May 30, 1835, EAPSB.

[32] EAP to Thomas W. White, September 11, 1835, EAPSB.

[33] Cited in EAP to Maria Clemm, August 29, 1835, EAPSB.

[34] EAP to Maria Clemm, August 29, 1835, EAPSB.

[35] EAP to John Kennedy, September 11, 1835, EAPSB.

[36] John Kennedy to EAP, September 19, 1835, EAPSB.

[37] Marie Louise Shew to John Ingram, May 16, 1875, quoted by John C. Miller, "Building the Poe Biography": 139, EAPSB.

[38] Quote from "King Pest the First": *Southern Literary Messenger*, September 1835.

[39] Quote from "Shadow. A Fable": *Southern Literary Messenger*, September 1835.

[41] T. H. White to Lucian Minor, September 8, 1835, quoted in *The Poe Log*, 167, G. K. Hall & Co., 1987.

[42] "Frogpondians": EAP to Frederick William Thomas, February 14, 1849, EAPSB.

[43] Ibid.

[44] EAP to Maria Clemm, April 7, 1844, Enoch Pratt Free Library.

[45] EAP to Washington Irving, October 12, 1839, EAPSB.

[46] Washington Irving to EAP, November 6, 1839, EAPSB.

[47] EAP to William Burton, June 1, 1840, EAPSB.

[48] Henry W. Longfellow to EAP, May 19, 1841, EAPSB.

[49] EAP to Henry W. Longfellow, June 22, 1841, EAPSB.

[50] Charles Dickens to Daniel Macalise, March 12, 1841.

[51] "namby-pamby character": EAP to Frederick William Thomas, May 25, 1842, EAPSB.

[52] Ibid.

[53] "Griswold's American Poetry": EAP, *Boston Miscellany*, November 1842, EAPSB.

[54] EAP to F. W. Thomas, September 12, 1842, EAPSB.

[55] *Saturday Museum*, January 28, 1843, EAPSB.

[56] "The Black Cat": EAP, *United States Saturday Post*, August 1843.

[57] "The Doom of the Drinker": Thomas Dunn English, Clarke's Saturday Museum, 1843.

[58] EAP to Maria Clemm, April 7, 1844, Enoch Pratt Free Library.

[59] Ibid.

[60] "buggy" Ibid.

[61] Ibid.

[62] Quote from "The Premature Burial": *Dollar Newspaper*, July 31, 1844.

[63] "The Raven": *Evening Mirror*, January 29, 1845.

[64] N. P. Willis, Introduction to "The Raven": *Evening Mirror*, January 29, 1845, quoted in

"*Edgar Allan Poe: Life, Letters, and Opinions*"; John H. Ingram, Balentine Press, Inc., Vol I, 1880, 272.

[65] Virginia Clemm to EAP, February 14, 1846, Enoch Pratt Free Library.

[66] EAP to Virginia Clemm, June 12, 1846, EAPSB.

[67] Nathaniel Hawthorne to EAP, June 17, 1846, EAPSB.

[68] *Evening Mirror*, June 23, 1846, cited in *The Poe Log*, 647-648, G. K. Hall & Co., 1987.

[69] Cited in "*Friends and Enemies: Women in the Life of Edgar Allan Poe*": Richard P. Benton, *Myths and Reality*, 15, 1987, EAPSB.

[70] *The Poe Log*, G. K. Hall & Co., 689, 1987.

[71] "*Friends and Enemies: Women in the Life of Edgar Allan Poe*": Richard P. Benton, Myths and Reality, 8, 1987, EAPSB.

[72] Marie Louise Shew to John Ingram, May 16, 1875, quoted by John C. Miller, *Building Poe Biography*, 139, EAPSB.

[73] Quote from "The Pit and the Pendulum": *The Gift* for, 1842.

[74] Quote from "The System of Dr. Tarr and Prof. Fether": *Graham's Magazine*, 1845.

[75] Quote from "The Pit and the Pendulum": *The Gift* for, 1842.

[76] Quote from "The Masque of the Red Death. A Fantasy.": *Graham's Magazine*, May 1842.

[77] Quoted in letter of EAP to Sarah Helen Whitman, October 1, 1848, EAPSB.

[78] Text from letter of EAP to Sarah Helen Whitman, October 18, 1848, EAPSB.

[79] Sarah Helen Whitman to EAP, September 27-29, 1848, EAPSB.

[80] EAP to Sarah Helen Whitman, October 1, 1848, EAPSB.

[81] Sarah Helen Whitman to EAP, October 10, 1848, EAPSB.

[82] EAP to Sarah Helen Whitman, October 18, 1848, EAPSB.

[83] EAP to Sarah Helen Whitman, November 7, 1848, EAPSB.

[84] EAP to Sarah Helen Whitman, November 14, 1848, EAPSB.

[85] EAP to Sarah Helen Whitman, November 22, 1848, EAPSB.

[86] EAP to Sarah Helen Whitman, November 24, 1848, EAPSB.

[87] Ibid.

[88] EAP to Sarah Helen Whitman, November 26, 1848, EAPSB.

[89] Ibid.

[90] EAP to Sarah Helen Whitman, January 25, 1849, EAPSB.

[91] EAP to Maria Clemm, July 7, 1849, EAPSB.

[92] Essay in *Boston Evening Transcript*, "Poe's Last Days": Dr. John Sartain, 1893, EAPSB.

[93] EAP to Maria Clemm, July 14, 1849, EAPSB.

[94] Essay by Susan Weiss, *Scribners Monthly*, March, 1878.

[95] EAP to Maria Clemm, September 18, 1849, EAPSB.

[96] Ibid.

[97] Neilson Poe to Maria Clemm, October 11, 1849, EAPSB.

[98] Ibid.

[99] "Lord, help my poor soul.": quoted in letter from Dr. John J. Moran to Maria Clemm, November 18, 1849, EAPSB.

[100] Letter of Colonel J. Alden Weston, *The Baltimore Sun*, March 1909.

[101] Letter of Eugene L. Didier, *Appleton's Journal*, March 16, 1872.

[102] Letter of Colonel John C. Legg, Sr., *The Baltimore Sun*, March 1909.

[103] Maria Clemm to Neilson Poe, October 9, 1849, EAPSB.

[104] Neilson Poe to Maria Clemm, October 11, 1849, EAPSB.

[105] Sarah Elmira Royster Shelton to Maria Clemm, October 11,1849, EAPSB.

[106] Partial Letter of Dr. John J. Moran to Maria Clemm, November 15, 1849, EAPSB.

[107] Letter of Dr. Rufus W. Griswold under pseudonym, *New York Tribune*, October 9, 1849.

[108] Partial Letter of Dr. Rufus W. Griswold to Sarah Helen Whitman, Dec. 17, 1849, EAPSB.

[109] Sarah Helen Whitman response to Dr. Rufus Griswold, "Edgar Allan Poe and His Critics," 1860.

[110] Ostrom, 408, cited in: "*Friends and Enemies: Women in the Life of Edgar Allan Poe*": Richard P. Benton, Myths and Reality, 2, 1987, EAPSB.

[111] EAP to Annie Lock Richmond, November 16, 1848, EAPSB.

[112] Letter of Dr. Thomas Dunn English, *The Independent*, October 15, 1896.

[113] Letter of William Wertenbaker, *The Poe Log*, 76, G. K. Hall & Co., 1987.

[114] Marie Louise Shew to John Ingram, May 16, 1875, quoted by John C. Miller, "Building the Poe Biography," 139.

[115] EAP to John Allan, February 21, 1831, EAPSB.

[116] "The Death of Edgar Allan Poe": *Home Journal*, Nathaniel P. Willis, October 13, 1849.

[117] EAP to Dr. J. Evans Snodgrass, *Letters*, April 1, 1841, EAPSB

[118] EAP to Maria Clemm, July 7, 1849, EAPSB.

Printed in the United States
117997LV00002B/256/A